W9-BKG-359

A PRACTICAL GUIDE TO DATA BASE DESIGN

A PRACTICAL GUIDE TO DATA BASE DESIGN

REX HOGAN

PRENTICE HALL
Englewood Cliffs, New Jersey 07632

Library of Congress Cataloging-in-Publication Data

Hogan, Rex
A practical guide to data base design / by Rex Hogan.
p. cm.
Includes index.
ISBN 0-13-690967-1
1. Data base design. I. Title.
QA76.9.D26H64 1990
005.74—dc20 89-8786
CIP

Editorial/production supervision and
interior design: KERRY REARDON
Cover Design: WANDA LUBELSKA
Manufacturing buyer: RAY SINTEL

The publisher offers discounts on this book when ordered
in bulk quantities. For more information, write:

Special Sales/College Marketing
College Technical and Reference Division
Prentice Hall
Englewood Cliffs, New Jersey 07632

Printed in the United States of America

10 9 8 7 6 5 4 3 2 1

ISBN 0-13-690967-1

PRENTICE HALL INTERNATIONAL (UK) LIMITED, LONDON
PRENTICE HALL OF AUSTRALIA PTY. LIMITED, SYDNEY
PRENTICE HALL CANADA INC., TORONTO
PRENTICE HALL HISPANOAMERICANA, S.A., MEXICO
PRENTICE HALL OF INDIA PRIVATE LIMITED, NEW DELHI
PRENTICE HALL OF JAPAN, INC., TOKYO
SIMON & SCHUSTER ASIA PTE. LTD. SINGAPORE
EDITORA PRENTICE HALL DO BRASIL, LTDA., RIO DE JANEIRO

Contents

Preface

As the name suggests, this book describes a practical approach to performing logical and physical data base design. It describes how to use entity/relationship diagrams as the basis for deriving a physical design for any type of data base management system, as well as for simple file structures. In other words, it is intended for users and programmer-analysts who are working together to design a data base system.

This book has evolved from the author's experience in providing data base support in a large IMS shop, while teaching night school classes in data base design at a major midwestern university. As a result of this background, the book reflects a blend of the analytical processes that need to be accomplished in data base design, together with a no-nonsense approach to accomplishing these tasks in a minimum amount of time. Feedback from the author's students over the years has consistently confirmed the bottom-line applicability of this approach.

The book describes a process where user group representatives and members of the application development team work together first to identify data requirements for the new system, and then to derive access path requirements going against these data. Finally, a first-cut data base solution is derived for those access requirements. The book establishes a framework where those who know the data best—members of the user community—can be assisted by application specialists to perform the required analysis in a minimum amount of time.

How is this different from all the other books on the market?

- It begins with practical, usable definitions of the various stages of normalization, backed up by complete examples illustrating what to do at each stage of the normalization process.
- The normalized data are then used to draw a data model reflecting the data relationships identified. This data model is then reviewed for completeness and accuracy.
- The process of usage path analysis is illustrated. On a program-by-program basis, access paths are developed to reflect how the data model would be accessed to satisfy requirements for data.
- It then illustrates how to transform the results from the usage path analysis into a first-cut solution for a physical data base design. Such information, when shared with a data base specialist for the particular data base management system to be used for physical implementation, provides sufficient information to permit that specialist to create an accurate and detailed physical data base design in a minimum amount of time.
- There are additional chapters included to discuss other pertinent management issues which affect data base systems. The topics include application development strategies, issues pertaining to data administration, and finally, backup and recovery strategies from the data center's perspective. Each topic is reviewed from a real-world perspective, including a review of pertinent issues involved, with suggestions on alternative approaches to each problem area.

The content of the book is divided into the following sections.

1. The first phase of analysis places its emphasis on the accurate identification of data requirements for the new application. Each phase of the normalization process is described, then illustrated by examples. Typical problems encountered are illustrated, along with their solution. This analysis results in the derivation of a data model, or relational view, of the data elements identified and their relationship to each other.
2. Next, the data are analyzed in terms of how they will be accessed or used to satisfy the requirements of each program in the system being designed. This phase verifies that the data model is complete in terms of data definition, and frequently used access paths are identified as possible candidates for performance optimization in physical design.
3. Each of the three types of data base management systems (network, hierarchical, and relational) are reviewed to establish an understanding of the design options typically available within each.

   For users of network data bases, the fundamentals of network structures are reviewed in enough detail to understand the implications of performance options which are typically available.

For hierarchical data bases, IMS data base structures are reviewed in a fair amount of detail. The emphasis, once again, is on building a basic understanding of how various functional capabilities are supported through physical implementation options.

Relational data bases are reviewed to help the reader establish an understanding of how data access is provided, in spite of a lack of internal linkage mechanisms to tie together related data elements.

4. The final phase of the design material describes how to map the results of the usage path analysis into a first-cut solution for a data base design for each of the three types of data base managers.
5. Additional material is also included regarding peripheral management issues in the areas of data administration and application development strategies. Each of these topics reviews the problem areas in today's environment, and practical alternatives are reviewed for handling those problems. Finally, data center backup/recovery operations are covered, using as a basis for analysis the various functions and utilities in an IMS environment, and describing how they can be used to design an effective data base recovery plan.

Each phase of the analytical process is illustrated by complete and detailed examples. In addition, Chapter 8 is a complete review of each phase in the logical and physical design process, using as a basis a real and sophisticated data model taken from the manufacturing environment.

In summary, this book is a practical, down-to-earth guide for the design of data bases. It tells you what you need to know to quickly and effectively perform an analysis of data requirements for an application system, leading you to a first-cut solution for all types of data base or file management systems in a minimal amount of time. And it works.

1

Why Data Base Management Systems?

1.1 BACKGROUND

Most large data processing shops have already concluded that a data base management system (DBMS) is, in fact, necessary, and have at least one installed. A lot of small-to medium-size shops, however, have been using some combination of traditional file systems (sequential, indexed, or direct access files) for a number of years, and have been doing a perfectly satisfactory job with them, usually for batch processing. A data processing manager in one of these shops, in trying to keep current by reading the various data processing magazines, will be bombarded by the typical ads for DBMS systems, each professing how that particular product will solve all his or her problems. Development time will be dramatically reduced, production will go up, and users will be delighted and view the DP staff as heroes.

Well, even if you haven't been in the DP business for 30 years, I'm sure you've been exposed to enough silver-tongued salesmen to be cautious of the grand and glorious claims. Yet somewhere there *just may be* a grain of truth (or hope)! Perhaps, in some way, a more sophisticated file management program (usually called a data base management system, or DBMS) really *does* possess the potential to provide significant savings to your operations.

Here I have some good news, and some bad news. First the good news. If your data processing environment has any degree of sophistication at all in the number of files and the interrelationship between those files, then yes, a DBMS does have the potential for saving time and money in your day-to-day operations. The bad news comes in two ways.

First, notice the use of the word "potential" in the preceding paragraph. Like so many things in life (much less the data processing business), a technology exists that can make life easier; that is, often data processing operations can be made more efficient with the proper use of a DBMS. The DBMS, however, is not in itself the answer. Inefficient file structures, when placed under the control of a DBMS, just become more inefficient and require a longer time to run. The original problems still exist, only now we must go through the additional overhead of a DBMS to get to the data.

The second piece of bad news relates to the choice of data base systems. Data bases are very much in vogue, so any vendor wishing to sell "state of the art" software will try to claim their product relates somehow to a data base system. A true DBMS, however, possesses certain characteristics or capabilities that separate it from the traditional file management system. These capabilities, if they exist and are used properly, can often make data processing operations more efficient and save your company some money. The trick, then, is to select software that has these features, and not be fooled by vague vendor claims.

To do this, you must understand the characteristics of data base management systems, and how they differ from traditional file systems. The remaining part of this chapter addresses these issues. Subsequent chapters cover various topics that involve the design and management of data base systems, including:

1. Normalization, an easy-to-use data analysis technique that facilitates end-user involvement in developing a data model representing data requirements. This technique also simplifies designing record structures that store data "where they belong."
2. Usage analysis, a technique for analyzing user access requirements against the data model in preparation for physical design;
3. A review of how several network, hierarchical, and relational data base management systems store and manage data records and data relationships;
4. Structural design, a technique for mapping user access requirements into a first-cut solution of a data base design;
5. Additional topics from a manager's perspective that are involved in the design, implementation, and maintenance of an application's data base systems.

It's important to note that the analytical techniques used apply to any type of DBMS or file structure.

In summary, the objective of this book is to cover the skills and techniques necessary to enable the application staff and end users to work together and arrive at an accurate, first-cut data base design that meets the user's requirements. To obtain a final data base design solution, the design team would then share the results of their analysis with a data base specialist within their company. This specialist would assist in determining implementation details for the particular DBMS to be used, to insure no mistakes or oversights were made.

To begin, let's look at some of the most common file management techniques.

1.2 TRADITIONAL FILE MANAGEMENT SYSTEMS

When designing applications using a simple file management system, you can choose to access data records in one of several ways.

The simplest structure, a sequential file, requires that the file be read (or written) one record at a time, where each record follows its predecessor physically on the storage device (as with a tape file). The data records are usually sorted in some sequence, although that is not necessary. Normally the entire file is "passed" whenever processed; in other words, each record is read or written.

Other file structures support direct, random access to individual data records. These structures, using techniques such as indexing or relative record access, allow programs to specify, one by one, the record desired. This flexibility increases performance over sequential processing by providing access to only those records that are required to accomplish a specific objective.

To illustrate how these files might work, Figure 1.1 shows an employee file implemented under sequential, direct access, and indexed file structures. Note the three-digit employee id (emp id) field in each example.

In studying this example, note also the effect of not having an employee with an id of "102." In Figure 1.1(a), the file is sorted by emp id, and the employee record for 102 is simply missing. Figure 1.1(b), however, is based on a direct access scheme that equates the emp id to the record number to be accessed. Therefore, record number 102 exists in the file, but is unused at this time as indicated by having a "zero" value stored in the emp id field.

Finally, Figure 1.1(c) shows these same data stored in an indexed file structure. Note how the system maintains a key for each record in an index component of the file, which is linked to the corresponding data component. Here, as in a sequential file, only records for active employees appear.

Such forms of file structures have several important things in common. First, all records within a given file "look alike"; that is, the same fields exist at the same location or offset within each record. In addition, the file descriptions are explicitly declared in each program. In each case, the program must issue I/O commands directly to the appropriate system access method for all read/write requests, using the required format for the command desired.

As a result, even minor changes in record layout or blocksize—as in increasing the size of the physical record when adding new data fields—require that each program which accesses that file be changed and tested, even if it doesn't use the

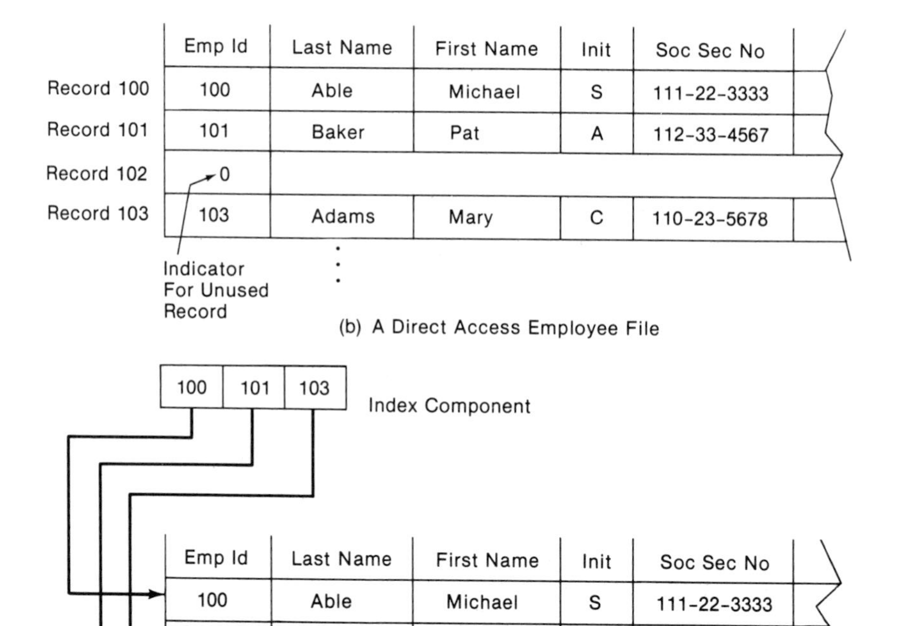

Figure 1.1 Employee File Implementations with Simple File Structures

new data fields. All such programs must then be controlled so that the production copies are simultaneously updated at the same time that the file is changed. Although this may sound like a simple task, it takes time, and care must be taken to prevent surprises in the way of production run-time failures caused by a forgotten or overlooked program not being updated with the others (otherwise known as a “significant emotional event”).

Another more subtle cost or problem with "flat files" lies in the hidden or imbedded relationships that might exist across records. Any such interdependence, as in the case of employee and deduction files, must be implemented within application code or logic. For example, employee records might be stored in a direct access file where the employee id equates to the file's record number, while deduction records would be sorted by employee id and stored in a sequential file. In this case, while the employee records may be randomly accessed when needed, sequential read requests against the deduction file must be issued to locate the first record for a specified employee. Consecutive reads would then be issued until a deduction record is found with another employee id. Application logic must control when and how to access these various records when data are to be added, modified, or deleted.

To ease the overhead of gaining access to data when needed, a common technique in file design is to store critical, often-used data fields redundantly across several files. For example, storing the employee name field within the deduction record would prevent the need to access employee records when simply listing deduction information. This reduces the overhead of accessing data in many instances but increases the size and number of maintenance programs required to update the replicated copies. More programs are required, additional CPU time is required to run the multiple updates, and disk storage requirements are higher than if the data were stored in only one location. Finally, think for a moment about the probable inconsistencies across the replicated data fields. If the same piece of information is stored in six places, which of the six copies is correct at any single instant in time?

I don't want to imply that all flat files are inefficient. If record structures are created to store data "where they belong," these problems will be eliminated (or at least minimized). Unfortunately, I've seen too many times when records are designed based on data requirements of a collection of reports or programs, which are all subject to change. The techniques described in Chapter 2 not only solve this problem, but are applicable to any file or data base management system.

Traditional file management systems

Advantages:

- Easy to create and simple to use
- Require minimal overhead to access and use

Disadvantages:

- Any change in structure or content requires simultaneous changes to all programs
- Relationships across files must be imbedded within application logic
- Encourage the proliferation of redundant data

Let's take a look at what a DBMS is and how it differs from a traditional file management system.

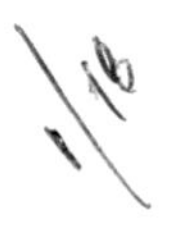

1.3 DATA BASE MANAGEMENT SYSTEMS

A data base management system is, in the simplest possible terms, an ultra-sophisticated file manager that has the capability to store and manage different types of records within one data set. A data base, on the other hand, is the physical implementation of a specific set of data records, the access to which is controlled by the DBMS. When a data base is first defined, the various types of records to be implemented are described to the DBMS in terms of their length, key field, and data fields, as well as any relationships that exist across records. Later, when records are added to the data base in response to application requests for data services, it's the job of the DBMS to manage any relationships (or, if applicable, linkage paths) that exist across the various records in the data base. As a result, application programs can be written without any knowledge of the physical attributes of the data base, and changes to the data base at a later time can be made transparently to these programs.

The three classical types of data base management systems are hierarchical, network, and relational. As illustrated in Figure 1.2(a), a hierarchical system has the general shape or appearance of an organizational chart. A node on the chart, representing a particular record type, is subordinate to only one record at the next highest level just as, on an organization chart, an employee reports to only one boss. This kind of structure is often referred to as an "inverted tree," with the top-most record referred to as the "root."

As shown in Figure 1.2(b), a network structure is somewhat similar, but has one major difference. Subordinate record types, depicted by arrows on the network diagram, may participate in as many subordinate relationships as desired. Therefore, a much more complex diagram may be used to represent the structure of the data base. Networks provide more flexibility than a simple hierarchical system in the data relationships that may be maintained.

Finally, a relational data base consists of a collection of simple files or tables, each of which has no structural or physical connection such as those typically used in hierarchical or network systems, as in Figure 1.2(c). The various records possess the interrelationships as depicted by a network-like diagram, but these relationships are based on the data content of the records involved, not by pointer chains or other types of structural connection techniques.

Figure 1.3 illustrates how a data base containing employee, weekly deduction, and payroll summary records might look under each of these types of data base management systems. In each case, ignoring internal limits of data set size for the sake of discussion, there can be as many occurrences of any record type as needed. In each case, as records are added or deleted, the DBMS maintains any relationships between and across these records.

Let's now review in more detail the benefits obtained through the use of a DBMS.

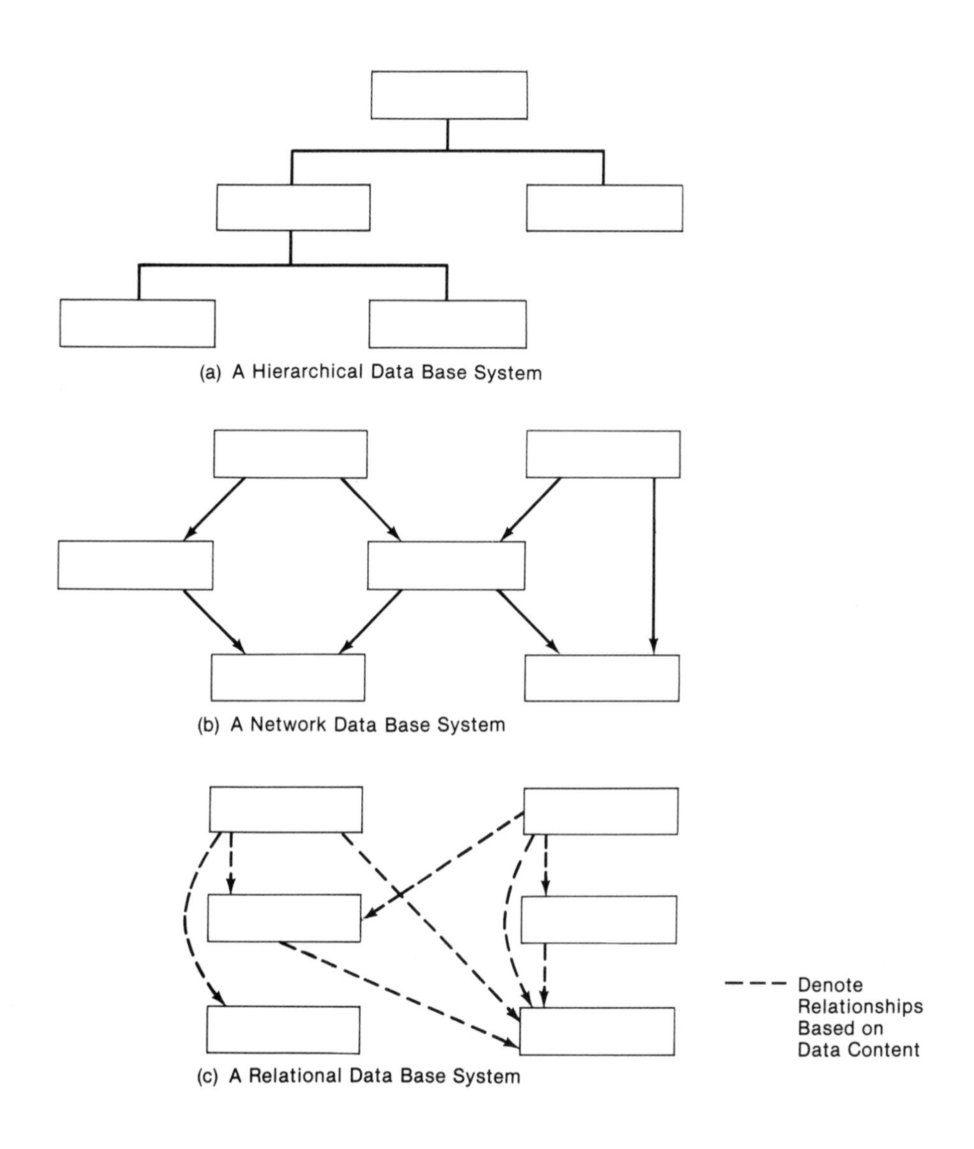

Figure 1.2 The Three Types of Data Base Systems

1.3.1 Advantages of Data Base Systems

1. Data Independence. To add a record to a data base, an application program first stores the appropriate information in its I/O area, and then makes a call to the DBMS to store the data. The DBMS determines where to physically store the record, based on parameters specified when the data base was first defined. For

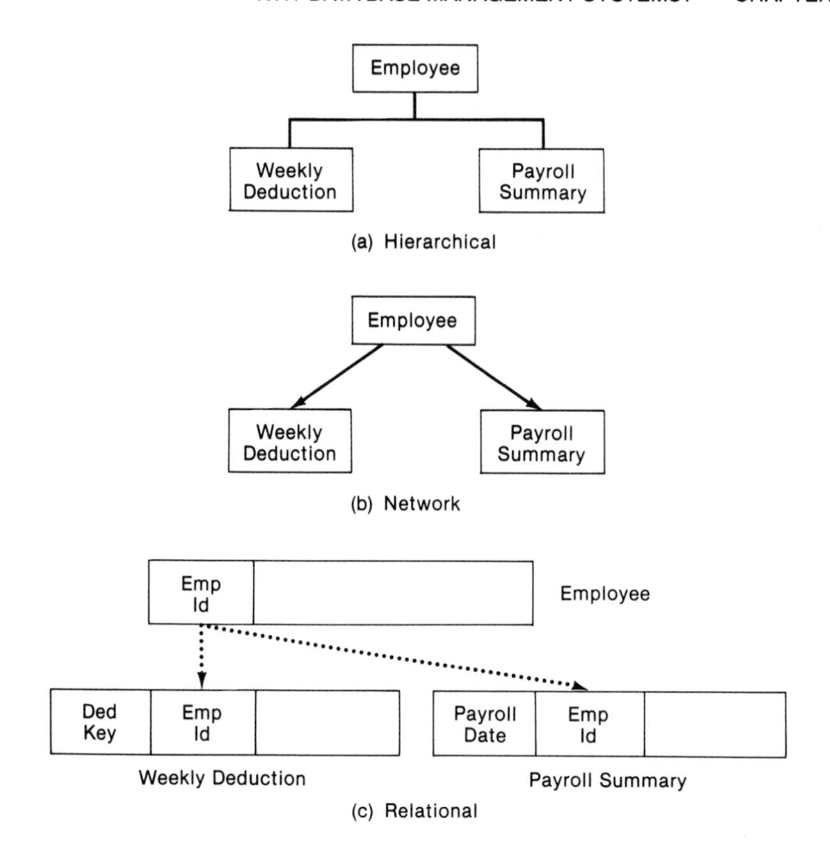

Figure 1.3 Hierarchical, Network, and Relational Versions of an Employee Payroll Data Base

data retrieval, the application program asks the DBMS for a record, specifying the record type desired and optionally the value for a key field(s). The DBMS will then invoke, as required, calls to the appropriate system access method to retrieve the block or page that the data are stored in, and then to locate the required information within the block.

In other words, the application program doesn't know (or care) about any of the physical attributes of the data sets involved, or how the individual data records are arranged within any given data set. That's the job of the DBMS. This is called "data independence," where the application programs using the data are insulated from these concerns by the DBMS. Figure 1.4 illustrates how, in effect, the DBMS sits between the application programs and the actual data sets that make up the data base.

In hierarchical or network systems, periodic tuning adjustments are often necessary to alter linkage paths, to adjust the amount of unused space in the data base, or to simply adjust blocksizes for better utilization of disk space. In making

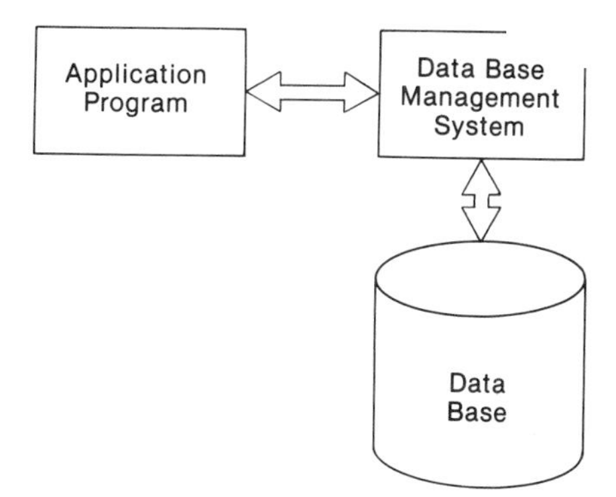

Figure 1.4 Data Base Systems Insulate Application Programs from Details of Physical Storage

such changes, you must typically unload the data base, update the description of the data base to the DBMS, and then reload the data base using the new definition. For relational systems, many tuning changes can be made without requiring this unload/reload process. This greatly increases their flexibility while reducing the "care and feeding" required by the data center. But regardless of the type of DBMS being tuned, application programs run unchanged and unaffected, except through changes in run time as a result of the tuning efforts.

2. Support Complex Data Relationships. Another major advantage of a hierarchical or network DBMS is that fairly complex data structures can be designed which allow various ways to logically view or access the data. This complexity greatly enhances the ability of a designer to put a piece of data in one place, "where it belongs," and provide a path to that data whenever needed.

A relational DBMS provides the same capability for flexibility in data access, but does not incur the burden of maintaining linkage paths. Because of this, users can dynamically define new record types, or add fields to existing record definitions, simultaneously with the data base being updated by application programs. New data fields may then be populated and used immediately as the means of bridging newly established relationships across records in the data base.

3. Sophisticated Data Security Features. Typical system-level security measures use password-based mechanisms to control access to resources (logon passwords, for the execution of programs, or for access to data sets). Normally such mechanisms control access to a resource as a whole. If granted read access to a file, the user may see each record in the file, and every data field it contains.

Data base security mechanisms typically go much further in adding more extensive security features. Access intent of each application program (read, write, update or delete) can be specified by record type. In addition, an application program's view of data records may be controlled to the field level. These features permit you to create complex record structures and definitions and still restrict the access of each program to only those data elements required.

y. Backup/recovery capabilities often distinguish be- and a software package that only claims that name. A true ıg or recording mechanism that captures information on changes within a data base under its control. If, at a later time, a data base ult of a hardware failure, the DBMS would have a utility capable of t by using a backup copy of the data and the log of changes as input. contrast, some products require the user to retain all input data and, if the data base requires recovery, to reprocess all update programs that have executed since the last backup. This is not recovering the data base, but merely reprocessing lost work.

5. Advanced Capabilities. Data base management systems also normally include other advanced features such as sophisticated on-line communications systems and ad hoc reporting capabilities. These extra support packages provide functions and capabilities that greatly enhance the value and usability of a DBMS. However, the ability to provide data independence, to create data complex data structures, to provide security for the access of data, and to provide backup/recovery capability are the primary requirements of a data base management system.

1.3.2 Disadvantages of a DBMS

If data base management systems are as powerful as described, why aren't more in use? Moreover, why have there been failures or disappointments in converting systems to a data base environment?

1. Additional Overhead is Required to Access Data. Think of it this way. Envision an inefficient process that, in its current form, reads tape files. So your management decides to "fix the problem" by putting the application under a data base. After all, data base systems are the answer to everything, aren't they?

But then, of course, there are the needs of the business. So, being faced with a very big job, too few people, and too little time, management makes the only rational (?) decision possible. Your programming staff takes the existing code and converts all of the read and write commands to data base calls.

Would you be surprised to find that this doesn't work?

What has happened? An inefficient process was made worse by imposing the additional overhead of going through a DBMS for I/O.

Let's go back to the basics. A DBMS can support a complex view of data, and provide multiple access paths to data to satisfy program requirements. A good design will take advantage of sophisticated structures to minimize data redundancy, hopefully (and ideally) placing a given data field in only one place, "where it belongs." Then and only then will maintenance requirements be reduced.

In other words, to take advantage of a data base management system's capability, you have to plan. More research, knowledge, and time are required.

Other less obvious problems are:

2. Application Programmers Require More Training to Code Efficient Programs That Will Run Under a DBMS. Data base systems generally have the ability to handle a number of variations in the way data retrieval may be requested. There is the distinct possibility that inadequate training or experience of application programmers will lead to the creation of grossly inefficient data base calls. The same data requirement, stated in a slightly different way in the call to the DBMS, can make a "night and day" difference in performance. Quite often, the problem might not be found until the program reaches production status.

SQL, which is widely recognized as *the* standard language for relational data base management systems, is no exception. It's not uncommon that, in one instance, a data requirement can be satisfied by a few records (or, in relational terms, rows) being retrieved using an index on some data field (or column). With a seemingly trivial change in the SQL parameters, the revised call can require a scan of the entire data base.

3. Rushed Data Analysis Can Result in an Incomplete or Incorrect Data Structure. A later change in structure, forced by changing requirements, can be costly in terms of conversion and testing of existing programs. Hierarchical data base systems are, in particular, more sensitive than network or relational systems toward this kind of problem, and implementing changes costs a great deal.

Relational systems, by their very nature, have a tremendous advantage over the more traditional hierarchical and network DBMSs. They were designed explicitly to support the highest degree possible of flexibility in terms of changing and expanding the internal content of a data base. On the other hand, this flexibility should not be relied on as a crutch to resolve problems that arise as a result of an incomplete analysis of user requirements.

4. Data Must Be Considered a Corporate Resource. The data in a company's data bases no longer belong to one organization alone. True, one organization or application normally has the primary responsibility for creating or updating the data. However, as data base systems mature, more companies are recognizing that there will be an increased need to share data across applications.

5. Data Structures Need to be Fully and Consistently Defined in a Data Dictionary System. In order to share data across application systems, or to simply give end users the ability to identify the location of information they need in order to do their jobs, the internal data content of a company's data bases needs to be documented in a consistent manner.

To satisfy these requirements, most companies that have migrated to a DBMS have also installed a data dictionary system. This software package stores information describing the internal content of a company's data structures. It could describe, for example, the makeup of each field of the payroll data base, including a full definition of each field, and potentially even cover the update rules applicable to that field.

In addition, the capability exists to identify whenever a given field is stored within multiple data records, which in turn may be in two or more data bases. A report of this type is particularly valuable if we need to change, for example, that field's length. The data dictionary can tell not only every different location where the field is stored, but also produce a list of programs that access these data.

While the data dictionary can be very useful, the only problem is that this capability isn't free. All of this information must first be identified or captured, and then entered into the data dictionary system in a consistent manner. That takes time, which is generally in short supply.

An even more significant problem concerns field definitions. If you wish at a later date to identify each record that contains a field representing "zip code," you must insure at the time the field is defined that the field name is entered with a consistent set of rules or standards. Has it already been defined? What was the name chosen? What rules do we use to construct the field name and definition? Without these rules, you can never at a later point come back into the dictionary and hope to find all locations where zip code is used; that is, if you don't know how it was entered, you cannot hope to find it with a query.

This is a *very* significant issue. It takes an enormous amount of time to create, use, and enforce standard naming conventions for the consistent entry of data elements to the data dictionary. Your company must carefully assess the costs and requirements for these standards, and make early and long-term decisions on how to handle this issue. If no uniformity is established at the front end, years later it will be too late to change.

If you think we needn't be prepared for change, remember that zip codes were always supposed to have five digits. Think about how many places that you store zip codes within your systems. In addition, the year 2000 is just around the corner. How many data records contain "year" as part of a date? How many programs will be affected if this field is changed?

These and other issues are reviewed in a subsequent chapter on Data Administration.

1.4 SUMMARY

Data base systems have significant, positive potential for any shop having a sophisticated data environment. They are not, however, a utopia. Data base systems offer many benefits, but require careful planning and direction. Quite often, early top-down support is necessary to insure the allocation of adequate resources, and to approve implementation time frames. Above all, the key to a successful implementation lies in a proper expectation of what the technology can, and cannot, be expected to do.

Data Base Management Systems

Advantages:

- Application programs are removed from knowledge of physical implementation
- Support complex data relationships
- Provide enhanced security mechanisms for access to data
- Provide sophisticated backup/recovery mechanisms
- Normally have advance access capability for on-line and ad hoc access

Disadvantages:

- Require additional system overhead
- Additional training required for application programmers
- Ease of changes to data base content will vary based on the type of DBMS chosen
- Application staff must begin thinking of data as a corporate resource
- Issues regarding identification and meaning of data elements must be dealt with

DISCUSSION QUESTIONS

1. What type of file system does your shop currently use? Would you classify it as a DBMS? Why or why not?
2. What is the future direction of your company in terms of DBMS technology?
3. For new systems to be designed within your company, do applications have a choice of which DBMS to use? If so, how is that decision made?
4. How have design reviews been used within your company to verify the accuracy of a new application system? What problems have you seen? What techniques has your company used to make them more effective?
5. What problems do you see in introducing data base technology for the first time within a company?

REVIEW QUESTIONS

1. What distinguishes the sequential, direct access and indexed file structures from each other? How do they differ from a data base management system?
2. Assume you are in a non-DBMS shop about to convert to data base technology. What problem or concerns are there in converting to the use of a DBMS? What steps should be taken in migrating to the new DBMS?

3. What distinguishes a DBMS from a non-DBMS file structure?
4. Assume that you are in a data processing shop using traditional file structures. Your management is considering implementing and converting to a DBMS. How can a new DBMS be justified? What are the major impacts anticipated to application systems and data center operations after the conversion is complete?
5. When reviewing the requirements for some new application system, how can you determine when data base technology is called for or should be used?
6. Assume that you are in a non-DBMS environment. Would a data dictionary system have any value to your company? Why or why not?

2

Normalization

2.1 INTRODUCTION

The first step in designing a data base is to identify the data requirements of the users. That sounds deceptively simple, and it *can* be, but it usually isn't because users rarely can clearly describe what they need. That's bad enough, but the problems are often compounded quite unintentionally by the data processing (DP) staff. These good folks, normally quite knowledgeable in the current system, know in detail what data exist, and how the existing programs work. However, what "is" rarely matches what *should be*. Often, in-depth knowledge of how the system functions causes tunnel vision in the DP staff as well as the users, and inhibits creative thought.

In short, the design team, composed of user representatives, some members of the DP staff, and the data base/data administration people, isn't able to communicate.

A process called normalization can solve these problems. Using this technique, users describe what their requirements are without the use of the buzz words and terms so common in data processing. The data processing and data administration staff participate in these discussions, serving as advisors in the analysis as well as providing their insight into what the new system might consist of. Afterward, when all data requirements have been identified, the technical staff can then decide on the details for a satisfactory physical data base design.

This analysis technique is not easy for end users to immediately understand and use. However, only a few basic concepts and definitions are required to begin. With the proper introduction and coaching, users can fully participate as members of the design team. Their input is so important to this process that many companies have created full-time user positions to translate requirements into entity/attribute specifications for the technical staff.

How is this technique different from others? The key is in communication. Users can, for the first time, concentrate on something they know and understand—a description of the information they use to perform their jobs—without using any technical terminology. The DP staff also benefits by hearing a description of the users' data requirements in the common language of normalization. At a later point in the design, these data requirements will be translated by the technical staff into a specific list of data elements required for each process (or program).

This technique is often referred to as *entity/relationship modeling.*

2.2 THE LANGUAGE OF NORMALIZATION

To review data and data requirements, the terms entity and attribute must first be defined.

An entity is something about which information is known. It describes or represents something, such as a person, a place, or a thing. Examples of an entity include Employee, Student, Town, and Department.

An attribute provides detailed information about an entity. It helps identify, describe or clarify the entity by providing a value for a quantifiable characteristic or trait. For example, for the Employee entity, appropriate attributes would be the employee's name, address, social security number, and phone number. Each attribute describes the employee by providing descriptive information about that person. For example, John Smith, SSN 111-22-3333, lives at 2505 Hillcrest Drive, and has a phone number of 846-2984.

Those of you with DP background have probably matched the terms *entity* and *attribute* with the DP terms *record* and *field*, respectively. That's exactly what they are. The only difference is that entities represent what you *might* do in terms of record structures; they by no means represent a physical design decision. It's far too early for that. Physical design decisions will follow after you have analyzed the overall impact of data access requirements. The entity/attribute terminology emphasizes the information content and meaning of the information being analyzed. At the same time, these terms help suppress the urge of the technical staff to prematurely jump into physical design decisions.

What, then, is normalization? For now, let's say it's a technique for reviewing the entity/attribute lists to insure that attributes are stored "where they belong." A more comprehensive definition is given later. For example, an Employee entity should contain only attributes that provide information about the employee. If, by accident or oversight, an attribute is incorrectly associated with employee, the normalization process will enable you to identify and correct the error.

In many respects, normalization is simply applied common sense. The end result of the analysis reflects the same type of logic analysts have used for years; this approach merely provides a set of formal rules to avoid mistakes or oversights. We review exactly what these rules are later in this chapter.

2.3 GETTING STARTED

Let's assume that you have formed a design team composed of representatives from the end user, application programming and data base support staff. Your team has agreed to use the normalization approach to data analysis, and has defined and discussed the terms *entity* and *attribute*. In getting started, what is done first?

As a starting point, search through existing reports or forms to identify data requirements. If part of the system is already automated, study the file layouts and the program I/O area definitions. If you have already automated some specific information, it's a pretty good bet that you will need these data in the new or expanded system. Ask the users what *else* they need to track. What other information will they want in six months? You want to keep future requirements in mind, even though the proposed data may not exist for six months or more.

On the other hand, recognize that requirements do change. Most of us who have been around the DP business for any amount of time can recall, for example, a report that's been produced for the last five years and is not used any more. You need to be careful to insure that the data are still relevant to today's (and *tomorrow's*) business.

Try brainstorming to identify data elements. Less experienced end users will find the discussion particularly useful because the DP staff can suggest "if you have these data elements, then you can perform these functions." For example, bill of material data for a shop assembly operation would include information on parts that are on order from suppliers. The anticipated delivery date of parts, along with the cost of each item, could be used to forecast accounts payable information for the finance department. As with any type of brainstorming session, accept all ideas and suggestions without question. Revise and refine later.

You will soon find that a massive volume of notes will be generated, along with the need to get this information organized in some way. The easiest thing to do is to treat these initial entity/attribute lists as hypothetical records and fields, storing the information in the data dictionary system. This provides an easy, mechanical way to store and print the current definitions and to make revisions as necessary as the analysis progresses.

Once these reports are available, review them to verify that an attribute is precisely and accurately defined. All team participants must agree on these definitions; disagreement often identifies the need for additional attributes to be created. Fortunately, the use of a data dictionary for this refinement process greatly reduces the administrative tasks required.

The following illustrates how employee information might appear in a report produced by the data dictionary.

Employee

field name	field description	picture
EMP-CLOCK-NUMBER	The unique identifier for each shop employee	3N
EMP-SOC-SEC-NO	The employee's social security number	9N
EMP-LAST-NAME	The last name of the employee	20A
EMP-FIRST-NAME	The first name of the employee	10A
EMP-MID-INITIAL	The employee's middle initial	1A
EMP-ADDRESS	The address of the employee	
EMP-PHONE-NO	The employee's phone number	7N
EMP-SALARY	The employee's salary	

A review of the previous report raises several questions. Is this the home or office address of the employee? The same question applies to phone number. Salary, on the other hand, has a more basic flaw. The original definition provided is so vague it has no meaning. These reports, used as an inspection tool, make it easy to present the current definition to the design team for review and analysis.

The following report contains modified definitions that resolve the questions in the previous paragraph.

Employee

field name	field description	picture
EMP-CLOCK-NUMBER	The unique identifier for each shop employee	3N
EMP-SOC-SEC-NO	The employee's social security number	9N
EMP-LAST-NAME	The last name of the employee	20A
EMP-FIRST-NAME	The first name of the employee	10A
EMP-MID-INITIAL	The employee's middle initial	1A
EMP-ADDRESS	The employee's office address	20A
EMP-PHONE-NO	The employee's office phone number	7N
EMP-SALARY	The employee's hourly salary	99v99

When an attribute is revised in this phase, there may easily be as many impressions of what it is or what it means as there are people on the design team. Designate in advance a discussion moderator who keeps your discussions from "going into a loop." Agree to spend no more than, perhaps, five minutes discussing or defining each new attribute that is identified. If a definition cannot be agreed upon in that time, the moderator needs to call a "time out." Action parties should be designated, as appropriate, for follow-up discussion, and then you can move on to the next item.

The "Order Entry" Model

Let's review the data environment that serves as the sample problem used to illustrate the data base design process.

Assume that you are part of the design team for a company which sells merchandise through magazine advertising. Customers who desire to place an order call a toll-free telephone number and place an order for the items that they want. This order is entered through an on-line terminal and is later filled and shipped by the stock room. The customer may pay for the purchase by credit card, or pay "collect."

The data model to be created will include data requirements to initiate orders from customer calls, to fill orders from the stock room, to monitor inventory quantities, and to update magazine ad information for the placement of new ads.

As part of the design team, consider the preceding overview of this environment, and try to come up with five or six entities that seem appropriate (for example, Customer). Using the format shown for the preceding dictionary report, try to define at least four attributes for each (as in Customer Name, Address, and Phone Number). Be sure to clearly define the meaning of each attribute that you identify.

When you have completed your list, compare your answer to that of Figure 2.1. This serves as a starting point for the next phase of analysis, as it contains several intentional errors which are resolved as part of the normalization process.

2.4 CLEANING UP THE ENTITY/ATTRIBUTE LIST

Before beginning the normalization process, the initial entity/attribute list must be checked for errors or oversights.

Problem Type 1—Synonyms

A synonym is created when two different names are used for the same information (attribute). If an attribute resides in more than one entity, insure that all entities use the same attribute name.

For example, the following attributes "SUPPLIER-CODE" and "SUPPLIER-ID" are both intended to represent the unique identifier (key field) for Supplier. Because they have been spelled differently, this represents an error.

```
Item                      Supplier
STOCK-NO                  SUPPLIER-ID            <== error
ITEM-COLOR                SUPPLIER-NAME
SUPPLIER-CODE    <==error
```

Using more than one name for the same attribute causes many problems, including a failure to recognize "one to many" (1:M) relationships when the data model is developed.

Item	Description	Domain
Customer		
CUST-TELNO	The customer's telephone number	10N
CUST-NAME	The standard spelling for the customer's name	30AN
CUST-ADDR	The mailing address for the customer	
CUST-CRED	The customer's credit rating	4A
ORDER-NO	An order no placed by this customer	5N
Order		
ORDER-NO	A unique identifier for each order	5N
CUST-NO	The standard customer identifier	10N
CUST-NAME	The standard spelling for the customer's name	30AN
ORD-DATE	The date the order was placed	6N
NUM-DAYS	The number of days since the order was placed	3N
CUST-ADDR	The address to which the order will be shipped	
CRED-CARD	A unique code for the credit card used	4AN
CARD-NAME	The name of the credit card used for purchase	20AN
CR-CD-NO	The credit card number to be billed	
COLL-IND	A flag that indicates a collect "shipment"	1A
STOCK-NO	A description of the item advertised	
Item		
STOCK-NO	The unique identifier for an advertised item	8AN
ITEM-DESCR	A description of the item advertised	20AN
SPORTS-FLAG	A flag setting to denote sports equipment	1A
AUTO-FLAG	A flag setting to denote automotive items	1A
WEIGHT	The shipping weight for the item as sold	
COLOR	The color of the item sold	
PRICE	The selling price of the item as sold	
ORDER-NO	An order no in which this item appears	5N
ISSUE-DATE	The month and year identifying a specific issue	8AN
Supplier		
SUPP-CODE	A unique identifier for a supplier of items	6N
SUPP-NAME	The standard spelling for the supplier	20AN
SUPP-ADDR	The supplier's address for orders to be placed	
STOCK-NO	The unique identifier for an advertised item	
Magazine		
MAG-CODE	A unique identifier for a publication with ads	4A
MAG-NAME	The standard spelling for a publication	20AN
MAG-ADDR	The mailing address for placing ads	
MAG-TELNO	The telephone contact number for ad information	
ISSUE-DATE	The month and year identifying a specific issue	8AN

Figure 2.1 The Initial Entity/Attribute List

```
Item                 Supplier
STOCK-NO             SUPPLIER-ID           <==
ITEM-COLOR           SUPPLIER-NAME
SUPPLIER-ID    <== correction
```

Problem Type 2—Homonyms

A homonym is the opposite of a synonym. Just as you can't use different names for the same attribute, you can't use the same name for different attributes. For example, the attribute "COMPANY-NAME" under the Customer entity would mean something different from "COMPANY-NAME" under Supplier. This is another error in data definition.

```
Customer
COMPANY-NAME        The name of the customer           <== error
Supplier
COMPANY-NAME        The name of the supplier           <== error
```

One or both of these attribute designators would need to be changed to reflect their differences.

```
Customer
CUSTOMER-NAME       The name of the customer           <==correction
Supplier
SUPPLIER-NAME       The name of the supplier           <==correction
```

Problem Type 3—Redundant Information

This problem, where the same information is stored in two different forms or ways, is a bit harder to spot. One way to check for it is to consider if the value of a particular attribute is known or is derivable through the other attributes defined. For example, storing an employee's age is redundant information when the birth date is also stored as an attribute under employee.

```
Employee
EMP-AGE          The age of the employee        <== error
BIRTH-DATE       The employee's birth date      <== error
```

In this example, removing EMP-AGE will eliminate the error condition.

Problem Type 4—Mutually Exclusive Data

Mutually exclusive data exists when attributes occur whose values, perhaps expressed as "yes/no" indicators, cannot all be true for any single entity. As an example, consider proposed attributes of "MARRIED" and "SINGLE" in an Employee entity.

```
Employee
MARRIED     A flag set if the employee is married   <==error
SINGLE      A flag set if the employee is single    <==error
```

Quite often errors of this type represent values of a larger category. Whenever possible, resolve the error by creating the larger categorical attribute. In this case, these two elements should be combined into a single attribute of "MARITAL-STATUS" which would have a value of either M (married) or S (single).

```
Employee
MARITAL-STATUS      An indicator of the employee's marital status
```

Study Figure 2.1 and see what suggestions you would make to correct any discrepancies as defined earlier. When you're finished, compare your list to the comments in Figure 2.2, and the revised entity/attribute list shown in Figure 2.3.

Problem Type 1—Synonyms
Note that the CUST-NO in Order and CUST-TELNO in Customer refer to the same field, but with two names. CUST-NO was therefore changed to CUST-TELNO.

Problem Type 2—Homonyms
In this case, note that CUST-ADDR appears in both Customer and Order, yet refers to different data elements. The one in ORDER was changed to SHIP-ADDR.

Problem Type 3—Redundant Information
In Order, NUM-DAYS was created to indicate the number of days since the order was placed. This is used to track the length of time since the order was created, and help identify those needing special attention or handling.
The same result is possible by simply using the ORD-DATE information to derive this information. Therefore, NUM-DAYS can simply be eliminated.

Problem Type 4—Mutually Exclusive Data
In Order, the COLL-IND and CRED-CARD elements reflect two different pieces of information which, for any single instance, both cannot be true. If we give a special value to CRED-CARD for collect shipments, we can eliminate the COLL-IND attribute completely.

In a different example, in Item, the SPORTS-FLAG and AUTO-FLAG elements cannot both be true for one item. This can be resolved by creating an ITEM-TYPE flag field whose value will identify which classification is assigned to that item.

Figure 2.2. Revisions to the Initial Entity/Attribute List

Item	Description	Domain
Customer		
CUST-TELNO	The customer's telephone number	10N
CUST-NAME	The standard spelling for the customer's name	30AN
CUST-ADDR	The mailing address for the customer	
CUST-CRED	The customer's credit rating	4A
ORDER-NO	A unique identifier for each order	5N
Order		
ORDER-NO	A unique identifier for each order	5N
CUST-TELNO	The customer's telephone number	10N
CUST-NAME	The standard spelling for the customer's name	30AN
ORD-DATE	The date the order was placed	6N
SHIP-ADDR	The address to which the order will be shipped	
CRED-CARD	A unique code for the credit card used	4AN
CARD-NAME	The name of the credit card used for purchase	20AN
CR-CD-NO	The credit card number to be billed	
STOCK-NO	The unique identifier for an advertised item	
Item		
STOCK-NO	The unique identifier for an advertised item	8AN
ITEM-DESCR	A description of the item advertised	20AN
ITEM-TYPE	A code denoting a specific classification type	6AN
WEIGHT	The shipping weight for the item as sold	
COLOR	The color of the item sold	
PRICE	The selling price of the item as sold	
ORDER-NO	A unique identifier for each order	5N
ISSUE-DATE	The month and year identifying a specific issue	8AN
Supplier		
SUPP-CODE	A unique identifier for a supplier of items	6N
SUPP-NAME	The standard spelling for the supplier	20AN
SUPP-ADDR	The supplier's address for orders to be placed	
STOCK-NO	The unique identifier for an advertised item	
Magazine		
MAG-CODE	A unique identifier for a publication with ads	4A
MAG-NAME	The standard spelling for a publication	20AN
MAG-ADDR	The mailing address for placing ads	
MAG-TELNO	The telephone contact number for ad information	
ISSUE-DATE	The month and year identifying a specific issue	8AN

Figure 2.3 The Revised Entity/Attribute List

2.5 NORMALIZATION

Now that a clean data model exists in which an attribute has one and only one name as well as a unique meaning, the normalization process can begin.

More formally stated, normalization is the process of analyzing the dependencies of attributes within entities. Attributes for each entity are checked consecutively against three sets of rules, making adjustments when necessary to put the entity in first, second, and finally third normal form. These rules are reviewed in detail in the next section, and provide a procedural way to make sure attributes are placed "where they belong."

Based on mathematical theory, normalization is the basis for relational data base systems; in practice, it is simply applied common sense. It means, for example, that you only put into an Employee entity (record) attributes (or fields) that describe the employee. If you should find an attribute that describes something else, put it wherever it belongs.

```
Employee
EMP-ID
DEDUCTION-AMOUNT    <== error
```

In this example, DEDUCTION-AMOUNT should not be associated with Employee, because it doesn't provide information about the employee as a person. Instead, it provides additional detail about a payroll deduction for that employee. A Payroll Deduction entity would be created, if necessary, and DEDUCTION-AMOUNT moved to it.

```
Employee                 PAYROLL-DEDUCTION
EMP-ID                   EMP-ID
                         PAYROLL-DATE
                         DEDUCTION-AMOUNT
```

Practical issues, typically related to performance, may later require you to use tricks of one kind or another when setting up physical structures. But you *aren't there yet*! Place your data in third normal form and do all subsequent analysis with that view of data. Later, when all requirements are known, and after considering usage requirements, decisions will be made regarding physical structures. If at that time nonthird normal structures are needed for reasons of efficiency, fine. For now, however, it is far too early to make judgments or decisions related to physical design.

The following procedures get the data model into, successively, first, second, and third normal forms. Keep in mind two points. First, the process works, and easily creates third normal form entities. Secondly, after you have done several of these, the result appears as common sense to you, and you will tend to "think third normal" and set up structures in this form initially. So, although the process appears to be tedious, in practice it really isn't.

2.5.1 First Normal Form

In his book *An Introduction to Database Systems*, C. J. Date gives the definition for first normal form as: "A relation *R* is in first normal form (1NF) if and only if all underlying domains contain atomic values only."[1] It is important to note that, in Date's discussion of this topic, it is implied that a relation has a primary key associated with it.

I prefer to rephrase this definition. An entity is in first normal form if it meets the following two criteria:

1. **All entities must have a key, composed of a combination of one or more attributes which uniquely identify one occurrence of the entity**; and
2. **For any single occurrence of an entity, each attribute must have one and only one value.**

Requirement 1—Keys to Create Uniqueness

For a specific value for the key attribute(s), there can be only one occurrence of the entity. For example, the attribute PART-NUMBER identifies one unique Part. Of course, the key should be unambiguous; there is no question or confusion on what PART-NUMBER signifies, and the key should be unchanging in value with time. If necessary, an attribute must be created to provide this key identifier.

There may, in fact, be more than one way within an entity to obtain uniqueness. In the Customer entity, either the CUST-NAME or CUST-TELNO identifies one specific customer. But, since lengthy names create problems when used as key fields, they are normally not a practical choice. The CUST-TELNO attribute provides uniqueness and is easier to use.

If you do find two candidates for keys, perhaps one can be eliminated. In some cases, however, both may be needed. For example, a Student entity might have candidate keys of STUDENT-ID and STUDENT-SSN. The social security number may be required for permanent transcript records as well as for other reasons, but STUDENT-ID might be used for data entry because of its ease of use in the keying and verification process of the input data. In this case, STUDENT-ID would be considered the primary key, and the STUDENT-SSN a secondary key.

Review the revised entity/attribute list in Figure 2.3 and try to identify keys for each entity. Then refer to Figure 2.4 for the "school solution," in which the key attributes are shown with an "**" indicator.

Requirement 2—Attributes Only Have One Value

The second requirement for first normal form is often stated as "an entity must have no repeating groups."

---

[1] C.J. Date, *An Introduction To Database Systems*, (Reading, Massachussetts, Addison-Wesley, 1985), p. 367.

Item	Description	Domain
Customer		
**CUST-TELNO	The customer's telephone number	10N
CUST-NAME	The standard spelling for the customer's name	30AN
CUST-ADDR	The mailing address for the customer	
CUST-CRED	The customer's credit rating	4A
ORDER-NO	A unique identifier for each order	5N
Order		
**ORDER-NO	A unique identifier for each order	5N
CUST-TELNO	The customer's telephone number	10N
CUST-NAME	The standard spelling for the customer's name	30AN
ORD-DATE	The date the order was placed	6N
SHIP-ADDR	The address to which the order will be shipped	
CRED-CARD	A unique code for the credit card used	4AN
CARD-NAME	The name of the credit card used for purchase	20AN
CR-CD-NO	The credit card number to be billed	
STOCK-NO	The unique identifier for an advertised item	
Item		
**STOCK-NO	The unique identifier for an advertised item	8AN
ITEM-DESCR	A description of the item advertised	20AN
ITEM-TYPE	A code denoting a specific classification type	6AN
WEIGHT	The shipping weight for the item as sold	
COLOR	The color of the item sold	
PRICE	The selling price of the item as sold	
ORDER-NO	An order no in which this item appears	5N
ISSUE-DATE	The month and year of a specific issue	8AN
Supplier		
**SUPP-CODE	A unique identifier for a supplier of items	6N
SUPP-NAME	The standard spelling for the supplier	20AN
SUPP-ADDR	The supplier's address for orders to be placed	
STOCK-NO	The unique identifier for an advertised item	
Magazine		
**MAG-CODE	A unique identifier for a publication with ads	4A
MAG-NAME	The standard spelling for a publication	20AN
MAG-ADDR	The mailing address for placing ads	
MAG-TELNO	The telephone contact number for ad information	
ISSUE-DATE	The month and year identifying a specific issue	8AN

Figure 2.4 The Revised Entity/Attribute List with Keys

To understand what a repeating group is, consider the ISSUE-DATE attribute within Magazine in Figure 2.3. For a given magazine, the attribute ISSUE-DATE possesses multiple values, since a magazine publishes new issues on a regular basis. ISSUE-DATE, therefore, is a repeating group. (Note that a repeating group is analogous to an "OCCURS" clause in a Cobol I/O area.)

As a second example, the ORDER-NO attribute under Item is also a repeating group, because any individual item is sold to many customers, each with separate order numbers. You cannot store as a single value the entire set of order numbers for that item.

```
Magazine                            Item    (from Figure 2.3)
MAG-CODE                            STOCK-NO
MAG-NAME                            ITEM-DESCR
MAG-ADDR                            ITEM-TYPE
MAG-TELNO                           WEIGHT
ISSUE-DATE   <== error              COLOR
                                    PRICE
                                    ORDER-NO   <== error
```

In contrast, consider CUST-TELNO in the Order entity. For any given order, there is only one value for CUST-TELNO. CUST-TELNO, therefore, is not a repeating group.

Whenever repeating groups occur, the repeating attribute must be removed and placed "where it belongs", under the entity that it describes. To see what that really means, let's look at a simple example. Here, Department has the repeating attribute EMP-NUMBER that is also shown within Employee.

```
Department                Employee
DEPT-NO                   EMP-NUMBER
EMP-NUMBER   <==error
```

To correct the error, perform the following:

Step 1. The repeating attribute must be removed from the entity with which it is associated, after assuring the attribute exists somewhere in the data model in first normal form.

You can't just throw the attribute away. Therefore, first assure yourself that it exists "where it belongs"; if necessary, create a new entity in first normal form with which to associate it. Consider what it describes, and create an appropriate entity. Finally, once a location exists for the attribute, the repeating attribute can be removed from where it appears.

In the Department/Employee example, after verifying that EMP-NUMBER is defined correctly under Employee, EMP-NUMBER can be removed from Department.

```
Department               Employee
DEPT-NO                  EMP-NUMBER   <== correction
```

Step 2. Next, study the relationship of where the repeating attribute came FROM and where the attribute went TO. Determine if the from-to relationship is one to many (1:M) or many to many (M:M).

In this example, the "from" entity is Department, and the "to" entity is Employee. To determine if the from-to relationship is 1:M or M:M, ask "for one department, are there one, or many, employees?" Then repeat the question in reverse by asking "for any one employee, are there one, or many, departments?" In this case, one department has many employees, but an employee has only one department. Therefore, the relationship is 1:M.

When the answer is 1:M, this is an acceptable relationship and no further adjustments are necessary. If, on the other hand, the answer is M:M, then one final adjustment is necessary, and you need to proceed to Step 3.

Before going any further, let's review the first two steps by correcting the repeating attributes ISSUE-DATE in Magazine and ORDER-NO in Item.

Does ISSUE-DATE exist correctly (in first normal form) in another attribute? The answer is no. Where does it belong, or what does it describe? After reading our definition, it would seem logical to create a new entity call Magazine Edition, with MAG-CODE and ISSUE-DATE as its key.

```
Magazine                 Magazine Edition
MAG-CODE                 MAG-CODE
MAG-NAME                 ISSUE-DATE   <==correction
MAG-ADDR
MAG-TELNO
```

What is the relationship between the "from" entity (Magazine) and the "to" entity (Magazine Edition)?

- Does one magazine have one or many magazine editions? (many)
- Does a magazine edition refer to one or many magazines?(one)

Therefore, the relationship between Magazine and Magazine Edition is 1:M and requires no further adjustments.

Now look at ORDER-NO. Following the same preceding steps, ask "does ORDER-NO exist correctly in first normal form in some other entity." The answer is "yes" (as the key of Order).

What, then, is the relationship between the "from" entity (Item) and the "to" entity (Order)?

- One item will appear on one or many orders? (many)
- One order contains one or many kinds of items? (many)

This presents a problem. The M:M relationship between Item and Order gives nowhere to store information about one item on a particular order—a lot of nice-to-know information, such as the quantity of items on that order, or the price of the items. Commonly referred to as "intersection data," this information could not exist if an M:M relationship were implemented.

```
Item          <<------------------------->>        Order
STOCK-NO            quantity ordered?              ORDER-NO

ITEM-DESCR          price paid?                    CUST-NO
```

When an M:M relationship is discovered, a third set of adjustments is necessary to correct the error.

Step 3. Convert each M:M relationship to two 1:M relationships by creating a new derived relation.

An M:M relationship poses a basic design problem because there is no place to store the attributes common to the two entities involved; that is, attributes which should lie at the intersection of the two entities. To solve this problem, create a new entity representing this intersection. This transforms the M:M relationship into two 1:M relationships, where the new entity provides the storage location for common information.

In the ORDER-NO example, create a new relationship called Item Ordered, which represents items on order. Create the key of the new relation automatically by concatenating the keys of the two original entities (STOCK-NO and ORDER-NO). Other attributes can then be added which are common to a particular item and order (the number required, unit price, and so on).

```
Item Ordered
ORDER-NO
STOCK-NO
NUM-REQD
UNIT-PRICE
```

This creates the adjustments necessary to correct an M:M error condition.

Study the revised list in Figure 2.4 and make a list of any adjustments you feel are necessary to put the entity/attribute list in first normal form. When you are finished, compare your solution to that shown in Figure 2.5.

2.5.2 Second Normal Form

Mr. Date's definition for second normal form is: "A relation R is in second normal form (2NF) if and only if it is in 1NF and every non-key attribute is fully dependent on the primary key."[2]

---

[2] C.J. Date, *An Introduction To Database Systems*, (Reading, Massachussetts, Addison-Wesley, 1985), p. 370.

```
Customer
 **CUST-TELNO
   CUST-NAME
   CUST-ADDR
   CUST-CRED

Order
 **ORDER-NO
   CUST-TELNO
   CUST-NAME
   ORD-DATE
   SHIP-ADDR
   CRED-CARD
   CARD-NAME
   CR-CD-NO

Item
 **STOCK-NO
   ITEM-DESCR
   ITEM-TYPE
   WEIGHT
   COLOR
   PRICE

Supplier
 **SUPP-CODE
   SUPP-NAME
   SUPP-ADDR

Magazine
 **MAG-CODE
   MAG-NAME
   MAG-ADDR
   MAG-TELNO

Item Ordered (Order-Item)
 **ORDER-NO
 **STOCK-NO
   NUM-REQD
   UNIT-PRICE

Price List (Supplier-Item)
 **SUPP-CODE
 **STOCK-NO
   SUPP-NAME
   ITEM-PRICE
   PRICE-DATE
   QUAL-ACCEPT
   ITEM-DESCR

Magazine Edition
 **MAG-CODE
 **ISSUE-DATE
   MAG-NAME

Advertised Item (Item-Mag Edition)
 **MAG-CODE
 **ISSUE-DATE
 **STOCK-NO
   PAGE-NO
   ADVER-PRICE

Corrections:
Order has STOCK-NO as a repeating group—M:M—created Item Ordered.
Item has ORDER-NO as a repeating group—Item Ordered already created.
Item has ISSUE-DATE as a repeating group—M:M—created Advertised
Item.
Supplier has STOCK-NO as a repeating group—M:M—created Price List.
Magazine has ISSUE-DATE as a repeating group—M:M—created Magazine
Edition.
```

Figure 2.5 The First Normal Form Solution—Order-Entry System

I prefer a slight modification by stating the additional requirement to move to second normal form.

For second normal form, each non-key attribute must depend on the key and all parts of the key.

If the value of an attribute can be determined only by knowing part of the entity's key, there is a violation of second normal form.

For example, the Magazine Edition entity in Figure 2.5 contains the attribute MAG-NAME. This is a violation of second normal form, because only part of the key (MAG-CODE) is needed to determine a value for MAG-NAME. The value for MAG-NAME does not depend in any way on ISSUE-DATE, the other component of Magazine Edition's key.

Any adjustments for second normal form violations follow the same steps covered for 1NF errors. First, insure that the attribute in error exists correctly in 1NF. In this example, MAG-NAME already appears within the Magazine entity. Next, check the relationship between the entity in error (Magazine Edition) and the one to which the attribute is correctly associated (Magazine). In this example, it has a 1:M relationship (one magazine has many magazine editions). The 1:M relationship is acceptable, and no further adjustments are necessary. If this last check *had* revealed an M:M relationship, a derived entity would be created to hold the intersection data.

Almost all violations of second normal form are found in entities having more than one attribute concatenated to form a key. It seems almost trivial to state that, for entities with a single key field, nonkey attributes must rely on that key. (For example, the entity Customer should have only attributes which tell us something about that customer.) If, when the entity/attribute list was created, keys were immediately identified and checks made to insure that only attributes dependent on that key were associated with the entity, you need check only entities having multiple attributes for keys at this point. If that initial check wasn't done, you should check everything, including entities with single attributes for keys.

Take a look at the first normal form solution in Figure 2.5 and determine what adjustments are necessary to go to second normal form. When you're finished, check your solution with that in Figure 2.6.

2.5.3 Third Normal Form

Finally, Mr. Date gives a definition for third normal form as: "A relation *R* is in third normal form (3NF) if and only if it is in 2NF and every nonkey attribute is nontransitively dependent on the primary key."[3]

---

[3] C.J. Date, *An Introduction To Database Systems*, (Reading, Massachussetts, Addison-Wesley, 1985), p. 373.

```
Customer
 **CUST-TELNO
   CUST-NAME
   CUST-ADDR
   CUST-CRED

Order
 **ORDER-NO
   CUST-TELNO
   CUST-NAME
   ORD-DATE
   SHIP-ADDR
   CRED-CARD
   CARD-NAME
   CR-CD-NO

Item
 **STOCK-NO
   ITEM-DESCR
   ITEM-TYPE
   WEIGHT
   COLOR
   PRICE

Supplier
 **SUPP-CODE
   SUPP-NAME
   SUPP-ADDR

Magazine
 **MAG-CODE
   MAG-NAME
   MAG-ADDR
   MAG-TELNO

Item Ordered (Order-Item)
 **ORDER-NO
 **STOCK-NO
   NUM-REQD
   UNIT-PRICE

Price List (Supplier-Item)
 **SUPP-CODE
 **STOCK-NO
   ITEM-PRICE
   PRICE-DATE
   QUAL-ACCEPT

Magazine Edition
 **MAG-CODE
 **ISSUE-DATE

Advertised Item (Item-Mag Edition)
 **MAG-CODE
 **ISSUE-DATE
 **STOCK-NO
   PAGE-NO
   ADVER-PRICE

Corrections:
SUPP-NAME, in Price List, relates only to SUPP-CODE; it was removed.
ITEM-DESCR, in Price List, relates only to STOCK-NO; it was removed.
MAG-NAME, in Magazine Edition, relates only to MAG-CODE; it was re-
moved.
```

Figure 2.6 The Second Normal Form Solution—Order-Entry System

Once again I prefer to phrase the requirement differently, adding the following to 2NF criteria:

A nonkey attribute must not depend on any other nonkey attribute.

If a nonkey attribute's value can be obtained simply by knowing the value of another nonkey attribute, you are not in third normal form.

For example, in the Order entity, you see the nonkey attributes CRED-CARD and CARD-NAME. There is an obvious dependency between the credit card code and the card name; if you know the value of the card number, you can determine the card name. A violation of third normal form exists, and CARD-NAME must be removed.

How do we make this adjustment? Once again, repeat the steps covered under first normal form adjustments. Make sure the proper entity exists, then check for 1:M versus M:M relationships. In this case, you would need to create a new entity called Credit Card, with CRED-CARD as a key and CARD-NAME as a nonkey attribute.

Start from the second normal form solution in Figure 2.6 and see what other adjustments are necessary to get to third normal form; then check your solution against that shown in Figure 2.7.

By the way, try this shortcut expression for the rules of normalization. For an entity to be in third normal form, each nonkey attribute must relate to "the key, the whole key, and nothing but the key, so help me Ted Codd."

The entity/attribute list is now in third normal form, and each attribute is "where it belongs." Nonkey attributes appear only once, in the entity which they describe. Attributes in key fields can (and do) appear in several related entities. These repeated occurrences establish the various one to many relationships that exist across entities. This redundancy is required for a relational DBMS, which provides data linkage based on data content only. For example, those entities related to Item (Item Ordered, Price List, and so on) must all have Item's key, STOCK-NO, stored in them to support linkage by STOCK-NO. In a hierarchical or network data base system, the apparent redundancy of keys will not necessarily be carried forward in physical implementation.

It's important to keep in mind that the final data base structure hasn't been created yet. The data model is just a logical view of data elements and how they relate to each other. The final decisions on data base layout and record structure will come later, after considering the results of how the data will be accessed; this is covered in the next chapter.

For now, there is one final step in this phase of the analysis, which clarifies your solution by drawing a picture of the data relationships that have been created.

```
Customer                     Item Ordered (Order-Item)
 **CUST-TELNO                 **ORDER-NO
   CUST-NAME                  **STOCK-NO
   CUST-ADDR                    NUM-REQD
   CUST-CRED                    UNIT-PRICE

Order                        Price List (Supplier-Item)
 **ORDER-NO                   **SUPP-CODE
   CUST-TELNO                 **STOCK-NO
   ORD-DATE                     ITEM-PRICE
   SHIP-ADDR                    PRICE-DATE
   CRED-CARD                    QUAL-ACCEPT
   CR-CD-NO

Item                         Magazine Edition
 **STOCK-NO                   **MAG-CODE
   ITEM-DESCR                 **ISSUE-DATE
   ITEM-TYPE
   WEIGHT
   COLOR
   PRICE

Supplier                     Advertised Item (Item-Mag Edition)
 **SUPP-CODE                  **MAG-CODE
   SUPP-NAME                  **ISSUE-DATE
   SUPP-ADDR                  **STOCK-NO
                                PAGE-NO
                                ADVER-PRICE

Magazine                     Credit Card
 **MAG-CODE                   **CRED-CARD
   MAG-NAME                     CARD-NAME
   MAG-ADDR
   MAG-TELNO

Corrections:
CUST-NAME, in Order, relates to CUST-TELNO; it was removed.
CARD-NAME, in Order, relates to CRED-CARD; it was removed.
```

Figure 2.7 The Third Normal Form Solution—Order-Entry System

2.6 THE DATA MODEL

The best way to view the results of this analysis is to draw a pictorial representation of the third normal form data, usually called a data model or a relational view. In this type of diagram, each entity is represented by a box, which is labeled with the entity's name. The "related" boxes are then connected with an arrow, such as:

In words, there is a one-to-many relationship between Customer and Order; or, for each Customer, there are many Orders.

This is a fairly easy diagram to draw. Begin by simply drawing and labeling a box for each entity. Then, for each entity, ask "Does the key of this entity exist entirely within another entity?" If so, connect them with an <----->> arrow.

To check your solution, insure that "the key of one appears in the many." In other words, the key of the entity with the single arrow appears within the entity on the double-arrowed side.

Draw the data model for the third normal solution shown in Figure 2.7. Compare your solution to that of Figure 2.8.

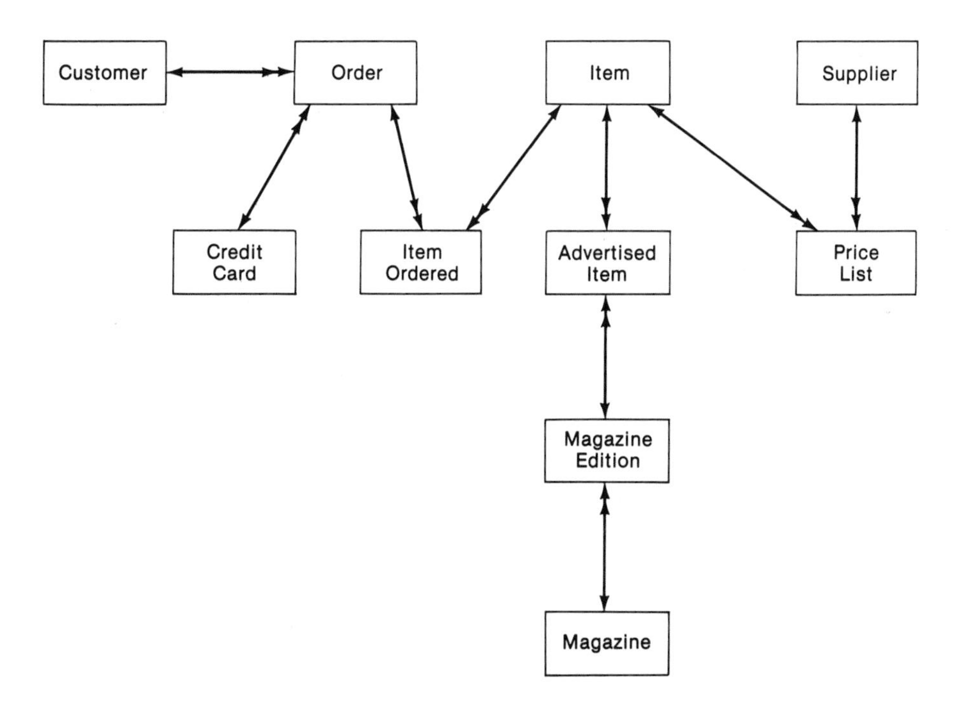

Figure 2.8 The Relational View (Data Model)

Use these hints to check the accuracy of your data model.

1. Use the "key of one..." rule previously stated when drawing the 1:M arrows, and draw them *only* if this relationship exists. Then, and only then, look at the diagram logically and see if it makes sense. For example, in a similar problem you might see that Item should be related to an Item Backordered entity, but you have not drawn a 1:M arrow. This suggests that STOCK-NO should have been placed in Item Backordered, but wasn't. Just add it, and draw the 1:M connection.
2. You should never have a data model showing an M:M relationship. If developed this way, you would have no place to store the intersection data between these two elements.
3. A 1:1 relationship exists between two entities if the key of the first appears totally in the second *and* the key of the second also appears totally in the first.

```
Patient                      Hospital Bed
**PATIENT-NO                 **ROOM-NO
  ROOM-NO                    **BED-NO
  BED-NO                       PATIENT NO
```

   This condition occurs on occasion, but is rare. If you see one in the data model, check the data carefully. Sometimes two entities are defined through oversight that refer to the same thing; if so, the two entities should be combined into one.
4. If two different entities are developed that happen to have the same key field(s), you have made an error. If these two entities refer to the same thing, combine them (as stated above). If, on the other hand, they refer to two distinctly different elements, change the key of one (or both) to reflect how they differ from one another.

Keep in mind that the information content of the data model is normally volatile. As the later stages of the design process are completed, new data requirements require continual modification to the 3NF definitions and the data model itself. You'll find that following this technique will provide the maximum flexibility to your data base design, regardless of the type of DBMS chosen.

Chapter 8 contains a detailed review of the complete normalization, usage analysis, and physical data base design steps for a much more complex data model. It may be useful to refer to this material as you review subsequent chapters for illustrations about how to handle more sophisticated data relationships and requirements.

DISCUSSION QUESTIONS

1. Define the criteria for first, second and third normal forms.
2. Have you used the normalization technique for the analysis of non-DBMS application systems? How successful was it?
3. Assume you are part of a system development team about to begin the analysis of a new system. How would you explain the following terms or concepts to participants in a meeting:
   (a) the meaning of entities and attributes;
   (b) the normalization approach;
   (c) the meaning of the data model.
4. Propose entities that might be appropriate for each of the following environments: a payroll system, a part inventory system, a mail-order supply house, and a doctor's office.
5. Propose attributes that would be appropriate for each of the following entities: Employee, Daily Time Record, Weekly Payroll Summary, Weekly Deduction, and Quarterly Payroll Summary.
6. Have you ever participated in the design of a system using this approach? How successful was it? What was the key to the success (or failure)?
7. How applicable is the normalization approach for use in designing micro-based systems? What problems do you envision in their use of this technique? How could these problems be handled?
8. What should be done if some performance problems are indicated in the data model?
9. Should the data model have any meaning to the user community?
10. What can be done to avoid "paralysis by analysis"?

REVIEW PROBLEMS

The following information describes various data environments that might be implemented under a DBMS. For each, derive the third-normal form entity/attribute list, and draw the corresponding data model. (Note that usage requirements for each will be given at the end of Chapter 3.)

1. An inventory system for goods sold. This is to include information on:
   (a) items in inventory, including the item description, selling price, size, color, quantity currently on hand, and their storage location in the warehouse.
   (b) the various suppliers from whom we can purchase items to be resold. This should include the name and address of the supplier, the name and phone number of our purchasing contact, the items available from that company, and the cost of each item.
   (c) information on each of our customers, including their name, address, and phone number. In addition, include information on items purchased, including the quantity of each and the date of the purchase.
2. A library system. This should include information on:
   (a) books and magazines available, including the title, author(s), quantity on hand, the file reference number, and the major subject category that applies to each.

- **(b)** for each author, the author's name, address, and occupation.
- **(c)** library patrons, including their names, addresses, and phone numbers.
- **(d)** material currently out on loan, including the patron who has the item checked out, with the date that it is due to be returned.

3. A project tracking system of employees and projects for a company that does custom design work. This is to include information on:

- **(a)** a table of possible skills of employees that are required to meet customer's design requirements. This is to include a skill code and a description of that skill.
- **(b)** the employee's name, address, department, and the skills that he or she possesses.
- **(c)** the projects currently active within the company, with a project number, description, and the skills required for the project. For each skill requirement, include the estimated hours needed for that skill, as well as the total hours worked, by skill, for each employee.

4. A magazine publishing house. This is to include information on:

- **(a)** each magazine published, with its name, publication interval, subscription price, and newsstand price.
- **(b)** subscribers for each magazine, including their names, addresses, and subscription renewal dates.
- **(c)** advertisers for each magazine issue, including their names and addresses, and the selling price of each ad.

5. A wholesale mail order house. This is to include information on:

- **(a)** the various magazines in which we have advertised.
- **(b)** the various types of equipment advertised for sale.
- **(c)** for each ad placed, the magazine and issue that the ad was placed in, with the page number and cost of each ad. This is to include the equipment and advertised price of each line item in each ad.

3

Usage Path Analysis

3.1 THE REQUIREMENT FOR USAGE ANALYSIS

The previous chapter reviews the normalization of entities and attributes, ending by creating a pictorial sketch of the data model illustrating all of the relationships between or across these data elements.

Is this information sufficient to begin making decisions about how to store records in a data base? To find out, let's consider design implications for each of the three major types of data base systems—hierarchical, network, and relational.

3.1.1 Hierarchical Structures

A hierarchical data base management system, such as IBM's IMS, has the appearance of a top-down organization chart. Each record type (or, in IMS terms, each segment) joins one and only one record or segment at the next highest level in the structure. Normally, the data base is entered by accessing the record (segment) at the top of the structure. The DBMS then follows the parent-child relationships or linkages which it maintains to get to the required data at a lower level in the hierarchy. This type of access (always entering at the top, or root, segment) restricts flexibility. For that reason, additional options are available within IMS to provide the capability needed by applications. These options are discussed in the chapter on IMS.

Well-designed IMS data bases can provide a relatively high level of performance; that is, they can retrieve the requested data with a minimum of I/O. In large part, this is due to the way IMS handles the storage of data segments. Related data elements are, as far as possible, placed physically together on storage.

To illustrate this, take the example of a data base containing information on customers of an equipment maintenance service. The data base contains information on customers, equipment which is warranted for service, historical information of service requests issued, and customer bills issued. Figure 3.1 shows the hierarchical structure as described to the DBMS, while Figure 3.2 illustrates three typical data base records in this data base. Finally, Figure 3.3 shows how IMS will automatically try to cluster these segments on disk.

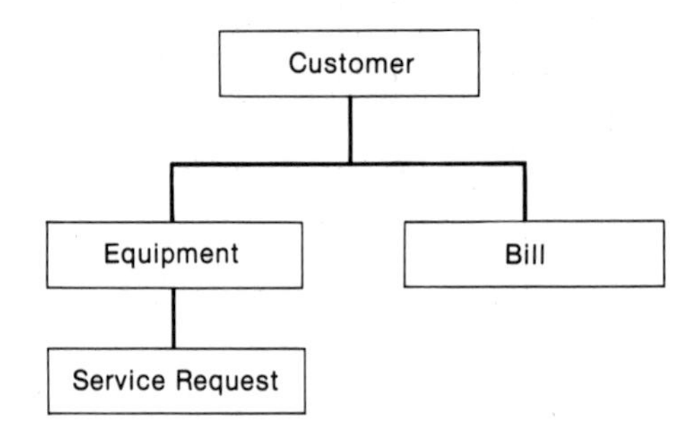

Figure 3.1 An Equipment Maintenance Data Base

As a result, an I/O done in response to an application request for data often retrieves data that will satisfy subsequent application requests "free of charge" (or at least free of I/O). The application program obtains the data it needs with minimal overhead, and performance is high.

In effect, then, to move from the data model created in the previous design phase to an IMS data base, you must know the sequence in which data will be accessed. For the Customer Service data base, the physical design needs to identify and balance several requirements. Access from Customer to Equipment and Service Request records must be provided on line, as well as access from Customer to Billing records during nightly batch processing. However, in the rush to complete the design phase of a data base project and begin coding, the temptation is to shortcut this phase by performing incomplete usage analysis, or skipping the analysis altogether.

Can a data base be designed without doing usage analysis? Certainly, but the results may not be worth much in terms of performance, or even general usability. Usage analysis is important for *any* DBMS, but it's critical for IMS.

3.1.2 Network Structures

A network system, such as the heart of Cullinet's IDMS/R, is similar to a hierarchical structure except that a subordinate record may be associated with any

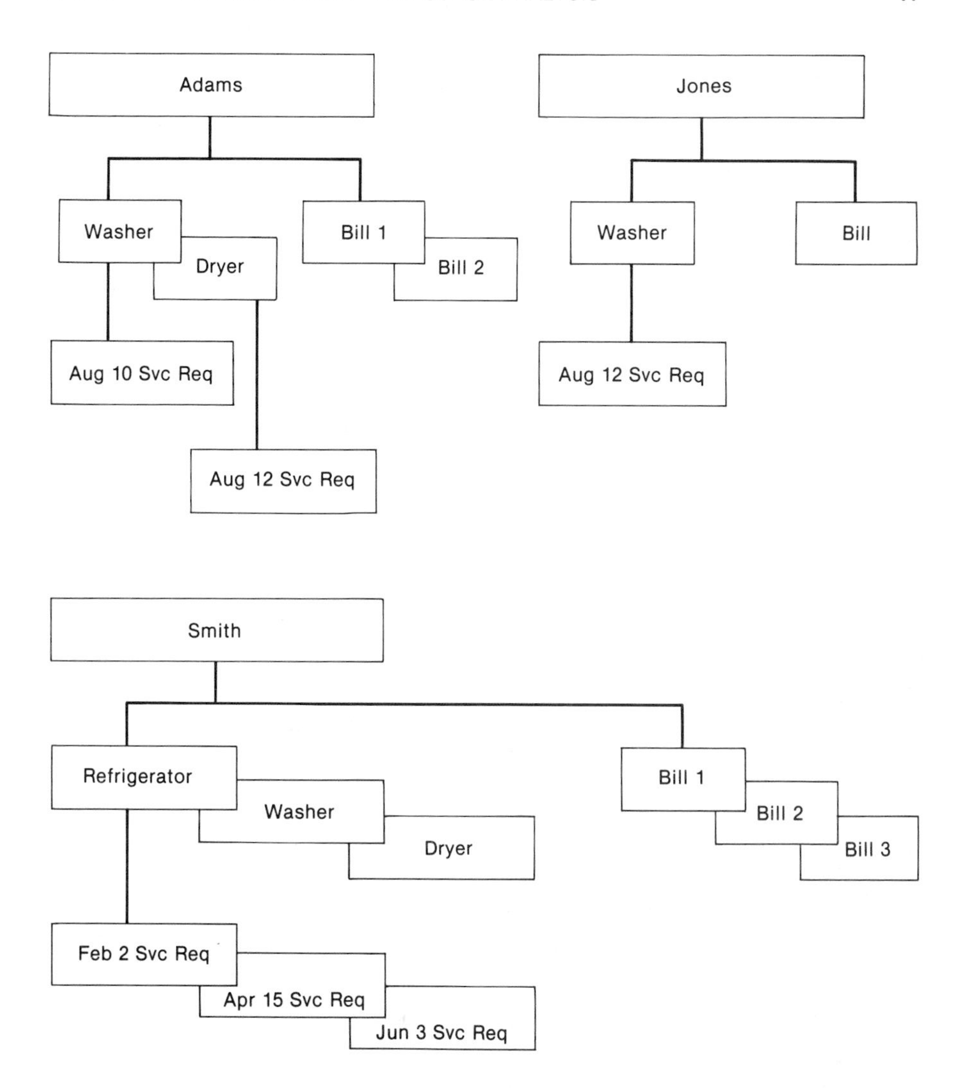

Figure 3.2 Three Typical Data Base Records in an Equipment Maintenance Data Base

number of records at the next higher level in the structure. Using the analogy of an organization chart, this is equivalent to saying an employee may have many supervisors. In fact, the general shape or appearance of a network can be identical to the data model diagram. A data model in third normal form could be implemented fully under a network DBMS, providing any access capability needed.

So why isn't this done as common practice, without concern for usage analysis? Hopefully the answer is obvious to you. Yes, a network DBMS can support requirements for as many of the data linkages as you wish. However, the

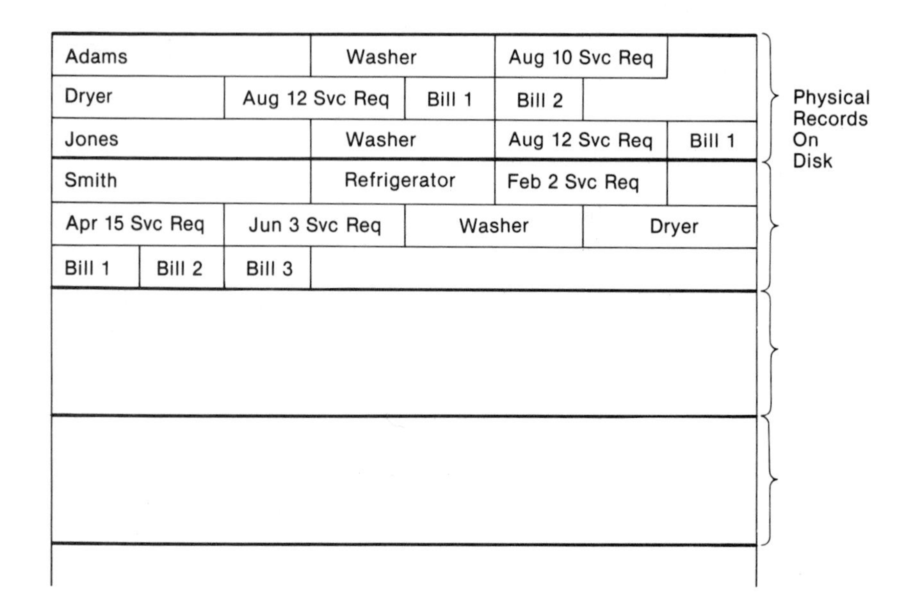

Figure 3.3 Clustering of Data Records on Disk

more you add, the more overhead is required. Each link generally translates to a pointer path that the DBMS must maintain; the more pointer paths implemented, the more work the DBMS must go through in terms of pointer maintenance with the insertion and deletion of records. Why, then, specify paths (and require overhead) that won't be used often, if at all?

In addition, networks have options where different record types may be clustered together on disk. As a result, just as in IMS, more required data can be retrieved with a single I/O, and the process runs faster. Once again, knowledge of data access requirements leads to a design with higher performance, and therefore greater user satisfaction.

3.1.3 Relational Data Base Systems

If you have read any current literature, I'm sure you know that relational systems are built around a more flexible, dynamic architecture which tends to deemphasize such things as usage analysis. You may create a relational data base immediately at the end of the normalization process, with the capability of easily modifying it later if needed.

Relational data bases can be thought of as a collection of flat files, or tables. There are no linkage paths or structural connections between associated records. Instead, the one-to-many (1:M) paths in the data model are implemented in a relational solution based on the data content of the records involved. Using IMS's parent/child terminology, this means the key of the parent must be contained in the child. In the example of Employee and Deduction records, the employee key must appear within the deduction, where it is considered a "foreign key."

So why do usage analysis for relational systems? If you know in advance that you need to cross that employee-to-deduction path frequently, there will normally be some kind of physical implementation option that can be used to provide a higher level of performance. For example, index mechanisms are available in most systems to permit access of records in alternating sequences. An index on deduction would permit direct retrieval of deduction records for a specified employee. Other options include clustering records on storage, or, in some systems, permit implementation of a pointer chain across 1:M paths. Of course, there are those who would argue that any DBMSs using pointer paths cannot, by definition, be considered relational.

Beyond these issues, to accomplish a specific task, access calls can be structured in several ways or sequences. If considered and reviewed as a group, a designer can, wherever practical, identify and use common paths to data elements. It's fairly easy to tune one path in making an access across related records. However, if through the lack of planning or foresight, you use ten different ways to move across those records, your tuning options for the other nine will be limited, if they exist at all, and the overall system's performance will suffer.

So—no matter what type of DBMS you use, it pays to plan. What, then, is usage analysis, and how is it done?

3.2 AN OVERVIEW OF USAGE ANALYSIS

Usage analysis can be defined as the study of access requirements for application programs or processes. (In this chapter, programs and processes are considered to be synonymous.) Wherever practical, these access paths need to be consolidated into common access paths and strategies. As a result, when physical data base structures are developed, the analyst can utilize the physical implementation options available to obtain the best possible system performance.

3.2.1 The Steps of Usage Analysis

The analysis itself is composed of the following steps.

1. Analyze each application process to determine its data requirements. For each process, look at all of the attributes required, and insure that each is currently in the data model. If attributes have not yet been defined, revise the data model to include the new requirements, keeping it in third normal form.

This phase of analysis confirms the completeness of the data model. If sufficient data elements exist to satisfy each application process, the data model is complete and meets the system's requirements. This verification, in itself, should be sufficient reason to perform usage analysis, even for those applications to be implemented under a relational DBMS.

2. Using the relational view as a guide, translate user data requirements into a list of accesses of entities in the data model. Here the data requirements identified in Step 1 are mapped into the data model. Which entities must be accessed to satisfy these requirements? In which sequence? Which of the possible paths of the data model will we use, and where do we want to enter the data model directly? The answers to these questions result in a list of entity accesses that are required to satisfy the data requirements of each process.

3. Consolidate usage path requirements into a diagram reflecting all access path requirements. The data model reflects all possible paths that a DBMS could be asked to support. After a list of accesses has been determined for each process, they are superimposed on a diagram of the data model to identify the composite of paths required.

4. Review and revise access path requirements to reflect common access paths. The objective of this phase is to identify, as far as possible, common and heavily used paths so that physical implementation choices can be made to provide performance edges for those paths. Because each application program can normally be satisfied by several variations in access paths, adjustments may be necessary in them to facilitate the use of common entry points to the data base whenever feasible. This leads to a simpler physical design with higher performance characteristics.

Some of this is simple to do, and some is not. The most difficult part is in resolving multiple path requirements in the "overlay" process.

Consider the following diagram illustrating two 1:M relationships (illustrated by <----->> connections). The 1:M arrow between Supplier and Price List says each supplier provides many parts. Similarly, the arrow between Part and Price List says that each part is available from many suppliers. Any single price list entry is the intersection of one supplier providing a particular part, containing the price of that part when purchased from that supplier, and so on.

Now assume that you have identified requirements to move from Supplier to Price List as well as from Part to Price List. Looking ahead a bit to physical implementation, you can provide fast access across Supplier and Price List records through a mechanism called *clustering*. To do this, you would choose physical implementation options to store each Price List record as close as possible to its Supplier parent, or owner, record. In IMS, this is done by making Price List a physical dependent of Supplier; IMS will cluster these automatically when selecting storage locations. In IDMS, the "VIA set Supplier-Price" location mode choice for Price List performs the same function. Some relational DBMSs also provide the capability to cluster records together on storage. These techniques are discussed in more detail in later chapters, but are mentioned here as examples of what can be done in terms of physical implementation.

The catch is that, using this technique, you can choose to store Price List records close to Supplier records or close to Part records, but not close to both. If Supplier-Price List is clustered, the opposite path, the Part-Price List, results in random I/O, which is relatively slow. In effect, these two access paths are competing for access to Price List. Access can be minimized across one, but not both, paths. The problem therefore is to identify the most important path.

To make this judgment you need to collect enough information in the analysis phase so that, at a later time, you can determine the relative importance of each path. The importance of a given path depends on:

1. How frequently the path will be crossed;
2. The number of programs that require that path; and
3. The path being required by on-line or batch processes.

All three of these elements must be taken into consideration.

3.2.2 Getting Started

To accomplish these objectives, you need to gather certain statistics for the process as a whole, as well as for each record accessed. For each process, you need to identify:

1. How frequently will it be executed?
2. Will it run in batch or on-line mode?
3. Are there any run-time requirements involved (a required on-line response time, or a batch time limit)?

At a lower level of detail, each time a given process accesses an entity (record), you need to ask:

1. Which entity is involved?
2. What is the access intent? (for example, find, add, modify, delete)
3. What search criteria are involved? That is, which attribute(s) determine the entity occurrence to be selected?
4. How many entity occurrences will be accessed in a single execution?

5. Which attributes are used? That is, are all attributes required already defined and in the data model?
6. What type of access is required? The possible types of accesses are:
   (a) *Random.* No ordered access required, and usually involves only one occurrence of an entity.
   (b) *Serial.* Multiple occurrences are required, but in no specific sequence; for example, consecutive retrievals of Supplier records, but not in any particular sequence.
   (c) *Sequential.* Multiple entities are required, and in some specified sequence; for example, retrieval of Item records in ascending sequence by STOCK-NO.

All of this may not be accurately known. Do the best you can. The more you know, and the more accurate this information is, the better physical implementation options can be identified and used.

Keeping in mind the need to gather information on all of the items just reviewed, I'd like to suggest one way in which the usage path can be recorded. I prefer this format because it identifies the most critical components of the information required, while being concise and easy to use.

For each process, develop a proposed list of entities accessed in the following format:

```
access intent  entity name  (attributes required for entity selection)
```

For example, "find customer information for a specific order" would translate to:

```
Find Order (ORDER-NO)           <returns CUST-CODE>
Find Customer (CUST-CODE)       <returns customer name, telephone
                                 number, and so on>
```

Keep in mind the other information that needs to be identified. Remember to include any new requirements identified during this phase in a revised data model. For example, you will find that program 3 which follows requires the addition of data elements to handle the program's requirements.

In describing usage paths, the term record is used. In this context, consider this to be synonymous with entity. At this stage, each access is against the hypothetical, or *possible*, record type noted, but does not necessarily reflect access of a physical record. These are first-cut, proposed accesses; no firm design decisions have been made.

Let's use the data model developed in Chapter 2 as a basis for creating usage paths for several programs.

3.3 EXAMPLES OF USAGE PATH DEVELOPMENT

Program 1. Take an order from a customer (on line)

A customer calls in using an "800" order number. As the clerk takes the order over the phone, the customer specifies each item desired by stock number and quantity, as well as the magazine name and issue date where the ad appeared. The clerk keys the order information into the system from their terminal.

Program Functions: Using the customer's telephone number as a key, the program reads the Customer record to check the credit rating and verify the address. For each new customer (about 20 percent of the calls received), the name, address, and phone number are obtained and a new Customer record is created.

An Order record is created. Then, for each item ordered, the stock number is used to read the Item record to verify the item's description. Using the magazine and issue date, magazine ad information is read to obtain the price of the item. A new Item Ordered record is created.

The translated usage path, in the macro language described earlier, is as follows:

```
Find Customer (CUST-TELNO)
<20%> Add Customer (CUST-TELNO)
Add Order (ORDER-NO)
Find Item (STOCK-NO)
Find Advertised Item (STOCK-NO, MAG-CODE, ISSUE-DATE)
Add Item Ordered (ORDER-NO, STOCK-NO)
```

Program 2. Check the status of an order (on line)

The customer calls in to check on the status of an order, and requests status information on unreceived items.

Program Functions: The order number is used to retrieve the order in question. All Item Ordered records are then read, and the information is displayed on the screen.

From past experience, you know that 10 percent of the customers calling in will not know their order number. For these cases, the customer record must first be read, which provides access to the Order record. The order date and the number of items on the order will be used to verify which order the customer is calling about. Once identified, the associated Item Ordered records are read, and the information displayed on the clerk's screen.

The translated usage path is as follows:

```
<10%> Find Customer (CUST-TELNO)
      Find Order (CUST-TELNO)
<90%> Find Order (ORDER-NO)
      Find Customer (CUST-TELNO)
Find Item Ordered (ORDER-NO)
```

When you are satisfied that you understand how these examples were developed, study each of the remaining program descriptions which follow, and develop a similar list of entity access requirements. Compare your list to the solution shown.

Program 3. Fill an order for shipment (on line)

Using a terminal, the stock clerk requests information on the next order to be filled. Items for that order are displayed, including the item name and the item's location in inventory. For items in stock, the stock level is adjusted automatically. Whenever inventory quantities are insufficient, the quantity backordered is indicated on the Item Ordered record.

Program Functions: The next order to be filled is accessed.

Looking at the third normal form solution, there is no way to determine orders that have been filled. A "status flag" attribute is therefore added to Order, which contains values distinguishing between new, partially completed, and completed orders.

The program then accesses each Item Ordered record and the corresponding Item record. After checking the quantity ordered against the inventory level, the quantity on hand is updated. The quantity backordered is calculated whenever necessary, with the status flag in Order set accordingly.

Several attributes required for this process are missing from Item. Further revisions in the third normal form solution are required, adding location, quantity on hand, reorder level, and reorder quantity to Item. Quantity backordered is also added to Item Ordered.

The translated usage path is as follows:

```
Find Order (STATS-FLAG)
Find Item Ordered (ORDER-NO)
Find Item (STOCK-NO)
Modify Order
Modify Item Ordered
Modify Item
```

Note that all adjustments are made keeping the data model in third-normal form. The revised entity/attribute list is shown in Figure 3.4.

Program 4. Update price information from a supplier (batch)

A new price list is received from a supplier. This information is used to create a batch input file, assumed to be available as input to this program, and which will be processed the night before prices are effective.

Third Normal Form Solution—Order-Entry System

```
Customer
 **CUST-TELNO
   CUST-NAME
   CUST-ADDR
   CUST-CRED

Item Ordered (Order-Item)
 **ORDER-NO
 **STOCK-NO
   NUM-REQD
   UNIT-PRICE
   QUAN-BACKORD

Order
 **ORDER-NO
   CUST-TELNO
   ORD-DATE
   SHIP-ADDR
   CRED-CARD
   CR-CD-NO
   STATUS-FLAG

Price List (Supplier-Item)
 **SUPP-CODE
 **STOCK-NO
   ITEM-PRICE
   PRICE-DATE
   QUAL-ACCEPT

Item
 **STOCK-NO
   ITEM-DESCR
   ITEM-TYPE
   WEIGHT
   COLOR
   PRICE
   LOCATION
   QUAN-ON-HAND
   REORDER-LVL
   REORDER-QUAN

Magazine Edition
 **MAG-CODE
 **ISSUE-DATE

Supplier
 **SUPP-CODE
   SUPP-NAME
   SUPP-ADDR

Advertised Item (Item-Mag Edition)
 **MAG-CODE
 **ISSUE-DATE
 **STOCK-NO
   PAGE-NO
   ADVER-PRICE

Magazine
 **MAG-CODE
   MAG-NAME
   MAG-ADDR
   MAG-TELNO

Credit Card
 **CRED-CARD
   CARD-NAME
```

Figure 3.4 The Modified Third Normal Form Solution

Process Functions: The program sequentially reads an input file with price information on it, sorted by supplier number and stock number. For each input record, Supplier is read, followed by Price List, and the price updated.

The translated usage path is as follows:

```
Find Supplier (SUPP-CODE)
Find Price List (SUPP-CODE, STOCK-NO)
Modify Price List (SUPP-CODE, STOCK-NO)
```

Program 5. Update ad information for new magazine issues (batch)

Each month, publications come out with ads for products offered. This program enters ad prices into the data base to make this information available for reference on line.

Program Functions: A sequential input file is available with records for all advertised items in each ad. The file is sorted by magazine code, issue date, and stock number. As this file is read, new ad records are created with the price of each item in a magazine ad.

The translated usage path is as follows:

```
Find Magazine (MAG-CODE)
Add Magazine Edition (MAG-CODE, ISSUE-DATE)
Add Advertised Item (MAG-CODE, ISSUE-DATE, STOCK-NO)
```

Program 6. Order items for inventory (batch)

On a weekly basis, inventory records are read to compare the quantity on hand with the reorder level. If the stock level is low, the supplier with the lowest price is found. A report is produced showing the item needed, the supplier selected, and the reorder quantity. This report is used to manually place orders for the required items.

Program Functions: Sequentially access each item and check its stock level against a reorder level. If the stock level is lower than the reorder level, available Price List records are read to identify the supplier with the lowest unit cost.

The translated usage path is as follows:

```
Find Item (STOCK-NO)
Find Price List (STOCK-NO)
Find Supplier (SUPP-CODE)
```

The usage paths just derived provides key input to the next phase, arriving at a first-cut data base design.

DISCUSSION QUESTIONS

1. How important is usage analysis for each of the three types of data base management systems? What are the potential dangers or costs if the analysis is incomplete or inaccurate? What can be done to minimize these problems?
2. How would your approach to usage analysis differ depending on the type of DBMS to be utilized?
3. With today's technology, end users developing systems for internal use would most likely choose relational technology. What would your recommendations be pertaining to usage analysis (what level of detail, the number of processes to be analyzed, etc)?
4. Assume that usage analysis for a particular high-performance program indicates an excess amount of I/O is required to retrieve the data elements as originally specified. What approaches might be considered in order to reduce the I/O required and increase performance?
5. Usage analysis can take a great deal of time to complete. What shortcuts or suggestions do you have to reduce the time and effort required, yet still achieve the objectives of the process?

REVIEW PROBLEMS

Each of these problems are a continuation of those first described at the end of Chapter 2. Refer to those descriptions for an overview of the data environment involved. For each of those problems, these access requirements must be supported.

1. Inventory system
   - (a) For each purchase, first verify a customer's credit status. Then record the sale of an item by decrementing the quantity on hand, and update the customer's history of items purchased (on line).
   - (b) Enter price data for items after price increases are received from a supplier (on line).
   - (c) For a specified item, check the price information for all suppliers, and identify the supplier with the lowest purchase price (on line).
   - (d) List the items purchased by each customer, including the item name (batch).
   - (e) List, for each supplier, the items available with the price for each (batch).
2. Library system
   - (a) Check to see what items a patron has currently checked out (on line).
   - (b) Record that a specified book or article is being checked out to a library patron (on line).
   - (c) Find all books and articles written by a specified author, or on a specified subject (on line).
   - (d) Produce a listing of all books and articles available in the library (batch).
   - (e) Search all subscribers to check for loaned items overdue by more than 30 days (batch).
3. Project tracking

- **(a)** List the skills that a specific employee possesses (on line).
- **(b)** Find all employees with a specified skill (on line).
- **(c)** Assign a specific employee to a project for a specified skill type (on line).
- **(d)** For each employee, enter project activity (by skill type) (on line).
- **(e)** List, by project, the skills required, the employees assigned, and the total hours worked by each (batch).

4. Magazine publication house
- **(a)** Enter new subscribers for magazines (on line).
- **(b)** Enter information on new ads placed by advertisers (on line).
- **(c)** Verify the credit rating of specified advertisers (on line).
- **(d)** Produce a list of subscribers whose subscriptions are about to expire (batch).
- **(e)** Produce a list of magazines available, and the advertisers placing ads within each (batch).

5. Wholesale mail order
- **(a)** When a customer calls in, check the price of desired equipment given in the specified magazine ad (on line).
- **(b)** Check the status of orders for customers (on line).
- **(c)** Enter new advertised items, given the magazine, issue, page of the ad, and the equipment advertised (on line).
- **(d)** List the status of customers and orders placed during the past month (batch).
- **(e)** For each type of equipment, list the details of each ad in which that equipment type is listed (batch).

4

Network Data Base Management Systems

4.1 INTRODUCTION

The terms and concepts discussed in this chapter refer to standards for network data base management systems proposed in a CODASYL (Conference on Data Systems Languages) report published in the early 1970s. Several network-based products have subsequently been developed based on the CODASYL guidelines. Software developers were, of course, free to choose the number of features to be implemented, as well as their own specific method of implementation. Rather than attempt to cover implementation details for each of these products, I use, as an example, Cullinet's IDMS/R. In the following material, all characteristics and functional capabilities are provided within IDMS/R, unless otherwise noted.

Let's look at the definition of some major terms used with network DBMSs.

4.2 DEFINITION OF TERMS

Owner record. When implementing a record relationship represented by a 1:M association in a data model, the owner record is the record type on the "one" side of the arrow.

Member record. When implementing a record relationship represented by a 1:M association in a data model, the member record is the record type on the "many" side of the arrow.

Network DBMS. Using the preceding terminology, a network DBMS is one in which a record may participate as a member in as many owner-member relationships as necessary. Each such relationship is established by declaring a "set" relationship between the record types involved.

This, then, is the most distinguishing characteristic between network and hierarchical data base systems. In a hierarchy, a record may be subordinate to only one record type at the next highest level in the hierarchy, where in a network, a record may be subordinate to (or may appear on the "many" side of a 1:M relationship) as many times as necessary.

A data model could, if desired, be implemented totally as depicted in its relational diagram using a network DBMS. This is not normally desirable, however. As described later, each 1:M linkage would be implemented as a pointer chain, which requires additional overhead and I/O as records in the chain are added or deleted. Implementation of all possible linkages into a network solution will result in making the DBMS work its heart out in maintaining linkages that aren't really necessary, resulting in a solution with poorer performance characteristics than one without the unnecessary overhead.

Set. A linkage path that joins a certain type of owner record to one or more types of member records. You'll see shortly how this linkage is implemented through the use of pointers.

Page. The amount of data transferred to or from DASD in a single I/O operation by the DBMS. (This is sometimes referred to as a block of data.) The DBMS would then locate the record required by the application program from within the page, and pass just that record's data contents to the program's I/O area.

4.3 NETWORK FUNDAMENTALS

Let's relate these definitions to a network implementation for the data model shown in Figure 4.1. Assume that all 1:M relationships shown in this diagram are required to satisfy application program access requirements.

The 1:M relationship between the Department and Employee records is created by defining a "set" between the owner record (Department) and the member record (Employee). As shown in Figure 4.2, this is supported by the creation of a pointer ring that links an owner record to its member records using a pointer field stored within these records. The owner record points to the first member, which in turn points to the next member, and so on to the end of the

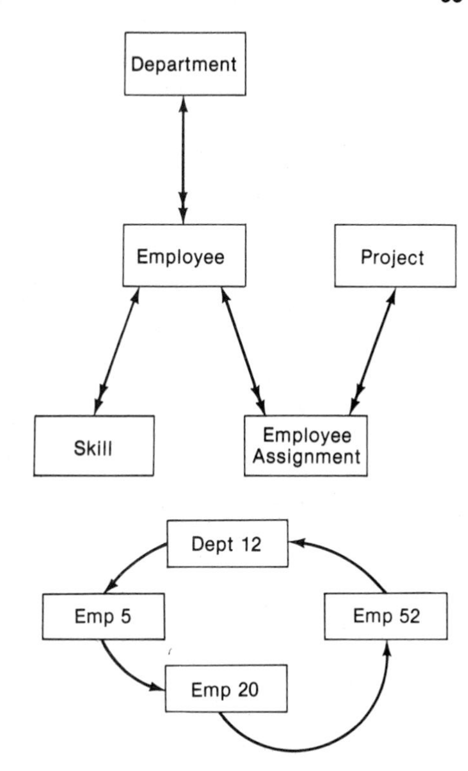

Figure 4.1 A Data Model for Employee-Project

Figure 4.2 The Dept-Emp Set as Implemented Through a Ring Structure

member chain. The last member in this example, Employee 52, ends the ring structure by pointing back to the owner record, Department 12.

Note that set linkages are "named" to allow a reference to a specific linkage path whenever required.

Let's expand the network solution to include each of the 1:M paths reflected in Figure 4.1. Figure 4.3 shows the network solution or structure that supports all of the 1:M paths in the data model, including a name assigned for each set.

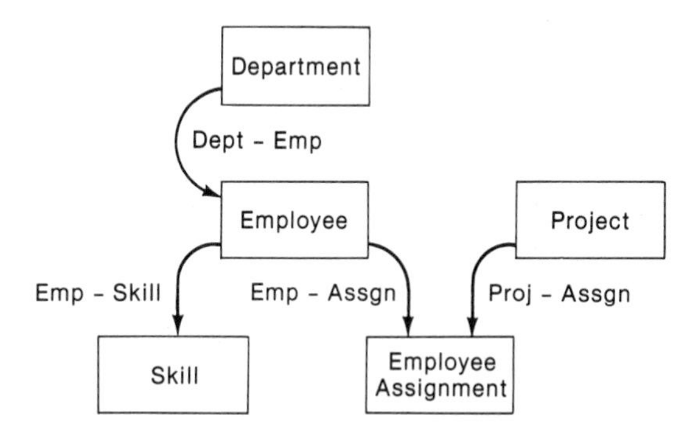

Figure 4.3 Set Requirements for the Employee-Project Data Model

Figure 4.4 illustrates the resulting linkage paths in this data base after it is loaded with data. Department 12 is shown having three employees (5, 20, and 52), each with various skills. Department 14 has Employees 12 and 18 assigned to it. Three of these five employees (Employees 52, 20, and 12) support projects 20 and 32.

Let's see how these various pointer chains can be used to move across or through the data base to satisfy requests for data.

As shown in Figure 4.4, if the data base were entered at Department 12, the Dept-Emp set causes the creation of a pointer ring from Dept 12 across each of the three employees in that department, and finally back to the Department 12 record. Therefore each employee record could be accessed until any desired employee record is found.

In addition, once any of the employee records are accessed, a path to that employee's skill records is available through the Emp-Skill set (or pointer chain). Each chain travels through the specific skill records for that employee, and ends with the original "owner" record.

Similarly, an employee's Employee Assignment records can be accessed through the Emp-Assgn set. After accessing any employee record, an application program can switch to this set to see what projects the employee is assigned to.

The Employee Assignment records are also members of the Proj-Assgn set, linking them to the appropriate project records. In our example, Project 20 has a Proj-Assgn pointer ring which shows three employees who are assigned to that project (Employees 52, 20, and 12). Project 32, on the other hand, requires only Employee 20.

Let's trace one specific path across these records. Assume that you must identify, for Project 20, all employees assigned as well as the departments for each. Referring to Figure 4.5, and following the Proj-Assgn chain from Project 20, you find the first assignment record, in this case for Employee 52. From there, following the Emp-Assgn pointer leads to the Employee 52 record where, switching to this employee's Dept-Emp set, the Dept 12 record is found. You have identified the department for the first employee assigned to Project 20.

In continuing to follow the original Proj-Assgn path for Project 20, you see the assignment record for Employee 20 (see Figure 4.6). After switching to the Emp-Assgn ring, eventually the actual employee record is found. By switching to that record's Dept-Emp pointer chain, this path leads back to Department 12's record, although the path (because of circumstances) is a bit longer. (If the performance implications of this path bother you, there are optional linkages which can provide a higher level of performance.)

Finally, continuing around the Project 20 Proj-Assgn set, you see the Emp 12-Proj 20 record (see Figure 4.7). Next, following the Emp-Assgn ring leads to the Employee 12 record where, by switching to the Dept-Emp set, you are led to Dept 14.

This example illustrates two primary points. First, individual pointer chains link a specific owner record across existing member records for that set. Second,

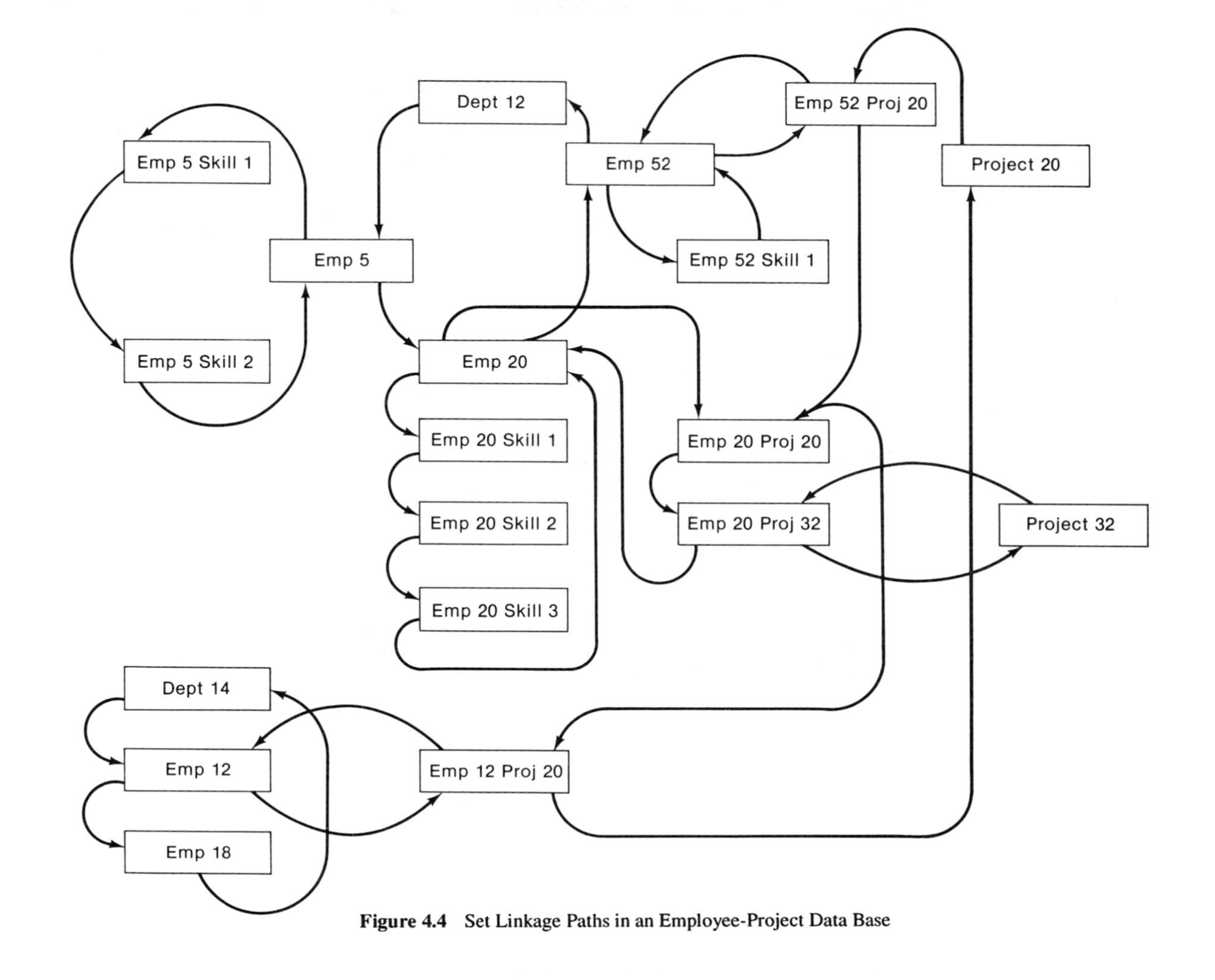

Figure 4.4 Set Linkage Paths in an Employee-Project Data Base

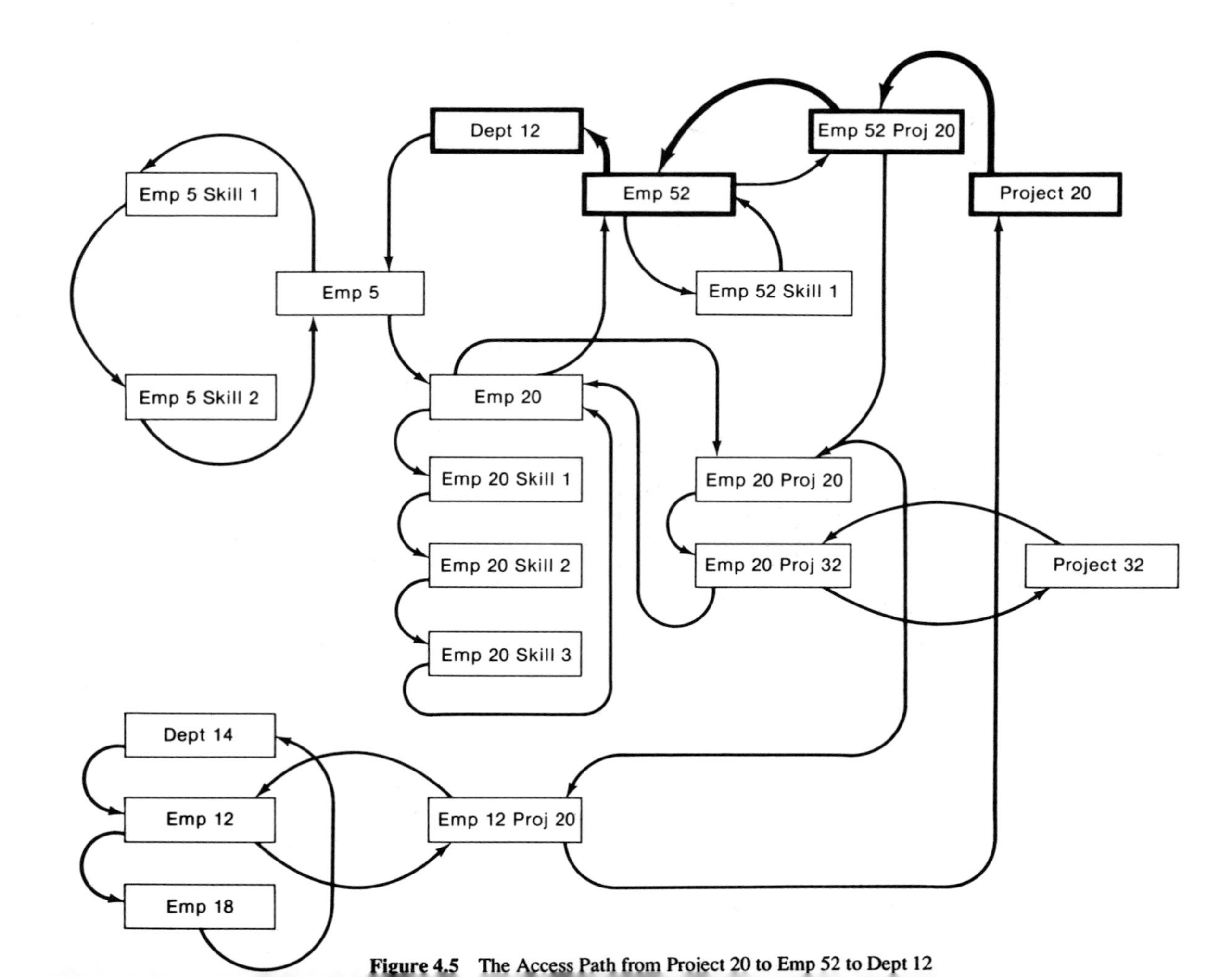

Figure 4.5 The Access Path from Project 20 to Emp 52 to Dept 12

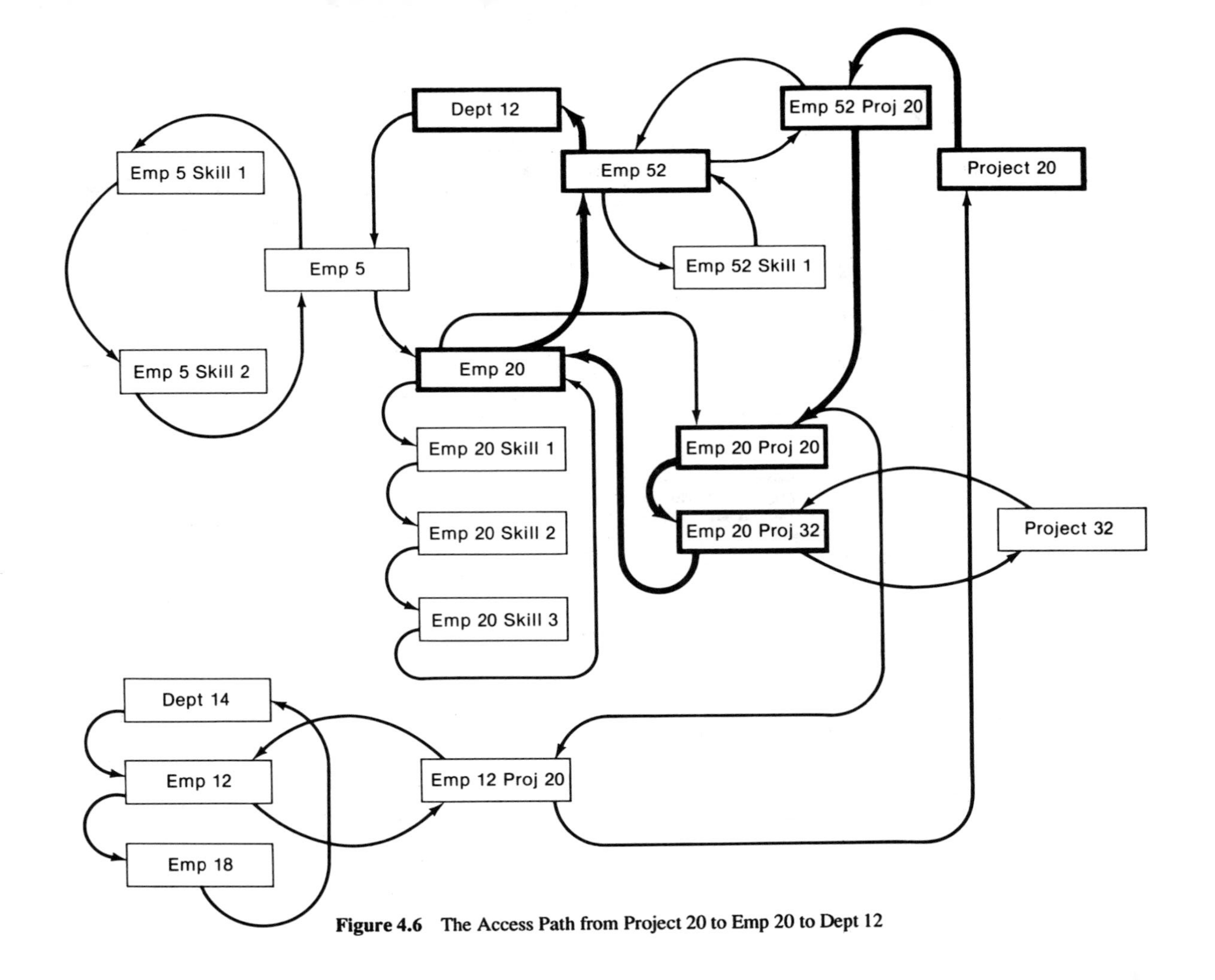

Figure 4.6 The Access Path from Project 20 to Emp 20 to Dept 12

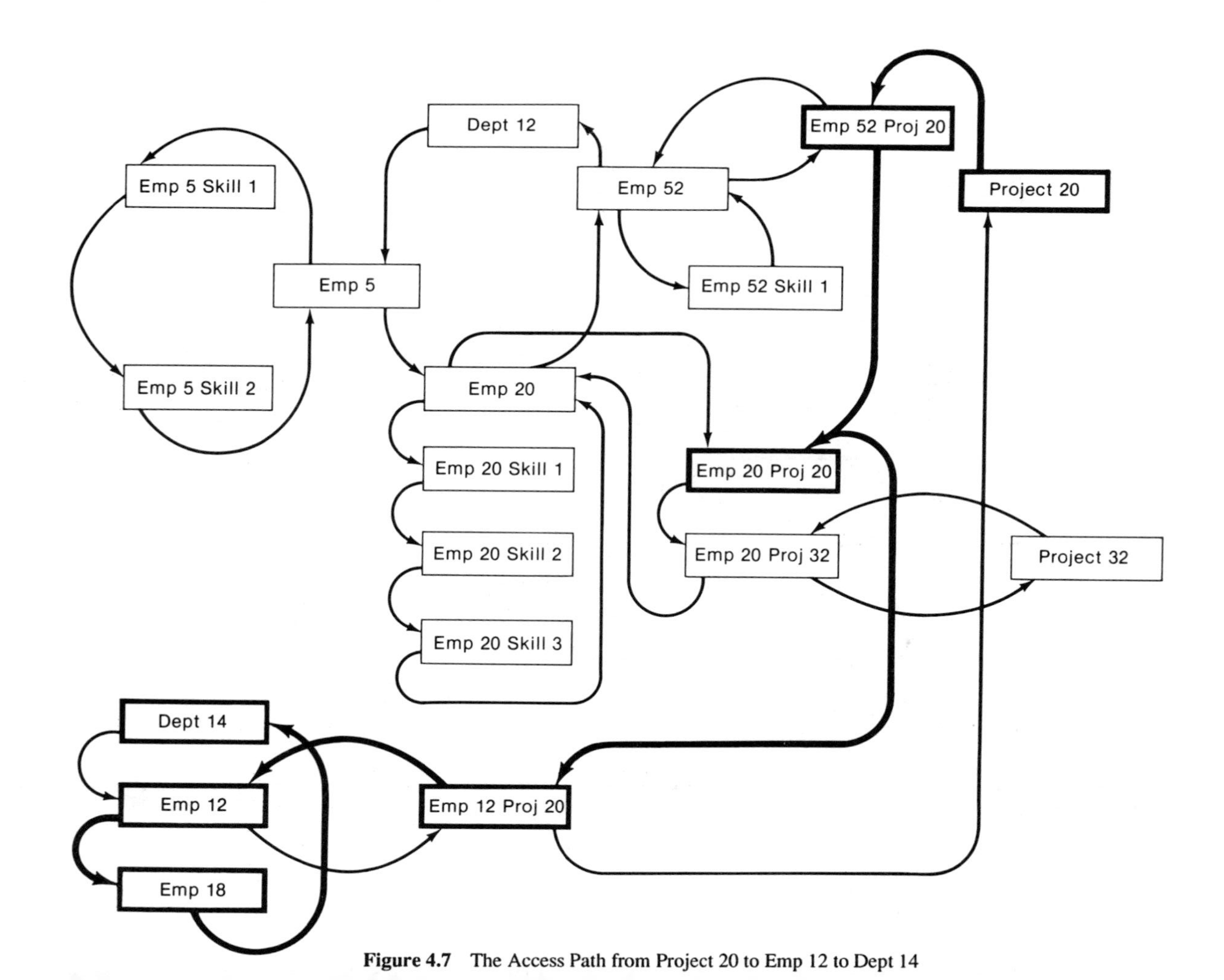

Figure 4.7 The Access Path from Project 20 to Emp 12 to Dept 14

with the implementation of the required set types, a program can navigate completely through the data base, switching use of set types when necessary to gain access to other record types.

The first phase of a network DBMS design, then, is fairly simple. The relational view, of course, must be developed and defined as discussed in Chapter 2. Then you must analyze usage paths as described in Chapter 3 to determine, from all of the possible 1:M linkages, those required for physical implementation. For all paths identified, set types should be defined, to give a solution as portrayed by Figure 4.3.

As you can see, network data bases are easy to design. However, in order for the network to provide efficient access to records, you need to be careful when making several design-related decisions.

4.4 IMPLEMENTATION OPTIONS

A network data base management system provides a number of choices to the designer in how data records may be accessed.

4.4.1 Choosing a Location Mode

In order for the DBMS to store or access data, a Location Mode must be defined for *each record type* being implemented in the data base. Each declaration of a Location Mode defines a set of rules for the DBMS to use to decide where to store (and subsequently where to look for) those records. That decision, when viewed against access path requirements, reflects very heavily on both flexibility and performance of the data structure. Unfortunately, this is an inverse relationship, for increased flexibility often causes reduced performance. To understand this, let's first define the Location Modes normally used in network structures. Afterward, the impact of these choices is viewed in terms of performance.

Depending on the particular product selected, a combination of the following are provided as choices for Location Mode.

1. CALC. The specification of CALC for a Location Mode tells the DBMS to randomly choose a page from within the data base to store (or retrieve) the specified record. Using the record's key field as the seed, a random number is calculated that translates to a storage address.

If the record is being added to the data base, this allows the DBMS to randomly choose a page to store the record in. For data retrieval, the randomization process always gives the same, repeatable answer to the randomization process, which permits the DBMS to determine the location of the desired record without having to incur the overhead of an index-based lookup.

Based on the nature of the randomization process, records stored with CALC as a Location Mode are not stored (or retrieved) in key sequence.

2. INDEX.[1] The INDEX specification causes these records to be stored as a "sorted set," accessible through an index structure based on the record's key field. As such, records can be randomly retrieved via the index, but can also be retrieved in key sequence.

3. VIA SET. "VIA SET name" may be specified for the member record participating in a set relationship, where "...name" is the name of the set linking the owner and member records. This option causes a clustering of owner/member records on storage. When member records are added to the data base, they are placed as closeby as possible to the owner record for that set. As a result, subsequent access across this set will be fast, since multiple record occurrences will normally be retrieved in a single I/O.

Remember that when defining a network data base, each type of data base record must have a Location Mode assigned. In referring back to Figure 4.3, you might choose CALC for Employee and Project, and VIA SET EMP-ASSGN for Employee Assignment. As there can be only one Location Mode for each record, selecting VIA SET EMP-ASSGN for Employee Assignment prevents direct entry to the data base on that record type. In this example, access to Employee Assignment records is only possible by first accessing either Employee or Project records, then using either the EMP-ASSGN or PROJ-ASSGN set to gain access to records participating in that set. Of course, as Employee and Employee Assignment records will be clustered on storage as a result of specifying VIA SET EMP-ASSGN for Employee Assignment records, this path would provide a relatively high level of performance, with slower access when accessing Employee Assignment records as members of the Proj-Assgn set.

4. DIRECT. The choice of DIRECT places the decision on where to store records in the hands of the application programmer.

With the implementation of the appropriate controls, documentation and procedures, this can be an effective way of managing data. However, it should be obvious that the entire application staff needs to be "in sync" on what these rules are. For this reason, some vendors have decided that this is not a wise thing to do and, to keep their customers from making a mistake, they have simply not implemented this capability.

5. SYSTEM.[1] This final option leaves the location of the record entirely up to the DBMS. There is no specification of a record key, and the programmer is not involved in any way with the decision.

---

[1] IDMS/R does not explicitly support INDEX and SYSTEM choices for Location Mode. However, indexes can be created by implementing an index based on a data field within a record. The index is specified as the member, and the system as the owner, in a set relationship.

The two most fundamental tasks in designing a network data base are identifying the sets required and specifying the Location Modes for each record type. There are, however, additional options available.

4.4.2 Pointer Selection

The preceding review of set declarations covers how pointer chains are created linking the owner and member occurrences for that set. This linkage requires, at a minimum, the use of a NEXT pointer to allow a forward pointer path across the various records in that set. The preceding diagrams were drawn showing only NEXT pointers for all sets.

Quite often, the NEXT option is paired with a PRIOR pointer to provide both forward and backward pointers across a set. This option is used to provide programs with the capability to follow sets in a backward direction.

In addition, the selection of OWNER pointers can significantly reduce I/O requirements when moving across multiple set types in the data base. Using Figure 4.4, let's assume that you need to produce a list of employees assigned to Project 20, including information on each employee's department.

Using only the NEXT pointers shown in this diagram, you have already traced the path in the data base to produce this information (Figures 4.5—4.7). This path starts with the specified Project record, and follows the Proj-Assgn set to the first member record. The Emp-Assgn chain is then followed to access the Employee record. Finally, the Dept-Emp set is used, chasing that pointer around the set until finally the ringed pointer chain accesses the Department record for that particular employee.

If, on the other hand, the Dept-Emp set was implemented with NEXT, PRIOR, and OWNER pointers, the number of member accesses required would be minimized, resulting in a reduction of I/O and therefore providing a higher level of performance (see Figure 4.8). Note that other paths would also be candidates for these options. However, for the sake of simplicity, Figure 4.8 only shows the Dept-Emp set in this way.

4.4.3 Managing Pointer Maintenance

The final options to be reviewed determine when pointer updates are to take place. The first specifies when pointer maintenance is to be done for new records being added to a set. The choices are:

1. *Automatic*. The DBMS automatically makes the appropriate pointer adjustments in the set when the record is added.
2. *Manual*. New member records are not automatically added to the set. The DBMS makes these pointer adjustments only when directed by the application program.

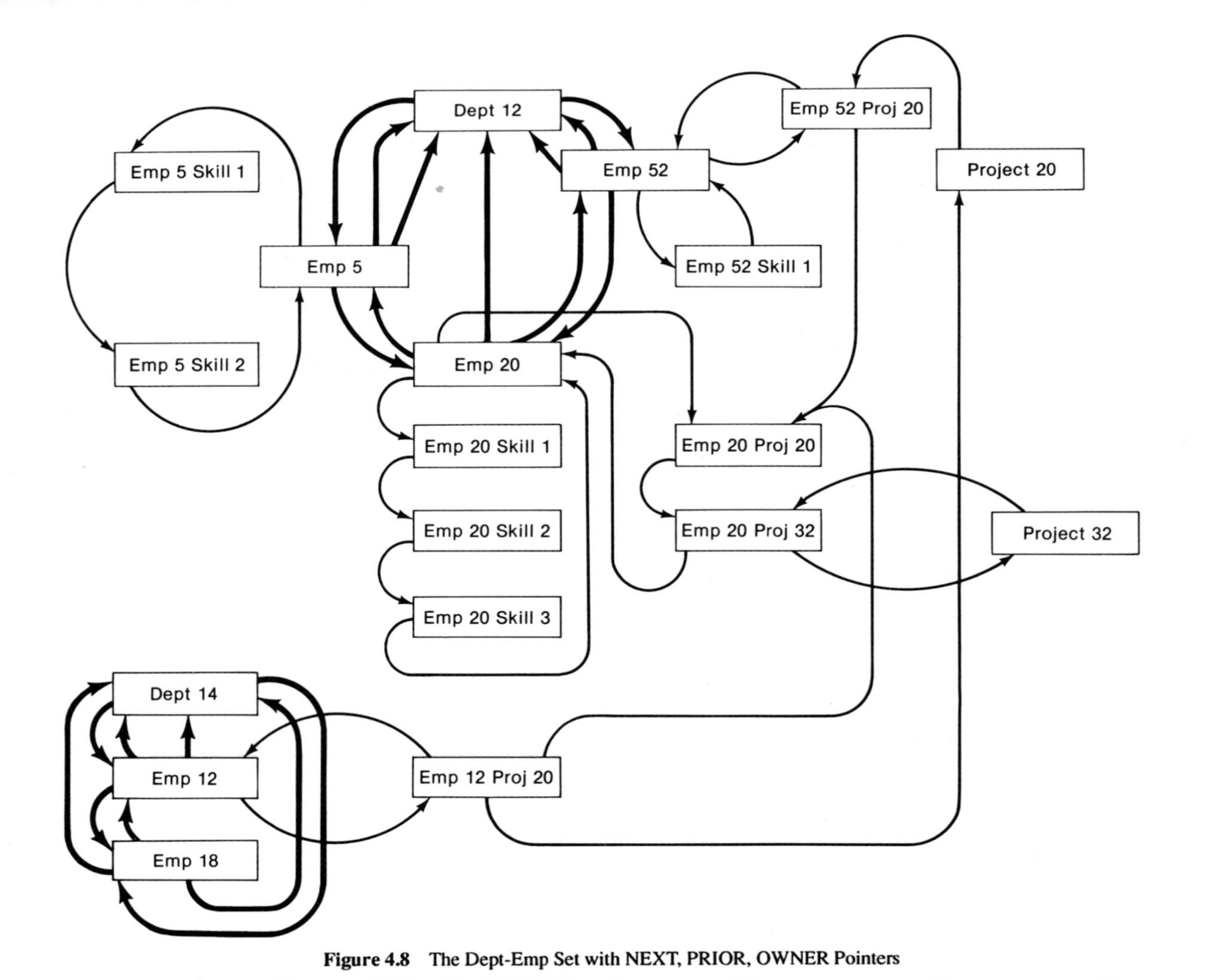

Figure 4.8 The Dept-Emp Set with NEXT, PRIOR, OWNER Pointers

In a similar manner, the point in time when records are removed from a set can be specified in two ways. These are:

1. *Mandatory.* The record is retained as a member of the set until the record is deleted.
2. *Optional.* The application may disconnect a record from a set without deleting it. In this way, a member record can be disconnected from one set and added to another without causing the DBMS to incur the overhead of space management adjustments in back-to-back "delete" and "add" processes.

The designer may choose various combinations of these options in defining a data base. Depending on which options are chosen, the potential does exist for loss of data records. If application logic were permitted to create "loose" or disconnected records for any period of time and a data base reorganization occurred in the same time period, a loss of data could occur, probably without anyone's knowledge. A combination of AUTOMATIC and MANDATORY options would prevent this from happening.

Under some circumstances, however, another combination might be desirable. For example, consider a record type that participated as a member in five different set relationships. If the record's contents change frequently (reflecting changes in owner-member relationships), it would be much more practical to allow application logic to disconnect a record from a set, change the I/O area, and reconnect that record to a new set without requiring insert/delete logic and the resulting simultaneous alteration of each of the five different sets. Therefore, with the appropriate internal standards and checks in application design, specifications of AUTOMATIC, MANDATORY can be chosen for the VIA SET path, and MANUAL, OPTIONAL chosen for all others.

4.5 IDMS/R's INTERNAL STORAGE FORMAT

Now that the general concepts of location modes and set declarations have been reviewed, let's take a look at how IDMS/R implements these mechanisms.

As depicted in Figure 4.9, when data records are stored in a page, IDMS/R assigns to each an address in terms of a page number and a line number, with line numbers assigned incrementally as data records are loaded. The line number is tied to a position in a table at the bottom of the page. Each entry in the table contains 8 bytes of control information giving, for that line, the record type, the record's displacement in the page, the record length, and the prefix length. As shown in Figure 4.10, the prefix is stored at the beginning of each record, and contains the pointers required to support the set linkages for that record type.

IDMS/R uses this table of control information to perform dynamic space management. As records are deleted, all remaining active records are dynamically

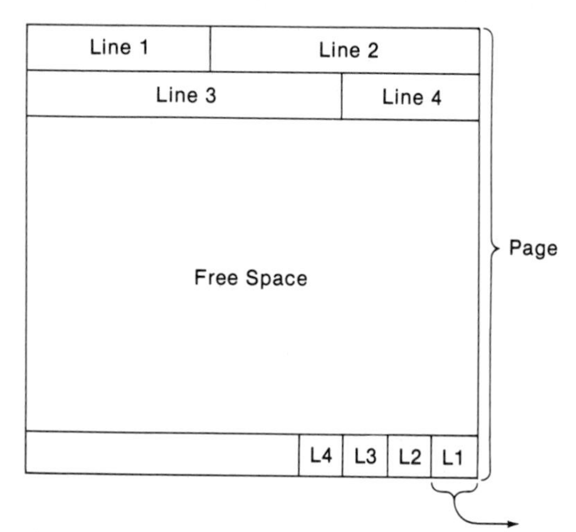

Figure 4.9 How IDMS/R Loads Data into a Page

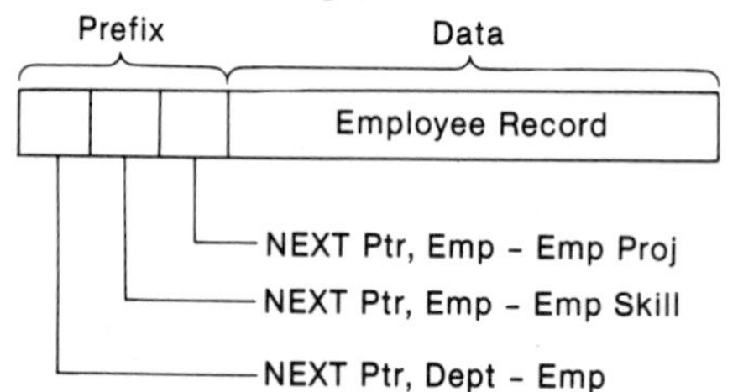

Figure 4.10 The Layout of an Employee Record in the Employee-Project Data Base

compressed to the top of the page, with new offset values assigned in the control table. In this way, addressing, based on page number and line number values, remains unchanged, yet all available free space in each page is in one contiguous piece.

Figure 4.11 illustrates in more detail how records are chained together across pages, omitting the detail of the control tables. This example, taken from Figure 4.4, shows how Department and Employee records are linked within the Dept-Emp set with NEXT pointers. The Department 12 record has a NEXT pointer to page 1000, line 2, where the record for Employee 5 is found. It, in turn, has a pointer to the Employee 20 record, stored in page 1020, line 1.

Hopefully this review of IDMS/R's internal storage format reinforces how flexible network structures can be. After developing the data model and performing usage analysis, any required 1:M linkages can be created by defining a set relationship across the appropriate record types, creating the linkage path(s) requested. Remember, however, that this increased flexibility has a price. The more linkage paths defined, the higher the associated overhead will be in terms of I/O to maintain those linkages when inserts and deletes of records occur. This is simply another example of the classic conflict between flexibility and performance.

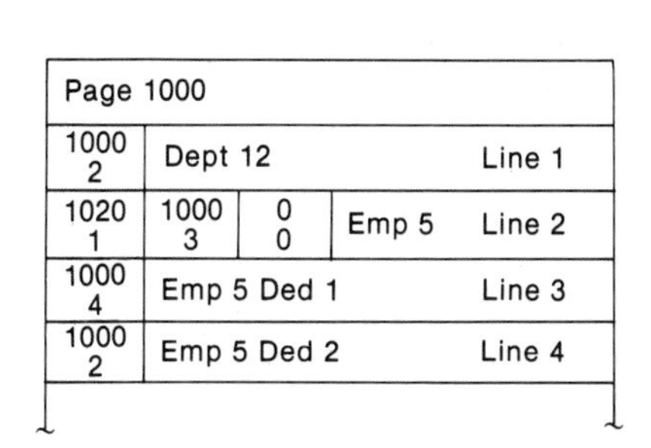

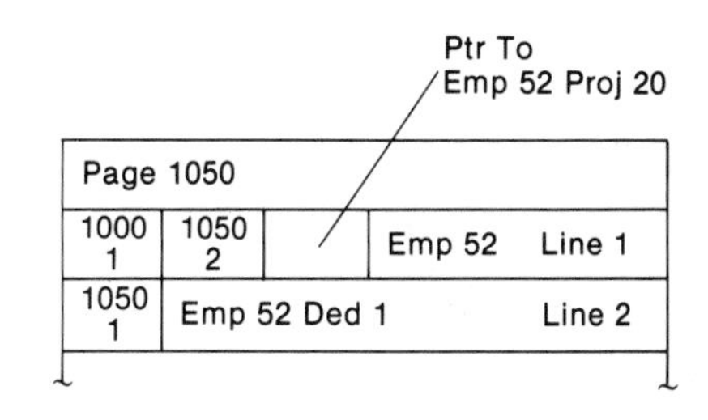

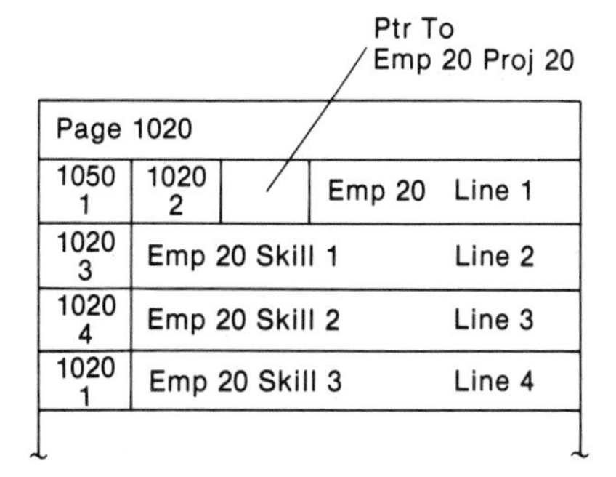

Figure 4.11 Records Chained Across Pages

4.6 SUMMARY OF DESIGN STEPS

1. Develop the data model (or relational view).
2. Using the data model developed, perform a usage analysis for the required application programs.
3. Compare the usage analysis results to the original data model to identify heavily-used 1:M access paths. For each such path, create a set relationship to provide that linkage in the network data base solution.
4. Refer again to the usage analysis to identify those record types which must support direct entry points to the data base.

    If there is significant key-sequential processing requirements for this record type, the Location Mode of this record should be INDEXED.

    If there is no significant key-sequential processing requirements for this record type, the Location Mode of this record should be CALC.
5. Consider using PRIOR pointers for any member chain with significant delete activity. Consider using OWNER pointers whenever a member record, accessed from another path, requires subsequent access to the owner of the set.

If done properly, the preceding analysis should result in a good first-cut solution to the design problem. This information, of course, should be shared with a local technical review staff in a design review to insure no oversights were made, as well as to provide additional technical tips for efficient use of the particular software used in your shop.

REVIEW QUESTIONS

1. Consider the choices of Location Modes of CALC, INDEX and VIA SET for designing a network DBMS. What guidelines would you use in deciding which to choose?
2. In considering the Location Mode for a member record, compare the two choices of CALC and VIA SET in terms of flexibility and performance.

REVIEW PROBLEMS

The following problems are a continuation of those first described at the end of Chapter 2. Refer to those descriptions for an overview of the data environment involved, and derive a network solution for each. Your solution should indicate a Location Mode for each record type, as well as which set relationships are required.

1. Inventory system
   - (a) For each purchase, first verify a customer's credit status. Then record the sale of an item by decrementing the quantity on hand, and update the customer's history of items purchased (on line).
   - (b) Enter price data for items after price increases are received from a supplier (on line).
   - (c) For a specified item, check the price information for all suppliers, and identify the supplier with the lowest purchase price (on line).
   - (d) List the items purchased by each customer, including the item name (batch).
   - (e) For each supplier, list the items available with the price for each (batch).
2. Library system
   - (a) Check to see what items a patron has currently checked out (on line).
   - (b) Record that a specified book or article is being checked out to a library patron (on line).
   - (c) Find all books and articles written by a specified author, or on a specified subject (on line).
   - (d) Produce a listing of all books and articles available in the library (batch).
   - (e) Search all subscribers to check for loaned items overdue by more than 30 days (batch).
3. Project tracking
   - (a) List the skills that a specific employee possesses (on line).
   - (b) Find all employees with a specified skill (on line).
   - (c) Assign a specific employee to a project for a specified skill type (on line).
   - (d) For each employee, enter project activity (by skill type) (on line).

(e) List, by project, the skills required, the employees assigned, and the total hours worked by each (batch).

4. Magazine publication house
   (a) Enter new subscribers for magazines (on line).
   (b) Enter information on new ads placed by advertisers (on line).
   (c) Verify the credit rating of specified advertisers (on line).
   (d) Produce a list of subscribers whose subscriptions are about to expire (batch).
   (e) Produce a list of magazines available, and the advertisers placing ads within each (batch).

5. Wholesale mail order
   (a) When a customer calls in, check the price of desired equipment given in the specified magazine ad (on line).
   (b) Check the status of orders for customers (on line).
   (c) Enter new advertised items, given the magazine, issue, page of the ad, and the equipment advertised (on line).
   (d) List the status of customers and orders placed during the past month (batch).
   (e) For each type of equipment, list the details of each ad in which that equipment type is listed (batch).

5

Fundamentals of IMS Data Bases

5.1 INTRODUCTION

This chapter reviews the concepts of hierarchical data base management systems. It is based on the features and capabilities of IBM's IMS DBMS, perhaps the most widely used DBMS for mainframe application systems.

The objective of this chapter is to provide a working knowledge of how IMS data bases work, as well as an understanding of the performance implications of various design choices. With this understanding, a design team should be able to propose reasonable first-cut data base solutions that satisfy a given set of access requirements.

With this in mind, let's look at some basic terms and definitions used with IMS.

5.2 TERMINOLOGY

A *hierarchical DBMS* is one that manages data such that each record is subordinate to only one record at the next higher level in the structure (see Figure 5.1), and has the general shape of an inverted tree.

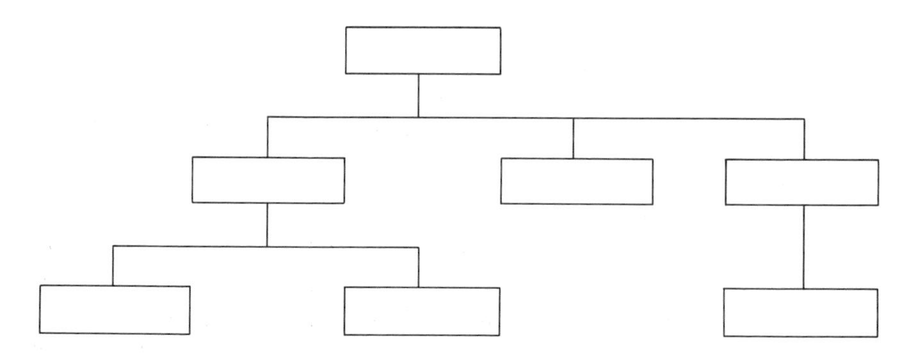

Figure 5.1 A Hierarchical Structure, or "Inverted Tree," as Used by IMS

Each node represents a different logical record type, or, in IMS terms, a *segment.* A segment is the typical amount of data retrieved by an application program when accessing the data base.

Data bases are first defined to IMS through assembler macros that are later used to create a *data base definition* (or DBD). DBDs are first created that reflect specific implementation options for segments and linkage options; they are referred to as physical DBDs because they contain physical implementation details. Other advanced options provide the capability of linking separate physical data bases together to give a more complex view. The DBDs used are referred to as logical DBDs because they provide access to data using a structural image that doesn't physically exist.

The terms *parent* and *child* are also used to describe relationships in the hierarchy. Each segment is the parent of segments immediately below it in the hierarchical structure, which are its children. They, in turn, will be parents of segments subordinate to them.

Twin segments are segments of the same type that have the same parent. They appear in the data base as a *twin chain.*

The segment at the top of the hierarchical structure is called the *root segment.* Normally, data segments in the data base are accessed first by entering the data base at the root level, and then moving through the data base record (the root and all of its dependents) to locate the specific segment desired.

The *hierarchical sequence* of the data base is the unload sequence of segments in an unload. This is referred to as the top-to-bottom, left-to-right ordering of data, and is simply the sequence by which data will be retrieved by IMS as a result of consecutive "Get Next" calls.

When the data base is defined to IMS, part of the control information created at that time will assign, in hierarchical sequence, segment codes or flags for each segment in the data base. For example, the fifth segment defined has a segment code of "05." These segment codes will become the first byte of data in each segment on physical storage. Then, when IMS locates an "05" segment after an

I/O request, the "05" segment code enables IMS to locate from the DBD all required information about the data just located (how long the segment is, if a key field is defined, the key's location and length, and so on).

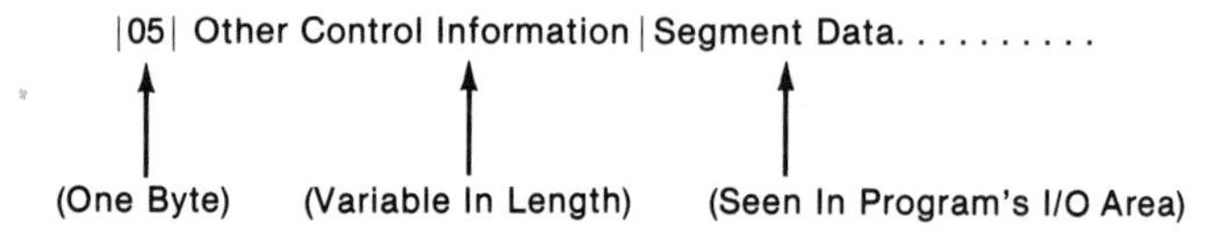

Figure 5.2 illustrates a hierarchical sequence in two ways. First, the segment codes assigned for this data base are shown on the first occurrence of each segment in the diagram. Second, for sequential processing, the numbers in the circles represent the order in which these segments will be retrieved.

The term *access method*, probably the most confusing term in IMS, refers to two different, yet related, types of accesses: system, and data base.

1. First, it commonly indicates the choice of system access methods reflected in the DBD. The system access method is invoked by the data base manager as a result of data base calls made by the application program. For example, you'll see that physical sequential data sets are commonly used in IMS. For these data sets, there are two kinds of system access methods that can be used: simple physical sequential data sets (referred to in IMS as OSAM), and the Virtual Storage Access Method's (VSAM) version of physical sequential, an Entry Sequence Data Set (ESDS).
2. Second, the term *access method* is also used to refer to the choice of *data base* access methods (for example, HISAM, HDAM, or HIDAM). These choices, specified in the DBD, determine the rules that IMS must follow to locate data within a logical record once the record is retrieved through an I/O request. These rules are explained in detail in the following sections.

To show how these two types of access methods relate together, Figure 5.3 illustrates the following sequence of events:

1. The application program makes a request to IMS for a segment; "From the employee master data base, get the employee segment whose payroll number equals 1785."
2. IMS, after checking the DBD for the proper system access method, issues the proper call(s). For indexed data bases (HISAM and HIDAM), IMS will issue either an ISAM or VSAM Key Sequential Data Set (KSDS) read request, depending on which was chosen to implement the data base. VSAM is by far the best choice for an index; assuming it was used in this example, IMS would issue a VSAM read with a key value of "1785."
3. VSAM, as the system access method, will issue the read request and retrieve a physical record from disk storage.

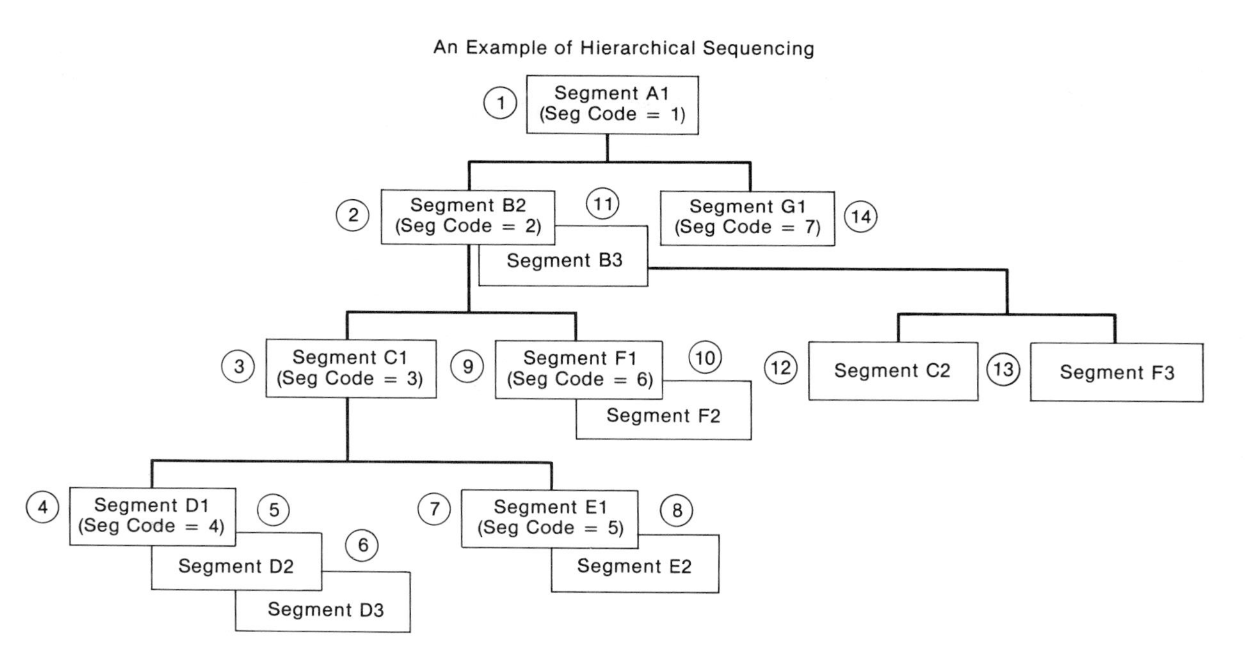

Figure 5.2 An Example of Hierarchical Sequencing

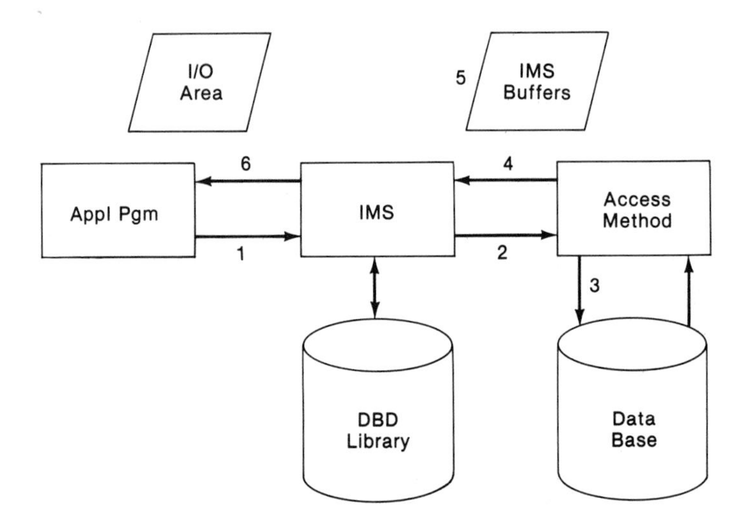

Figure 5.3 The Relationship of System and Data Base Access Methods in Retrieving Application Data

4. VSAM places this record in IMS's buffer pool.
5. IMS, using the rules for the particular IMS data base access method (for example, HISAM or HIDAM), will move through the logical record to locate the particular segment desired.

In this example, for an HISAM data base, the segment requested will be in the index record retrieved and Step 6 follows. If the data base were implemented using HIDAM, in that case IMS must repeat Steps 2 through 5 to access data from the physical sequential component of the data base before completing Step 6.

6. IMS will move the data portion of the segment into the program's I/O area.

In other words, a data base must always have both a system access method, as well as a data base access method, associated with it. With that in mind, let's now look at how the various data base access methods work.

5.3 HSAM

HSAM (Hierarchical Sequential Access Method) is one of the earlier and more primitive access methods available. As the sequential name implies, it is meant for sequential processing. Figure 5.4 illustrates how the entire data base is stored, usually on magnetic tape, with the data segments marching along in hierarchical

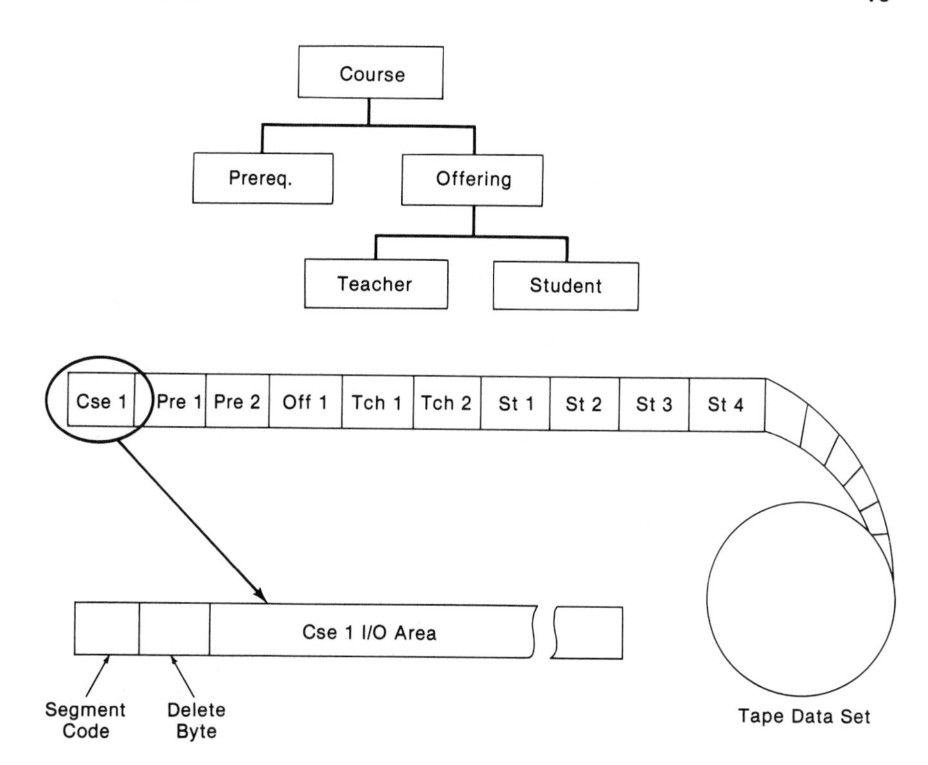

Figure 5.4 An HSAM Data Base

sequence. When accessing the data base, IMS scans the data in this sequence until locating the segment required. If updates are to be made, the program treats the data base in an "old master/new master" basis, reading the original data set as input and writing revisions to an updated version as output.

Keep in mind that the data base consists of a mixture of data segments (different record types) that are intermingled on storage. IMS has to have a way to interpret, on a segment-by-segment basis, what type of record (segment) is being accessed. To do this, each physical segment on storage begins with a two-byte "prefix." The first byte of each prefix, the segment code, serves as a record (segment) identifier. With the segment code, IMS knows from the DBD all of the required characteristics of the data (such as the length of the I/O area and the key field length and location). Given this information, IMS can move the appropriate offset to locate the next segment in hierarchical sequence where, finding its segment code, the process can be repeated.

As you can probably guess, because of the work contained in sequentially reading every segment, HSAM is not heavily used. However, you may choose this for archival files, to copy many different related record types to tape as a data base rather than, perhaps, multiple sequential files.

5.4 HISAM

The requirement of segment storage in hierarchical sequence is also used in the Hierarchical Index Sequential Access Method, or HISAM. Here, while segments are stored as in HSAM, an index is also used to provide random access capabilities to any data base record. Here's how it works.

As shown in Figure 5.5, an HISAM data base, when implemented with VSAM as the system access method, has an indexed component as well as a physical sequential component for overflow data (segments that will not fit into the index component). Note that each data set has a separately defined Logical Record Length (LRECL). When the data base record (a root segment and its dependents) is first created, IMS begins storing the root and dependents, in hierarchical sequence, in the physical record in the indexed side. Dependent segments, as in HSAM, begin with a two-byte prefix; the first is a segment code, which is followed by a delete byte. This continues until the record is filled (based on the value of the LRECL). IMS then gets a physical record from overflow, and continues storing dependents, in hierarchical sequence, until all dependents for that data base record are stored. This may require utilizing additional records in overflow.

In handling a request from an application program for data, IMS uses the key field specified for the root segment to retrieve the logical record from the indexed component. The root is the first element stored in this physical record. If the application program has requested a dependent segment, IMS starts with the root and begins searching, in hierarchical sequence, for the requested segment. Additional I/Os to the overflow data set may be necessary to locate the data requested.

What capabilities does HISAM support? Because of the index, programs can randomly retrieve data base records based on the root segment's key field. Dependent segments can then be read, inserted, or deleted. In other words, HISAM is a full-function data base with the ability to perform any type of data retrieval or update necessary. There are, however, a number of cases where HISAM may not be the best choice.

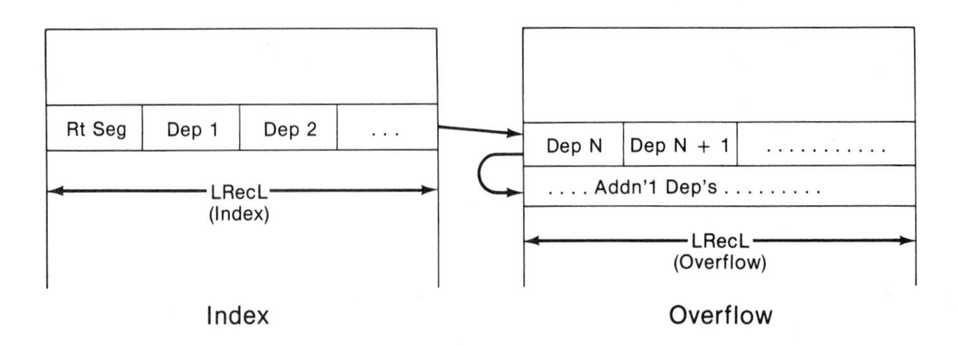

Figure 5.5 A HISAM (VSAM) Data Base

1. Note that all access requires starting at the root, followed by a sequential scan to locate dependents. If you have long data base records, this scanning can involve a lot of searching and I/Os to locate the desired segment.
2. For this technique to work, all dependents must always be stored physically adjacent to each other in hierarchical sequence. What happens if the application program issues an insert call, and the logical record doesn't have space to add the new segment where required to maintain the hierarchical sequence? Too bad. IMS *must* store the segment at the specified location, and must therefore move whatever data are required to make room. This can very easily trigger a snowball effect, where old segments at the right end of the record will be forced into the left end of the next overflow record in the chain. This, in turn, can cause other dependents to drop out of that record, and the cycle repeats.
3. There is an additional weakness with HISAM when handling dependent segment deletions. When this occurs, the delete byte in the prefix is turned on, and the deleted segment's space becomes frozen and unusable until reclaimed through a reorganization process. This creates a requirement for more "care and feeding" by the operations staff.

This sounds pretty negative, but it simply means there are conditions where HISAM is not a good choice. Specifically, HISAM is not efficient in handling long data base records, or for handling a high number of inserts or deletes of dependent segments. On the other hand, it is good for static, table-like data. There is also a variation of HISAM called SHISAM ("Simple HISAM"), that is exceptionally good for root-only data bases. SHISAM permits an index data base to be created without requiring the two-byte overhead for a prefix.

Because of the inefficiencies of HISAM, the "Hierarchical Direct" (HD) access methods were designed.

5.5 THE HIERARCHICAL DIRECT (HD) ACCESS METHODS

5.5.1 Fundamentals of HD Access Methods

Under HISAM you saw how problems arose because related segments must be physically adjacent on storage. Eliminating this problem, in fact, was a primary goal in the design of the new access methods—to have a method for locating related segment types without requiring physical adjacency. The solution was to use something called pointers, a new type of linkage mechanism where additional information is stored in an expanded prefix area.

Assume that a Customer segment for "Adams" exists in storage, and a twin is being added and is to be linked to Adams by this type of pointer. As shown in Figure 5.6, IMS will store the data for Baker as close as possible to that for Adams.

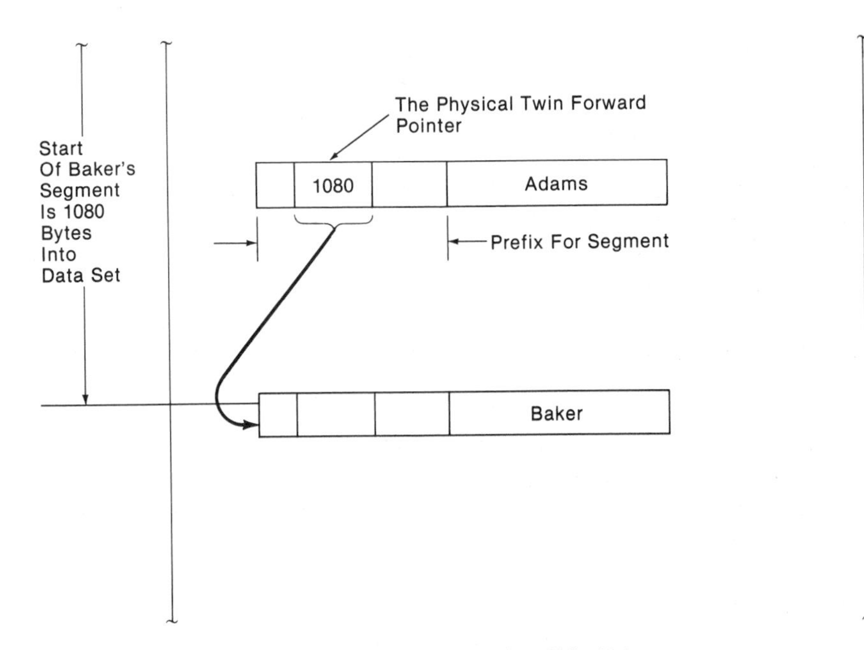

Figure 5.6 Segment Connections Using Pointers

Once the location is decided, the address (or location) of the Baker segment is calculated as being equal to the number of bytes into the data set that you must move to find the first byte of the segment. If you recall, this is the location of the segment code. This address or offset, here having the value of 1080, is stored in a special field in the prefix for Adams as a physical twin forward pointer.

Different types of pointers can be implemented. Using the previous example, keep in mind that any pointer referencing, or "pointing to," the segment for Baker will have the value of 1080.

Figure 5.7 illustrates how various pointer options are used to connect segments. These pointer options, selected in the design phase, include:

1. *Physical Child First (PCF).*[1] This is used to move from the parent to the first occurrence of the indicated dependent segment type (as in A1 to B1).
2. *Physical Child Last (PCL).* Similar to the PCF pointer, this points from the parent to the last occurrence of the indicated segment type (as in A1 to D1).
3. *Physical Twin Forward (PTF or TF).*[1] This is used to move from one segment occurrence to the next occurrence of the same segment type existing for the same parent (as in B1 to B2);

[1] If no pointer options are specified in the DBD, IMS will choose these as defaults. These options will guarantee a forward path to every segment in the data base.

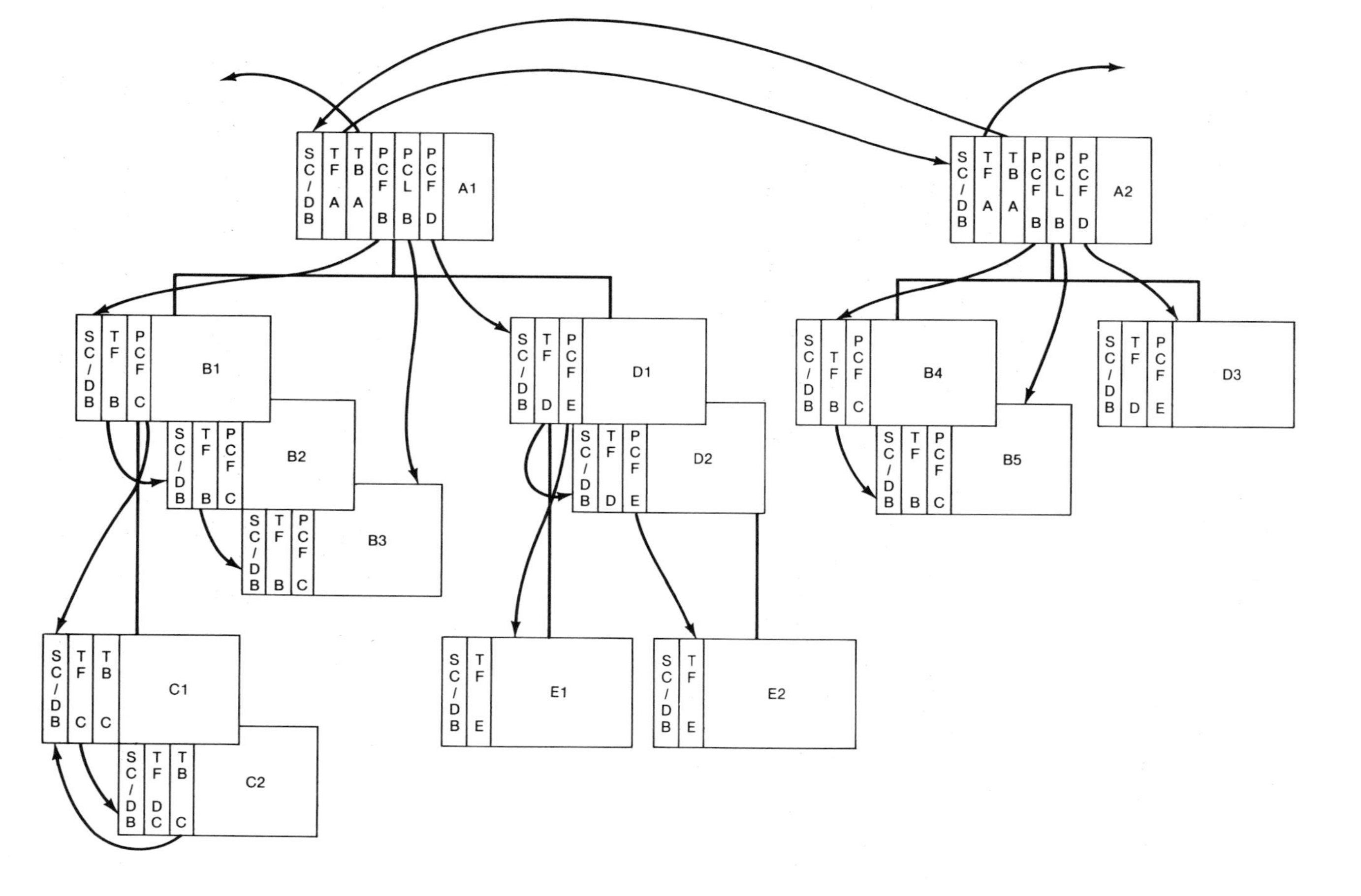

Figure 5.7 Two Sample Data Base Records

4. *Physical Twin Backward (PTB or TB).* Similar to the PTF, this chains segments in a reverse direction (as in C2 to C1);
5. *Hierarchical Forward (HF).* An option to PCF/PTF pointers, this connects a parent and its dependents with one pointer chain in a hierarchical fashion. As an example, an HF link from D to E segments would replace the PCF pointers from D to E, as well as the PTF pointers on E;
6. Hierarchical Backward (HB)—similar to the HF pointer, only connecting the segments in a reverse hierarchical sequence.

Note that every occurrence of a segment on physical storage has a prefix that is identical in length and definition to every other segment of that type. For example, in Figure 5.7, the prefix of every "A" segment is identical to other "A" segments, "B" segment prefixes are identical to each other, and so on.

Although it's not my intent to make you an expert on the fine points of pointer selection (your local data base specialist will help you with that), here are some general guidelines:

- *backward* pointers are generally chosen to improve delete performance for dependent segment chains;
- *last* pointers are used to provide fast access to the last segment of an unsequenced twin chain when storing new segments, rather than run down the twin chain each time to find the end; and
- *hierarchical* pointers are chosen for parent/child segments when the parent/child data are always accessed together. In practice, this option is seldom, if ever, chosen.

If you have any prior data base experience, you may have heard of processing problems involving "bad pointers," representing data integrity errors. Let's consider for a moment what a "bad pointer" (or pointer error) means.

1. Every pointer field, as previously discussed, exists for a specific linkage requirement based on the type of pointer defined. For example, a PTF pointer residing in an '02' segment should point to another '02' segment.
2. Because each segment always begins with the segment code representing the appropriate segment type, the first byte of the segment being addressed in the preceding paragraph should contain the value '02'. This is the only acceptable value at this offset; any other value indicates a "bad pointer," an error condition for IMS. Usually this results in abnormal termination of the application program executing at the time.

That's where the fun begins. The immediate questions, under these circumstances, are normally how *many* bad pointers are there, followed by how did this happen? This whole topic could be (and is) the subject of another book.[2] Anyone who has been around IMS for any amount of time, however, has at least heard of "bad pointers," and you need to understand the meaning behind that expression.

In summary, to gain access to dependent segments, IMS must first access the root segment, then follow a combination of PCF and PTF pointers to move down and across the data base record to access the segment requested by the application program. In the case of extremely long twin chains or complex data base structures, quite a lot of searching (and a high amount of I/O) will be required. For that reason, although technically IMS is capable of handling very large and complex hierarchies, most of what you see in practice are relatively small and simple structures. Typical data bases contain no more than ten to fifteen segment types, and are no more than three or four levels deep. Smaller structures allow application programs to "get in and get out" quickly, with a minimum of I/O, and provide higher performance characteristics (with a correspondingly high amount of user satisfaction).

In other words, keep it simple...

5.5.2 Storage Efficiencies

In the preceding discussion, the unstated assumption was that all segments of the same type look alike on storage. In general, that's true. There are methods, however, of defining segments that can vary in terms of physical storage, based on data content at a given moment.

One such technique allows the application program to view a segment's I/O area as having, in COBOL terms, a variable OCCURS clause. The program can, at execution time, determine how much data are to be stored, and set (under program control) a two-byte length field to reflect this value (the first two bytes of the I/O area). Thus, physical storage requirements are controlled by the application program within limits of minimum and maximum values specified in the DBD.

Another technique allows the application program to always "see" a fixed-length segment in its I/O area. In other words, there is no length field to set; a segment defined to be 1,000 bytes will always have 1,000 bytes in the I/O area. However, in this case, you can advise IMS in the DBD that the segment is to be "compressed" with a specified compression routine. If this segment contains character data, there are any number of techniques that can reduce storage requirements. For example, a repeating character string, such as a series of spaces, can be reduced to only two bytes. IMS will automatically invoke the compression routine in moving the segment to or from the buffer pool and the application

---

[2] Hogan, Rex. *Diagnostic Techniques for IMS Data Bases* (Wellesley, MA: QED Information Sciences, Inc., 1986).

program. As a result, a 1,000-byte segment as seen by the application might only require 200 or 300 bytes of physical storage. Less disk space is required for a given amount of data, more segments are stored within each block, and most processes run with higher performance. It's a "win-win" situation, when used appropriately.

A (maximum) 1,000-byte segment might require only 300 bytes when first added to the data base, but what will happen if the application program makes an update and it now requires 400 bytes of storage? No matter which technique is used, IMS has a way of handling segments whose lengths fluctuate. There could easily be insufficient room to put it back to its original location. Yet IMS can't move the segment, for there will be pointers that address this segment at its original location.

As shown in Figure 5.8, IMS handles this situation through a compromise of what must be done. First, the original segment's prefix stays in the original location. Next, IMS uses the first four bytes of the old I/O area to store a variable-length segment pointer. This is simply another type of pointer which, in this case, takes us to where the data are now stored. IMS places the modified segment wherever necessary to meet the new space requirements. You might also note the special delete byte flags set when a segment is split on storage to identify the different pieces of a separated segment.

Of course, the most important point here is not necessarily the technical details of what is happening or how, but to realize the more sophisticated storage mechanisms that may be implemented, as well as the processing efficiencies which they provide.

Hopefully at this point you have a reasonable understanding of how IMS can move into and across data base records, following appropriate pointer chains. The following discussion addresses the two different HD mechanisms (or set of rules) which dictate how IMS locates the actual root segments. Keep in mind that once a root has been located, all access to dependents occurs as described. The two

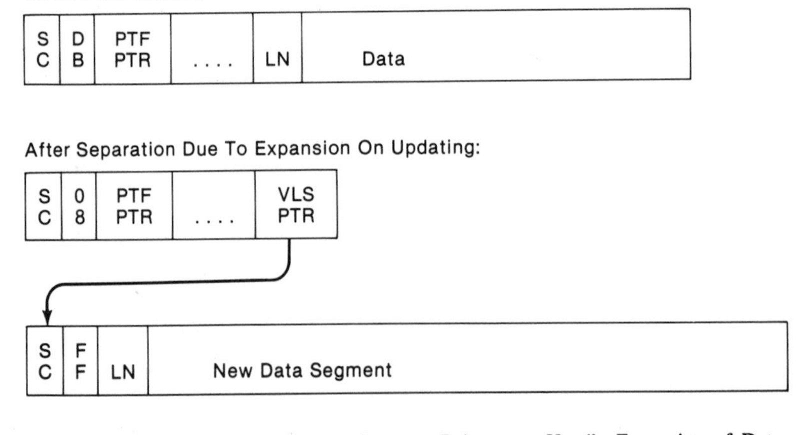

Figure 5.8 Using Variable-Length Segment Pointers to Handle Expansion of Data Segment

access methods differ in the way the root is located, but look and work alike "from the root down."

5.5.3 Accessing Data Base Records

In the Hierarchical Direct (HD) access methods, IMS provides two types of capabilities of accessing root segments. The first to be reviewed, HIDAM (Hierarchical Direct Indexed Access Method), uses an index mechanism, as its name implies.

Figure 5.9 illustrates how this index records information about root segments. Note that the data base consists of two separate physical data bases. The data component is simply a physical sequential data set. Based on the choice of system access methods, it is either a simple physical sequential data set (or to IMS, OSAM), or it is VSAM's version of physical sequential, a VSAM Entry Sequence Data Set (ESDS). Regardless of which "flavor" of system access method is chosen, at load time or in a reorganization (an unload/reload sequence, or "reorg"), data segments are loaded into this data set in the hierarchical processing sequence described earlier. As each segment is loaded in storage, a prefix is created for this segment containing all of the pointer connections called for in the DBD. Pointer values are established as segment locations are assigned by IMS in the load/reorg process.

As the load progresses, IMS stores information on where root segments are located in the index component. As each root segment is loaded into the data base, IMS creates an index entry "pointing to" the root. The index record consists of a delete byte, a four-byte pointer giving the location of the root segment on the data side, and finally the key of the root segment itself. After the load is complete, IMS handles an application request for a specific root segment by first requesting an

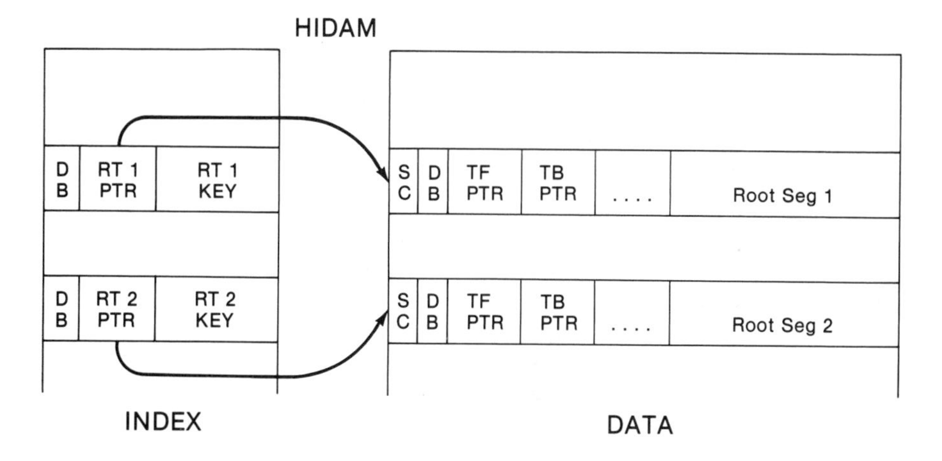

Figure 5.9 A HIDAM Data Base Configuration

index lookup of the index record (based on the root's key field), and then uses the pointer value indicated to retrieve the proper record (block) on the data side.

When using HIDAM, a data base designer should choose the twin backward option for the root segment. As a result, after the retrieval of a specified root based on its key field, IMS can move directly to the next root in key sequence in response to the appropriate application call. It will do so without incurring additional I/O to the index component of the data base. However, if only twin forward pointers are used for the root in HIDAM, they are *not* chained in sequence by the forward pointer, requiring IMS to use the index to move from one root to the next.

In any case, HIDAM provides a direct lookup capability for roots based on their key field, and, in sequential retrieval, returns roots in key sequence.

The second HD access method is HDAM, standing for the Hierarchical Direct Access Method. Here, roots are located based on a randomization scheme, therefore avoiding the I/O of index lookups. As such, HDAM is faster than HIDAM, being designed for high-speed random access. Figure 5.10 illustrates the storage structure of HDAM.

1. When the data base is set up, a parameter in the Data Base Description defines how much address space (a total number of blocks) across which IMS has to randomize roots. Assigning a value of 100 says IMS may choose a random block between 1 and 100 for this root. This parameter is called the Root Addressable Area.

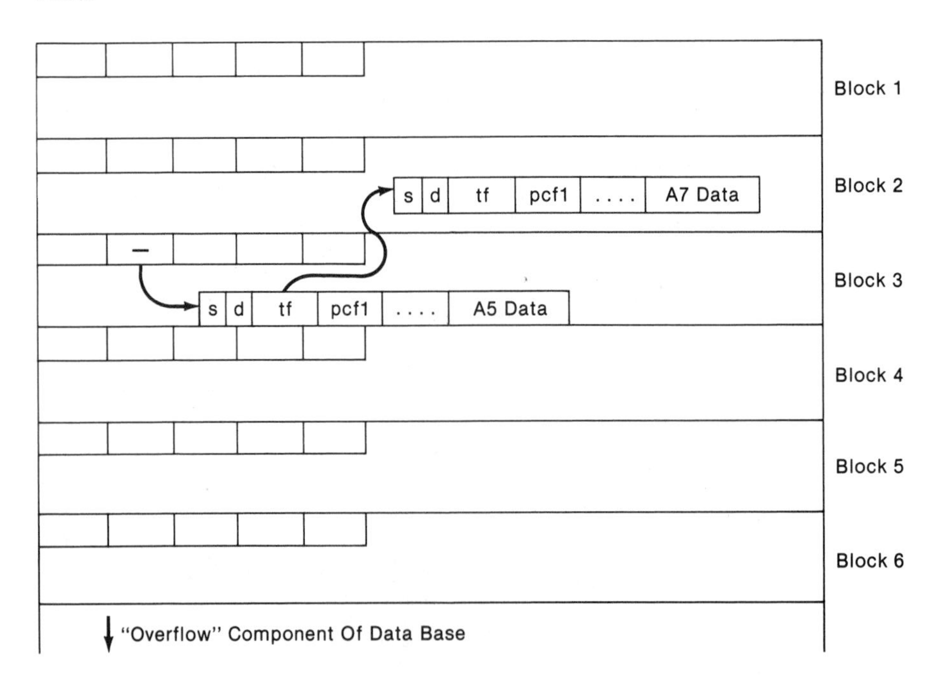

Figure 5.10 An HDAM Data Base Configuration

In Figure 5.10, this HDAM data base has six blocks in its Root Addressable Area.

2. Picking a random block in which to store a root is a good start, but is rather inexact. A block typically is 4K to 12K in size; therefore, an additional mechanism needs to exist to aid in selecting the root location. This mechanism can be thought of as a series of "mailboxes" which can contain the address of a root segment. Each mailbox is a special type of four-byte pointer.

In Figure 5.10, the data base has six blocks in its Root Addressable Area, with five mailboxes stored at the beginning of each block. In effect, then, IMS has a total of (6 × 5) 30 unique points across which to randomize root keys.

As another way to think of this, in handling a specific root key, IMS may choose a random number from 1 to 30. The particular mailbox indicated then holds the address of where the root is stored. In this example, the root having the key field "A5" is assumed to randomize to block 3, mailbox 2.

The IMS term for what has been termed a mailbox is a *root anchor point*, or RAP.

3. When using a set of values (in this case the keys for root segments) to generate random numbers, there is the distinct possibility that two different keys will generate the same random answer or result. IMS handles this situation automatically. All roots randomizing to the same block and RAP combination are called synonyms. The mailbox (RAP) will point to the root chaining to this location which has the lowest valued key. The physical twin forward pointer in that root will then point to the synonym with the next highest key; that root's PTF pointer will point to the next highest root, and so on. This is illustrated in Figure 5.10, where both A5 and A7 randomize to block 3, RAP 2.

That's pretty much it. Knowing in advance how many data base records are to be stored, it's fairly simple to properly size a Root Addressable Area that will provide good performance. When properly tuned, HDAM should give the fastest performance of these access methods; IMS figures out what block the root should be in, accesses that block, and it should be there. However, if improperly tuned, massive synonym chains can result, which can require many I/Os to retrieve a single root. In these instances, it can be much slower than the other access methods.

Regardless which of the two HD access methods is used (using randomization or an index), both work the same "from the root down." The access method defines a set of rules which IMS must follow in locating the root segment. Once the root is located, IMS locates dependents in the same way, through the use of physical child and twin pointers.

5.5.4 Space Management

Unused space in an HD-type block is automatically tracked and maintained by IMS as free-space elements, which may be used to store new segments added to the data base at a future time. As a performance option, unused space is normally reserved at load or reorg time by specifying, in the Data Base Description, free space as a percentage of every block, or as every nth block. In addition, when application programs call for data to be deleted, the newly liberated space is added to the free-space chain.

When making inserts to the data base, IMS automatically clusters new segments on storage as close together as possible. IMS tries to store new data within the block that contains the segment with the forward pointer to the one being inserted. If there is no room within that block, IMS stores the new segment as close as possible to the preferred block, within the range of another parameter called the scan limit. It specifies how far on either side of the preferred block IMS may search before storing the new segment at the end of the data base.

The objective, of course, is to balance free space with insert/delete activity to keep dependents as close as possible to their parents on storage. Subsequent retrieval of data segments can then be performed with minimal I/O, resulting in a system with higher performance and higher user satisfaction.

5.5.5 Secondary Data Set Groups

As an additional performance option specified within the DBD, the various segment types defined in a data base can be stored within one or several data set groups. Using physical child and twin pointers, data set groups can be established for essentially any grouping of segment types desired. Typical groupings may be in terms of segments that are used exclusively by batch or on-line processes, or segments that will always be accessed together whenever required by application programs.

Another typical use of secondary data sets relates to a mechanism called a bit map. The bit map is a scoresheet which IMS maintains on a one-bit-per-block basis, showing if that block does, or does not, have enough contiguous free space to hold the largest data base segment within the data set. This enables IMS to quickly find a block, when necessary, to hold a new segment in the data base without doing random I/O to look for space.

Problems arise if one segment in the data base is much longer than the other segments defined. The bit map, by definition, is maintained on the largest segment in the data set, and under these circumstances will mask, or not reflect, blocks where free space for smaller segments is available. If, on the other hand, the larger segment(s) are isolated in their own data set, each data set will have its own bit map, and free space is more effectively managed.

Data set groups are also a technique to handle large data bases. Space limitations exist on how large individual data sets may be. By dividing the segments in a data base across more data sets, more data can be stored in the data base.

Data set groups also have disadvantages. Following pointers across data sets always results in more I/O. Furthermore, backup/recovery functions work at the data set level; the more data sets there are to the data base, the more pieces there are to manage in backing up or recovering the data base. On the other hand, the fact that there are multiple pieces to back up or recover provides opportunities to simultaneously execute these jobs in parallel, and complete that function much faster than if everything were in one data set. Finally, performance gains from clustering data are only possible if parent/child segments are stored in the same data set.

5.6 ADVANCED TECHNIQUES—LOGICAL RELATIONSHIPS

5.6.1 An Overview of Logical Relationships

Previous sections reviewed various ways of creating physical data bases along with the rules under which data segments are stored or retrieved. Such techniques provide the capability for storing or retrieving data, but with a basic limitation. Access to data must begin with the root segment and continue with subsequent movement to the appropriate dependent segment type(s) required. Unfortunately, this isn't always enough.

Consider a data model involving data relationships between Part and Supplier entities. The intersection, or derived, entity Part-Supplier would be created as a result of the original M:M relationship between Part and Supplier, creating instead two 1:M relationships to the new intersection element, as depicted in Figure 5.11.

With this data relationship, application access requirements commonly cross these paths in both directions. For example, for a specified part, you need to find all suppliers. Conversely, for a specified supplier, you need to identify all parts that the supplier provides. Given such requirements, if you had nothing but the access capabilities previously described, the only solution is to make the application responsible for maintaining duplicate information in the two separate Part and Supplier data bases.

Logical relationships are designed to handle this kind of problem. With this capability, you can define a segment that contains the intersection of, in this case,

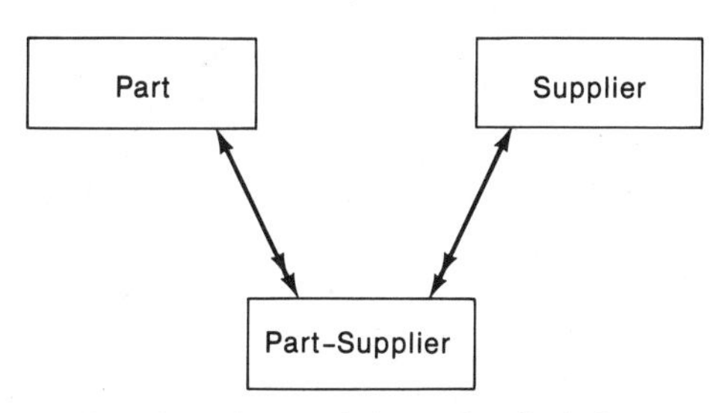

Figure 5.11 Intersection Data in a Part-Supplier Relationship

one part and one supplier. This intersection information, containing such things as the price of that part when purchased from the indicated supplier, is stored in one segment that also serves as a logical link between the two physical data bases. This segment type is called the logical child, because it creates a logical bridge between the physical parent (the true parent in the data base where the segment is physically stored) and the logical parent, which resides in the opposite, linked data base.

5.6.2 Implementation Options

Logical data bases can, in fact, be set up (or linked) in three different ways, depending on the requirements of the application. Figure 5.12 illustrates the differences between these choices.

Uni-directional

In Figure 5.12(a), the application requires crossing the two related data bases in only one direction. For example, you often need to find suppliers for parts, but don't need to identify all of the parts that a particular supplier provides. In this uni-directional implementation, the logical child provides a link in one direction only. In this example, the logical child would be stored physically in the Part data base, where each occurrence of Part-Supplier links that specific part with a supplier segment in the Supplier data base. Note that there is no capability to go from a supplier to the parts that it provides.

However, application requirements involving intersection data typically require access of these data from both directions. There are, in fact, two different ways to handle this type of requirement. Figure 5.12(b) shows the first such technique, where the logical child is physically stored in both data bases. This implementation option is appropriately named the bi-directional, physically paired method.

This may look a lot like a "home grown" application solution where data are redundantly stored in two physical data bases. It certainly appears this way, because the information contained in the logical child (such things as the price and delivery time for the part) are redundantly stored in each physical data base. The big difference is that IMS knows of this duplication and automatically keeps the two copies in sync when updates take place. The application programmer maintains only one update program. When any change is made to either copy, IMS automatically makes the corresponding change in the "clone" of the logical child in the other data base. (By the way, *clone* is a term I use to refer to this relationship; it is not an IMS term.)

If one goal in moving to logical relationships is to eliminate redundant data, you won't be satisfied with a physically paired implementation. The second bi-directional option, a "bi-directional, virtually paired" implementation, addresses this issue. As shown in Figure 5.12(c), the logical child appears only once

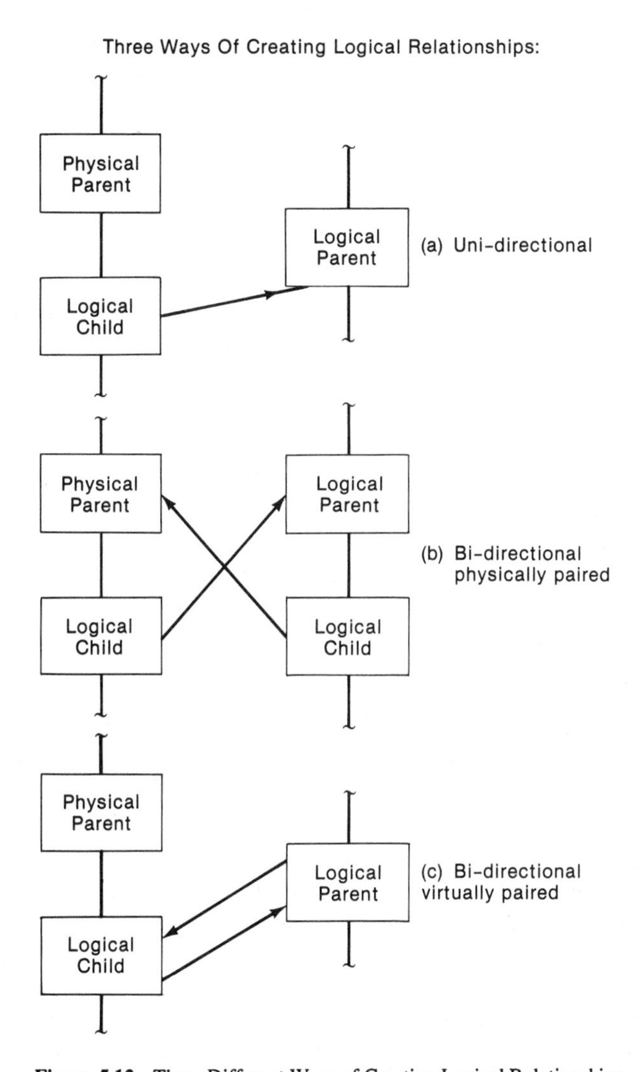

Figure 5.12 Three Different Ways of Creating Logical Relationships

and is linked in a reverse direction by a special logical pointer chain. Therefore, the bi-directional access capability exists, although there is only one physical copy of the data.

In this bi-directional implementation, note that the logical child may be placed in either physical data base. You can store the Part-Supplier information in either the Part data base, linking Part to Supplier, or in Supplier, linking Supplier to Part. Place the logical child in the data base having the most frequent access requirements. For example, you might frequently need to find suppliers for a given part, but very rarely care about parts from a given supplier. Therefore, by storing Part-Supplier in Part, IMS automatically clusters on storage the Part and Part-Supplier segments, and therefore retrieves as many of these segments as possible on a single I/O. Access from Part, then, is fast; access from Supplier is still possible, but is much slower.

5.6.3 Rules for Creating Logical Relationships

Logical relationships are a complex subject, with numerous pages of IMS manuals providing all sorts of detail. The major points, however, are:

1. A logical child is a dependent segment in a physical data base, and therefore has one, but only one, physical parent.
2. A logical child is a linkage mechanism between the data base in which it appears and one other physical data base. It therefore has one, but only one, logical parent. If a data base needs to be linked to more than one other data base, a logical child must be created for each.
3. A logical child can appear at any level of the hierarchy (other than at the root level).
4. A logical child cannot be the parent of another logical child.
5. A logical child can, however, have physical dependents. (One exception is that, in physical pairing, only one logical child can have dependents.)
6. A logical parent can have multiple logical children. This is the same as saying a data base can be involved in more than one logical relationship.
7. You need to be aware that rules options must be specified in the DBD, defining under what circumstances logical segments may be created or deleted. For example, when issuing a delete call, you may wish the logical child to be deleted from only the one path specified. To complete the delete function, you must later issue a delete from the opposite path.

   This is, in itself, a complex topic; consult the assistance of your local technical specialist when setting up your data base definitions.

5.6.4 Linkage Mechanisms

Previously you saw diagrams illustrating a logical child pointing to a logical parent segment. This logical linkage can, in fact, be provided in two ways.

1. *Use of Symbolic Pointer.* In this case, the literal key for the logical parent is stored physically as data in the logical child segment type. IMS can then use this key to do a direct lookup in the target (logical) data base whenever necessary to bridge that path.

2. *Use of Direct Pointers.* Here, a direct (four-byte) pointer type can be defined in the DBD. Each logical child, then, has a special pointer in its prefix which points to the logical parent.

This latter mechanism provides the fastest way to bridge these two data bases but requires extra work and overhead to be performed by maintenance utilities to rebuild the logical pointer chains every time either data base is reorganized. On the other hand, having the symbolic key in the logical child will, on occasion, keep IMS from having to perform unnecessary I/O. Quite often, logical data bases are implemented with both symbolic and direct pointers, giving the "best of both worlds."

5.6.5 Performance Implications

Let's review logical relationships by looking at examples that should illustrate the performance implications involved. The following illustrations are based on one part that is available by three suppliers. The following illustrations show how these data would appear for each of the various choices possible in implementing logical relationships.

Figure 5.13 illustrates this data relationship when stored as a Uni-Directional implementation. Note that there are three occurrences of the Part-Suppler segment, each providing a linkage to its respective Supplier segment. If you remember, this link could be made by a symbolic or a direct pointer, or both.

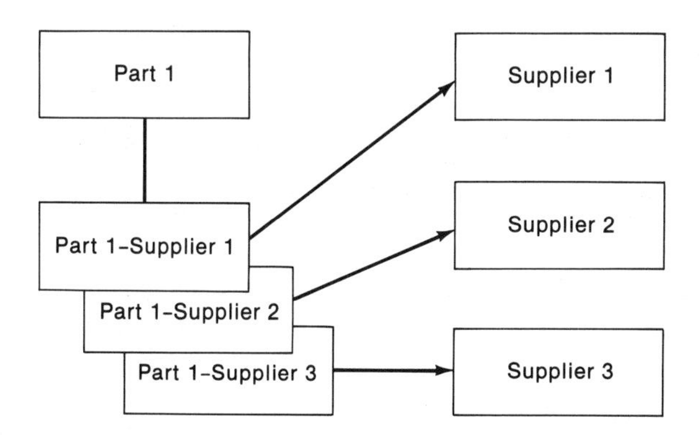

Figure 5.13 A Uni-Directional Implementation

Figure 5.14 shows these same data in a bi-directional, physically paired relationship. Note that this is essentially the same as the uni-directional solution, with the addition of the clone segments and paths to obtain bi-directional capability. Note also the redundant data segments required for this implementation.

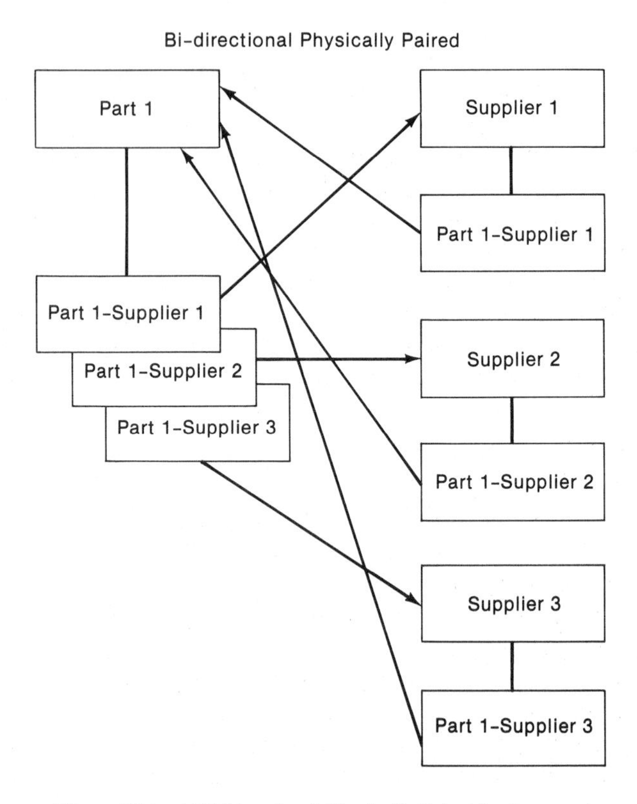

Figure 5.14 A Bi-Directional, Physically Paired Implementation

Figure 5.15, illustrating a bi-directional, virtually paired relationship, also looks similar to the uni-directional solution, modified to include the reverse pointer chains required for the opposite path. Keep in mind that IMS will try to store the various segments in the Part data base as close as possible on storage, thereby minimizing I/O in retrieving data from that direction.

Note, however, that if the decision had been made to store the logical child under Supplier, the performance characteristics of the solution would change significantly. Study Figure 5.16. This is another bi-directional, virtually paired solution for the same data configuration, but showing what would happen if the logical child were stored under Supplier. Note the reverse path from Part. A logical child first pointer connects Part 1 to its first logical child; from there, a logical twin forward chain can be seen connecting the various occurrences of the logical children for Part 1. This solution, clustering the intersection information close to the Supplier segments, provides fast access to these data from the Supplier side, but slower access from Part.

As the designer, you can use virtually paired relationships to provide fast access from one path, but with slower access from the opposite path. You must

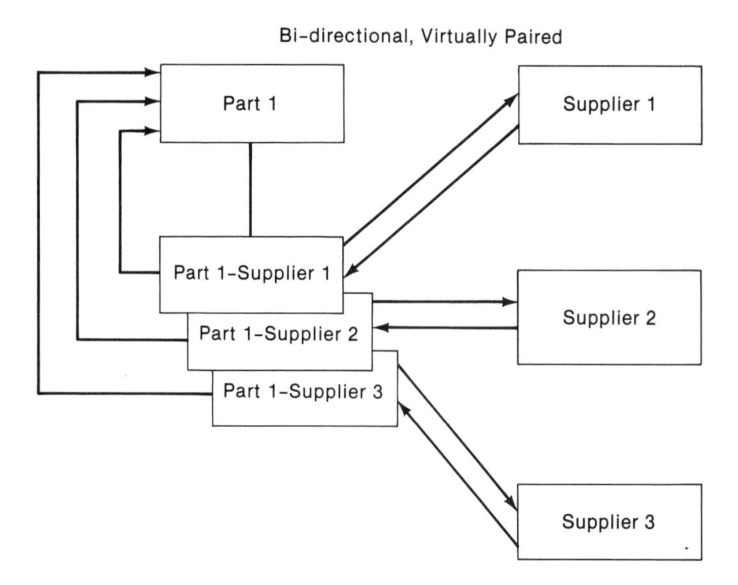

Figure 5.15 A Bi-Directional, Virtually Paired Implementation

decide, from an analysis of the usage path requirements, which of the two paths is more important to you, and then make your choice accordingly.

5.7 ADVANCED TECHNIQUES—SECONDARY INDEXING

5.7.1 Fundamentals of Secondary Indexing

In addition to logical relationships, secondary indexing also allows sophisticated access of data bases. Simply stated, a secondary index provides an alternate way of accessing or sequencing data base records.

To understand a secondary index, you must understand how a HIDAM data base works. Figure 5.17 shows how a Customer and Equipment data base would appear if stored in a HIDAM data base. The data component contains all of the segments in the data base. This data set is loaded in a physical sequential manner at reorganization time, placing the segments into the data base in hierarchical sequence. As each root segment is loaded in the data component, IMS creates a record in the index component of the data base containing the root's key field, along with a four-byte pointer, specifying the root segment's location in the data component.

Let's assume that you need to answer telephone queries on customer information, where the caller is unaware of your internal customer code, which is the key of the Customer segment. As shown in Figure 5.18, a secondary index can be

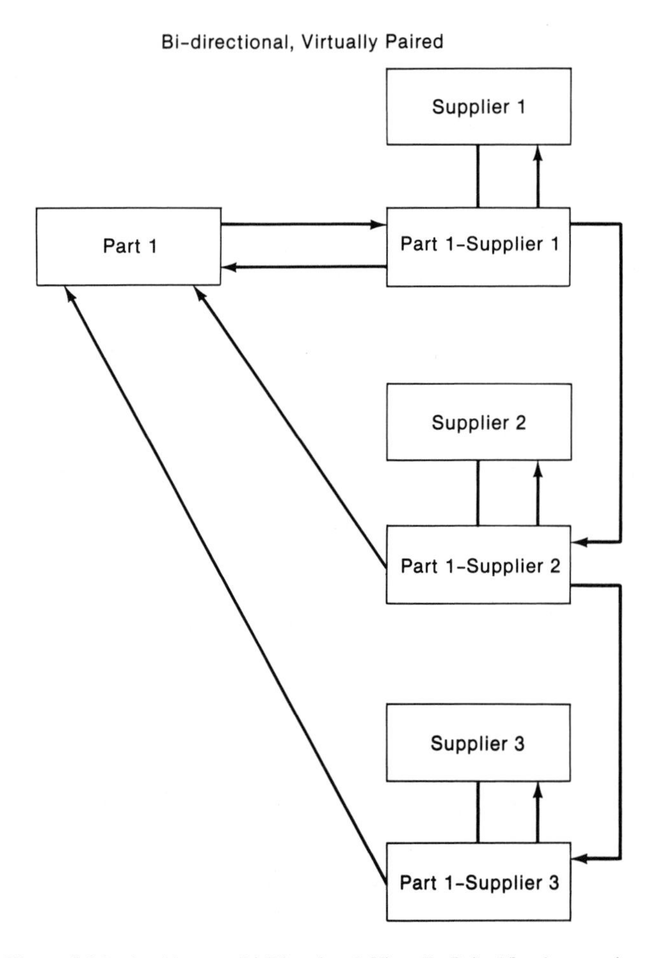

Figure 5.16 An Alternate Bi-Directional, Virtually Paired Implementation

created, based on customer name. Each record in the secondary index contains the key for the index (the customer's name), along with a four-byte pointer showing where the record is located. Therefore, given only the name, the application program can directly access the customer segment.

In summary, a HIDAM index sequences the data component of the data base on the root's key field, while a secondary index sequences the same set of data based on an alternate processing sequence.

Establishing secondary indexes on other data fields from the Customer segment would provide a wide variety of capability and function. One based on the Customer's telephone number would permit access to Customer records without the complexity of matching alphabetic names. If one were placed on the salesperson's code, each salesperson could be given on-line access to their Custo-

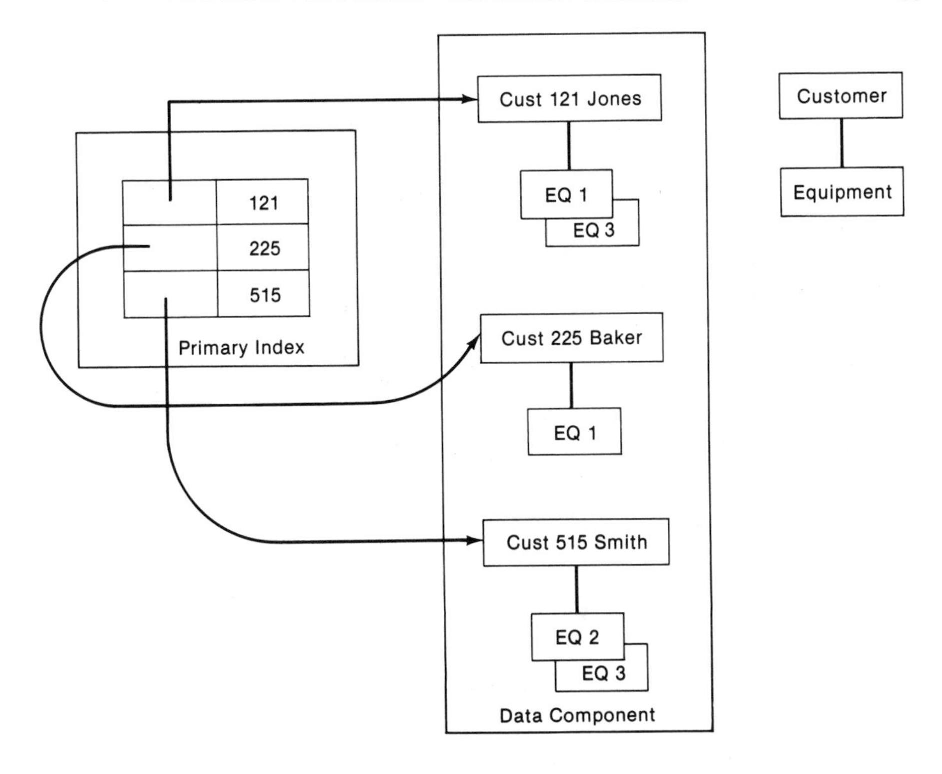

Figure 5.17 A Customer Data Base Implementation Using HIDAM

mer records while avoiding a scan of the data base. Finally, a list of customers with bad credit ratings could be produced by creating an index on a field having credit rating values.

Figure 5.18 shows another way in which indexes might be used. A secondary index has been created based on equipment type. With this index, you can access customers who have, for example, equipment type 1. Once again, the original data are being sequenced on a data field other than the root's key, which in this case resides in a dependent segment.

5.7.2 Terminology

IMS manuals use special terminology for secondary indexes.

Index Source Segment. The segment containing the source data fields used to construct the secondary index.

Index Pointer Segment. The segment in the secondary index which "points into" the primary data base.

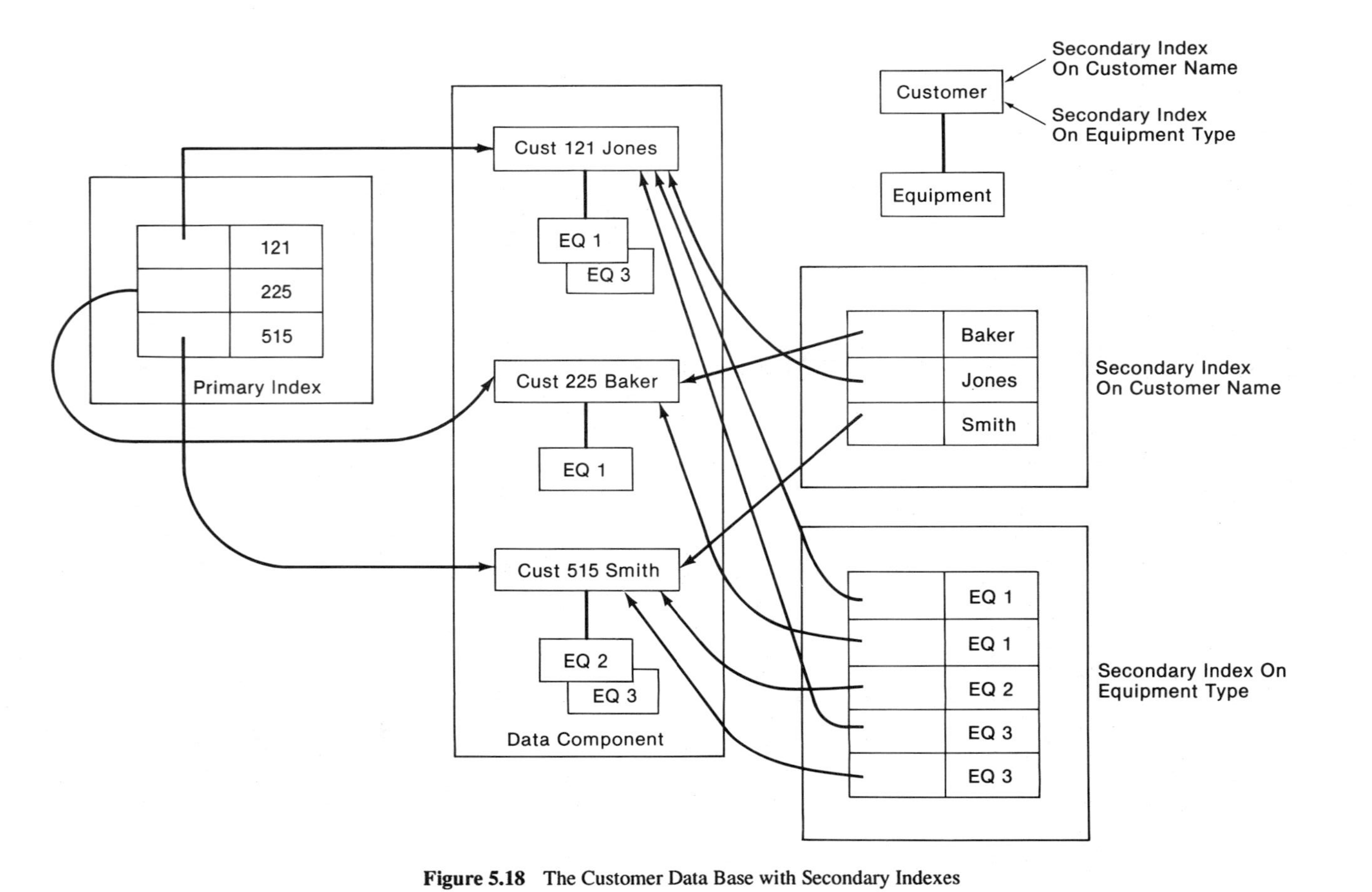

Figure 5.18 The Customer Data Base with Secondary Indexes

Index Target Segment. The root of the indexed data base as seen through the secondary index. In establishing secondary indexes, the designer chooses what is seen or addressed by the index itself. I recommend targeting the root of the original structure as a standard choice. Other options are also possible but result in an inverted structure, which changes the view of the data base as seen by the programmer.

In Figure 5.18, the Equipment index has been set up to point to the Customer having that equipment. Therefore, the Equipment segment is the source segment, the secondary index data base segment is the pointer segment, and the Customer segment is the target segment type.

5.7.3 Options for Secondary Indexing

Secondary indexes, like the subject of logical relationships, are documented across numerous pages in IMS manuals. Briefly, these are their major options:

1. A secondary index can be defined on HDAM or HIDAM data bases. It may also be defined on HISAM data bases with a single data set, although in the practical sense that is rarely done.
2. The source for the index can be constructed from one to five noncontiguous fields from the source segment type.
3. Sparse indexing options may be implemented in several ways. In one method, if a field is filled with a specified constant, the index record is suppressed. For example, a special flag could be set for Customer records having a special class of equipment which only 5 percent of the customers possess. Using this flag to control a sparse index, the secondary index would contain only records reflecting that rare 5 percent of customers who have that classification.
4. Other fields in the source segment may be duplicated by IMS within the index, making it practical for use in stand-alone processing.
5. The index may contain additional user data fields, which are the user's responsibility to maintain.

Finally, in addition to the preceding more classical usages, it is possible to use a secondary index as an alternative to implementing a logical relationship. As you recall, logical relationships generally require pointer chains to tie together two separate physical data bases. This creates a physical dependency across these two structures which, in turn, imposes limits on their availability and scheduling. Though normally not a problem, it does result in reduced flexibility for the data center in meeting special processing requirements.

A secondary index can also provide the same access capability as that obtained by a bi-directional, virtually paired logical relationship. Figure 5.19 provides the same functional capability as provided in Figure 5.15.

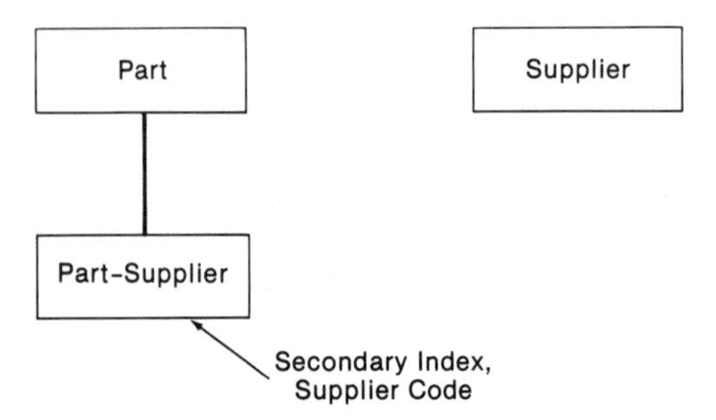

Figure 5.19 Using Secondary Indexing as an Alternative to Logical Relationships

5.8 SUMMARY OF ADVANCED IMPLEMENTATION OPTIONS

Hierarchical structures, by their basic nature, provide the fastest and most efficient access to data possible when usage requirements match the hierarchical sequence in which data are stored. These same data, however, can be accessed in other ways.

Using logical relationships, two physical data bases that share intersection data can be logically connected. This shared segment links these two data bases so a program may view them as one hierarchical structure. This link may be implemented in several ways to satisfy varying access and performance requirements.

Secondary indexes may be implemented to provide access to data in other than hierarchical sequence. They provide a great deal of flexibility to satisfy access requirements to any required segment type where the root key may not be known. They can, if desired, be used to provide the same functional capability as logical relationships while avoiding the use of pointer chains to tie physical data bases together.

Considering all the options and alternatives available, there is seldom just one IMS-based solution for a given design. The trick, then, is to identify and view requirements in such a way that the possible alternatives can be identified and considered, weighing when appropriate any high-performance or high-volume data requirements.

5.9 SUMMARY OF DESIGN STEPS

1. Develop the data model (or relational view).
2. Using the data model developed, perform a usage analysis for the required application programs.

   Keep in mind that, during this stage, any usage paths developed are simply first-cut solutions, and will probably change later when considering the composite of all usages. At that time, it will be important to identify and use common access paths for data, so the appropriate implementation options can be used to satisfy these access requirements. Therefore, these initial access paths will change as needed to conform to standard paths or sequences as they evolve.

3. Overlay the initial usage path requirements over the data model to identify first-cut linkage and entry point requirements. Special attention should be given in identifying entry points to the data base, particularly where access of segment types is not based on the segment's key field.
4. Review all proposed access paths and call patterns to devise, as far as practical, common paths to all frequently accessed data.
5. Make initial suggestions for physical implementation options. An HD-type data base would be chosen if one or more of the following circumstances exist (most data bases will fall in this category):
   (a) the data base has long or complex data base records;
   (b) the data base has any high amount of insert/delete activity;
   (c) access requirements call for the use of secondary indexes or logical relationships.

   If an HD mechanism is to be used:
   (a) Choose HDAM for data bases with no significant requirement for retrieval of roots in ascending order of the root key field. HDAM data bases should have TF specified for the root segment's pointer option.
   (b) Choose HIDAM for data bases with a significant requirement for retrieval of roots in ascending order of the root key field. HIDAM roots should have TB specified for the root segment's pointer option.
   (c) Use PCF pointers at a minimum for parent/dependent segment linkage.
   (d) Choose TB pointers for dependent segments having significant delete activity.

   Consider the use of HISAM or SHISAM for simple table-like structures.
6. Review this initial solution in a design review with appropriate support personnel.

Following these steps should result in devising a good first-cut design in a minimum amount of time. In support of this effort, use your technical support staff at appropriate times to prevent mistakes and make proper use of available techniques and options. The end result is a higher quality product, both in meeting user requirements as well as in performance.

REVIEW QUESTIONS

1. Envision Customer and Order records which are involved in a 1:M relationship. They can be implemented in a simple hierarchical structure, a tree structure with a secondary index, or two root-only data bases. Discuss the implications of these choices in terms of flexibility and performance.

2. HDAM and HIDAM are the most commonly used access methods for IMS. However, on occasion HISAM and SHISAM are also used. Determine decision criteria for conditions where each would be considered.
3. Part and Supplier data bases are to be related by either some type of bi-directional relationship or by a secondary index. Determine the implications of these two choices in terms of flexibility and performance.
4. Describe how the network Location Modes of CALC, INDEX and VIA SET relate to data base access methods in an IMS environment.

REVIEW PROBLEMS

The following problems are a continuation of those first described at the end of Chapter 2. Refer to those descriptions for an overview of the data environment involved, and derive IMS solutions for each.

1. Inventory system
   - **(a)** For each purchase, first verify a customer's credit status. Then record the sale of an item by decrementing the quantity on hand, and update the customer's history of items purchased (on line).
   - **(b)** Enter price data for items after price increases are received from a supplier (on line).
   - **(c)** For a specified item, check the price information for all suppliers, and identify the supplier with the lowest purchase price (on line).
   - **(d)** List the items purchased by each customer, including the item name (batch).
   - **(e)** List, for each supplier, the items available with the price for each (batch).
2. Library system
   - **(a)** Check to see what items a patron has currently checked out (on line).
   - **(b)** Record that a specified book or article is being checked out to a library patron (on line).
   - **(c)** Find all books and articles written by a specified author, or on a specified subject (on line).
   - **(d)** Produce a listing of all books and articles available in the library (batch).
   - **(e)** Search all subscribers to check for loaned items overdue by more than 30 days (batch).
3. Project tracking
   - **(a)** List the skills that a specific employee possesses (on line).
   - **(b)** Find all employees with a specified skill (on line).
   - **(c)** Assign a specific employee to a project for a specified skill type (on line).
   - **(d)** For each employee, enter project activity (by skill type) (on line).
   - **(e)** List, by project, the skills required, the employees assigned, and the total hours worked by each (batch).
4. Magazine publication house
   - **(a)** Enter new subscribers for magazines (on line).
   - **(b)** Enter information on new ads placed by advertisers (on line).
   - **(c)** Verify the credit rating of specified advertisers (on line).
   - **(d)** Produce a list of subscribers whose subscriptions are about to expire (batch).

(e) Produce a list of magazines available, and the advertisers placing ads within each (batch).

5. Wholesale mail order

(a) When a customer calls in, check the price of desired equipment given in the specified magazine ad (on line).

(b) Check the status of orders for customers (on line).

(c) Enter new advertised items, given the magazine, issue, page of the ad, and the equipment advertised (on line).

(d) List the status of customers and orders placed during the past month (batch).

(e) For each type of equipment, list the details of each ad in which that equipment type is listed (batch).

6

Relational Data Base Systems

6.1 INTRODUCTION

Today, relational data bases are infiltrating the mainframe environment, penetrating into application systems formerly dominated by the more traditional DBMS forms. Such applications cover accounting systems, inventory control, and are even being used for systems which require quick response, such as the banking industry. Beginning in late 1985, readers of data processing literature have become inundated with a variety of articles on relational systems; claims and counterclaims of what a relational DBMS is, and why certain products are, or are not, considered to be truly relational. Besides providing entertaining reading, these articles do raise a number of points on the positive and negative sides of selecting and using a relational DBMS. However, all too often readers are left to sift through the bits and pieces of claims and counterclaims to obtain a personal interpretation of reality, and to try to identify and apply the more pertinent points from the literature. The primary objective of this chapter is to provide a working knowledge of what a relational DBMS "is all about"; what capabilities it should have, how data are managed, and how to obtain a good first-cut data base design for your application. The internal storage structure of IBM's DB2 product is also briefly reviewed to give you an idea of how that product has been implemented.

6.2 DEFINITIONS

Relation. A two-dimensional array or table of data containing descriptive information about an entity which is, at a minimum, in first normal form. In this text, the terms *relation* and *table* are used interchangeably.

Column. An attribute defined within a specific table. Here the terms *column*, *attribute*, and *field* are used interchangeably.

```
Employee                       <=== the entity being described
     SOCIAL-SECURITY-NUMBER     =|
     EMPLOYEE-NAME               |
     HOME-ADDRESS                |====> attributes describing
     JOB-TITLE-CODE              |       the entity
     SALARY                     =|
```

Row. One occurrence of a record within a table. Here the terms *row* and *record* are used interchangeably.

```
Employee                                            <== An Employee table
123-45-6789 Sam Jones     123 West Willford Ave ... <== a row in the
234-56-7890 Mary Williams 1238 Cliffwood Drive ....   Employee table
```

Tuple. Another term for a row; a record.

Primary Key. In a relation, the attribute (or combination of attributes) that uniquely identify one row or record.

In the Employee table, SOCIAL-SECURITY-NUMBER would uniquely identify a unique employee, and could be used as the primary key. EMPLOYEE-NAME, on the other hand, is not unique, and could not be used as a key.

Foreign Key. In a relation, an attribute (or combination of attributes) that appears totally as a primary key within another relation.

```
Employee
SOCIAL-SECURITY-NUMBER     <=== primary key, Employee
EMPLOYEE-NAME
HOME-ADDRESS
JOB-TITLE-CODE             <=== foreign key relating Employee
SALARY                          to Job Title
Job Title
JOB-TITLE-CODE             <=== primary key, Job Title
POSITION-TITLE
```

Foreign key relationships are the basis for establishing 1:M relationships across tables in a relational data base.

Domain. The set of all possible values that a particular attribute may have.

In Employee, if SALARY represented an hourly rate, a DBMS providing domain support would know that salary figures could only be positive numbers of the form $99.99. Salary values would automatically be edited by the DBMS on data entry or modification, reducing the amount of work required by application code.

Join. The concatenation of two tables created from rows which have the same value for matching columns (a foreign key).

Cursor. In set-oriented processing, a mechanism which permits an application program to point to or address a single row from an entire set of rows.

6.3 PROPERTIES OF RELATIONS

A relational DBMS, by definition, must have certain inherent characteristics that form the basis for its underlying strength and flexibility. Because of these features, an application implemented with such a system is much more flexible and can be easily modified when alterations or enhancements to the underlying data model take place. These characteristics are:

1. No duplicate rows exist. No two rows can be identical. If they were, why would two rows be necessary in the table? Duplicate rows would also violate the definition of what a relation represents. As you recall, part of the first normal form requirements call for the existence of a unique primary key, which in itself says that no two rows will ever be totally identical.

2. The order of rows is insignificant. There is no ordering or sequencing of the rows in the data base. A relational implementation of the Employee table should support all required access based on nothing but data content, and must not be dependent on any specific ordering of the individual rows. It is not necessary to sequence the rows on the SOCIAL-SECURITY-NUMBER key.

3. The order of the columns is insignificant. The sequence in which columns are defined should have no significance when implementing the data base. A more subtle extension of this property is that columns can be dynamically defined and added "on the fly." The application may define new columns in tables while the data base is being updated by application programs. This flexibility has tremendous impact on the ease with which modification or expansion of the data base can be made.

4. Columns are all elemental, or atomic. At the lowest level, all columns are decomposed or broken down into their simplest elemental meaning or definition.

Combinations of these simple or elemental columns may be defined, but are just that—a composite or collection of elemental columns.

Dates provide a good example of elements that should be decomposed. A data element representing EFFECTIVE-SALARY-DATE should be broken down to reflect the individual elements of month-day-year. In that way you can later support salary surveys which require a selection of all rows matching a particular year, or perhaps a year-month combination. Failure to decompose the date will prevent performing this type of search.

More subtly, a column (or attribute) can possess one and only one value for the row to which it belongs. In other words, there can be "no repeating groups."

A relational data base, then, is a collection of associated tables where 1:M paths are maintained based on the data contents of the various rows, not by some means of physical implementation or structure.

A number of issues directly determine the overall effectiveness of a relational DBMS. Virtually every software vendor on the market claims to have a relational product. To perform any intelligent analysis of these products, you must be aware of the major features that distinguish a relational system from other products which simply lay claim to the name. The next section reviews the characteristics required in relational systems.

6.4 REQUIREMENTS FOR A RELATIONAL DBMS

Dr. Ted Codd originated the concept of the relational model for data base management systems in the early 1970s. Since that time, he has been a devoted advocate of relational concepts, emphasizing the necessity for vendors to provide products with capabilities consistent with the relational model. In two *Computerworld* articles, published October 14, 1985 and October 21, 1985, he defined a number of rules necessary for compliance to the relational model. In the following section, I have given my interpretation of the capabilities necessary to support these rules, along with the price developers must pay if that capability did not exist.

Backup/Recovery facilities

In beginning this topic, I'd like to add one basic and fundamental item that is sometimes overlooked in a review of current literature. A relational DBMS should first qualify as a data base management system, with its conformance to the relational model being an additional but separate matter. More specifically, as stated in Chapter 1, a data base system must include backup/recovery facilities.

Upon experiencing data loss or damage after a system or hardware failure, backup/recovery mechanisms provide for automatic recovery of a data base to the point of failure. This normally involves using a system log data set that records changes to the data base as the result of application processing. Recovery is performed by restoring a copy of the data base, and then overlaying that old copy with change information to bring the data base back to the point of failure.

A recovery process should never require reexecuting completed work. This is *reprocessing* lost data, not recovering it. Any data base system worthy of that name will provide recovery mechanisms to reconstruct lost data in a failure. Reprocessing work to reproduce lost data should only be done when, because of extreme circumstances, normal recovery mechanisms will not work.

When investigating this kind of capability, check to see if some type of system log tape is produced recording data base changes. Then see what kind of information is recorded on this log, and in what format. Finally, check to see what process or system utility would be invoked to restore the data base in the event of a system failure.

Active Data Dictionary

Most data processing shops have already found the need to use an automated data dictionary product. If properly used, a dictionary system can be used to store, in a standard, uniform way, descriptive information about data stored in your company's files or data structures. For each field, a dictionary contains a description of what the field represents, the program name(s) used by applications, the length and data type of the field, the record(s) in which the field is located, update or edit rules, and so on. This information is typically used to:

1. Generate standard I/O areas for any program requiring access to these files.
2. Provide an automated way to store entity/attribute list information for new or revised application systems.
3. Provide support for data administrators or end users in identifying the location of corporate data on specified topics. If data elements in the corporate data dictionary have been fully defined in a standard, uniform way, then you can find the location of information required for ad hoc reports.

Assume that you must perform a salary survey, and you need to know what kind of salary data are available, what they represent, and where they are stored. Using keywords that were used to describe data elements initially in the dictionary, you can run queries to produce reports describing fields related to salary.

These ad hoc reporting capabilities are extremely powerful, and are found in any full-fledged data dictionary system. However, relational DBMS packages without an active dictionary must still include a catalog structure to map data elements into whatever storage structure is used. These catalogs are too simplistic to include definitions of what the data elements really represent and do not support full dictionary-like services or facilities. In addition, if other software products are used for generating reports or application programs, they will also require their own definition or mapping facility to provide access to data elements.

The biggest problem, of course, is figuring out how to keep all of these in sync. This problem is compounded by the general ease in using a relational product's catalog, where new data elements can be easily and quickly defined "on the fly." This information also needs to be defined in the corporate data dictionary, and in more detail than that contained in the relational system's catalog. If the dictionary is considered to be the controlling mechanism, will users be satisfied to describe data first to the dictionary, then download it to the relational catalog (with an appropriate delay to allow for these things to happen)? If, on the other hand, the relational catalog is the controlling mechanism, will users faithfully keep track of all data elements defined directly to the catalog for later entry to the dictionary? The answers to both questions are probably "No."

An active data dictionary would avoid the problem of dual definition. Data can be defined in one place, totally and completely, as well as provide the real-time access control required in a relational environment. If a relational DBMS lacks this capability, users of that system must:

1. Identify data elements in two or more locations and bear the effort of keeping all of them in sync; or
2. Develop their own extension of the catalog to provide dictionary-like support.

Treatment of Null Values

As a relational system can define, dynamically, new columns for existing tables, the capability must also exist to recognize which rows have a value stored for new columns, and which have not.

It's also possible that certain data fields may never be populated. As an example, assume that the Employee table contains a field that gives the number of people supervised. Now you need to run a query to identify the average number of people supervised. What do you think should happen for those employees who have no subordinates? Should a "zero" value be included in each row, and be counted in the final average? Or should these rows be ignored, and only employees normally having a nonnull value for "number of employees supervised" be counted?

If you were dealing with a system that provided no support for null values, you must derive a scheme to make the query work as desired. In this particular example, you could define an additional data element to indicate a "manager" (that is, one who has subordinates) and include that qualification as part of the query.

Oh, a final thought on null values. Articles describing relational systems state that nulls should not be used as part of a primary key in a relation. Although this is technically correct, it seems redundant when considering the nature of a key. By definition, all components of the primary key are required to guarantee uniqueness.

How, then, could something be a part of the key and yet have a null value? So, if your particular relational DBMS does not provide protection against null fields participating as keys, this shouldn't be a problem because the unique key requirement will prevent nulls from being used as part of the key.

Provide Update Capability within Views

Users of a relational system think of the system as a collection of user views or tables. With the definition of a specific view of data, any process using this view (and possessing the appropriate authority) should be able to update the data base. If this is not supported, users loose much of the logical data independence which the data base system should provide.

Some relational systems allow viewing the result of two tables joined by a foreign key, but force the use of separate physical views of individual tables when applying updates. It would certainly be easier if all views would support updates.

Set-oriented Operations

Relational systems must, by definition, retrieve data records by returning *all* rows in the data base which satisfy the selection criteria specified. This is in direct opposition to the "record at a time" processing which most of us have used for years.

This does not say that the old "record at a time" processing is obsolete; there are many processes, particularly those implemented in an on-line environment, that still need to function that way, even when the data are stored in a relational environment. However, there are a number of times that set-oriented processing would make application logic much simpler. Without that capability, application developers must go to more effort to accomplish the same amount of work.

Physical Data Independence

Physical data independence is a condition where the application programmer does not know or care about the physical storage characteristics of the data base. This includes such things as the particular type of storage device, blocksizes chosen on DASD, and so on.

With physical independence, applications are totally unaffected by any changes made to the data base for tuning or to implement structural changes. However, if a DBMS uses pointer chains to bridge 1:M access paths, independence is greatly reduced, as an unload/reload operation is required to add or delete pointer chains.

Logical Data Independence

Logical independence calls for application processes to be unaffected by changes in the logical definition of the base tables in a relational data base. For example, a table might be split into two tables as the original design matures; or, conversely, two tables might be combined into one.

This feature provides the designer flexibility in the definition of the original base tables. Without this type of support, more time and analysis is required to insure that mistakes or oversights don't occur.

The Domain Concept

Each column of a table has only one domain, that is, only one legitimate set of possible values. On the other hand, a particular domain may be applicable to more than one column.

If domain support were available, it would be much easier to process updates to tables by having automatic editing for data values. Without domain support, application logic must bear more responsibility for editing. In addition, system designers must be careful to use consistent edits for attributes used as foreign keys.

Referential Integrity

Referential integrity enforces the idea that "the key of the one appears within the many."

Using an example of employees and deductions, referential integrity insures that the employee record exists before permitting new deduction records to be created. In network terms, this means an owner record must exist before creating a member.

Without this record capability, the application must itself perform the appropriate checks to insure that the value of the foreign key is correct.

6.5 PHYSICAL IMPLEMENTATION TECHNIQUES

To understand a physical implementation of a relational data base, remember that they are, loosely, "flat files" or tables of data, with no inherent structure. All 1:M relationships are managed based on foreign key data content, not by physical structure or pointer chains.

Figure 6.1 illustrates how employee and employee deduction records look in table form. Note the absence of pointer chains in linking those two record types. The key of the employee table, EMP-ID (employee id), appears as a foreign key in the employee deduction table, which has a key of EMP-ID, DED-CODE (deduction code). The data base system associates a particular employee record with its deduction records based on the fact that the employee key is stored physically in the deduction record.

Basically, four ways exist to bridge these 1:M relationships—searching, sorting, indexing, and pointers.

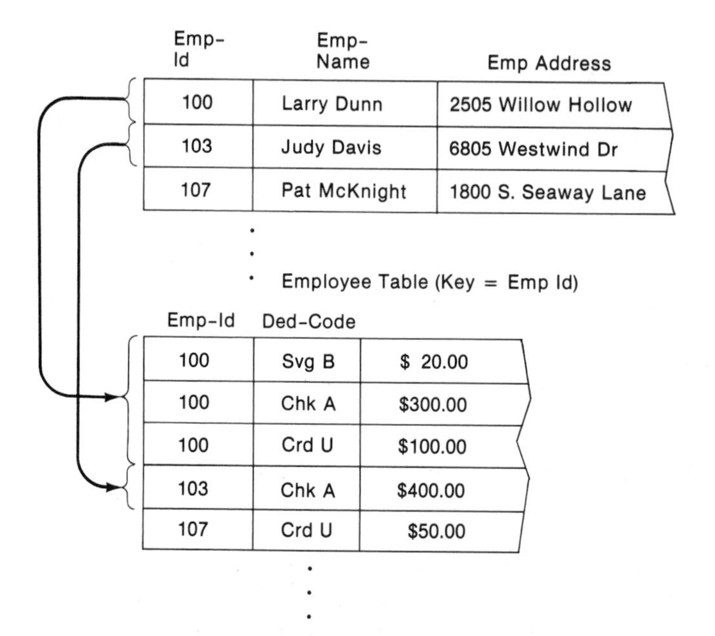

Figure 6.1 Employee and Employee Deduction Information in Relational Tables

1. Search for the data. This is the simplest of all mechanisms. To find all deduction records for a specific employee, the DBMS sequentially runs through the entire deduction file to locate deduction records having the required employee key (see Figure 6.2). Each record selected is added to the output set, the collection of records that reflect all deduction records for the specified employee. Note that since the file is from a relational data base, record order is insignificant, and therefore the DBMS must search the entire file.

This method is simple to implement and is flexible because the DBMS always searches for records based on data content. For large tables, however, this searching requires a considerable amount of I/O. If the employee system accessed deductions frequently, it should employ another mechanism with a higher level of performance.

2. Sort the data records. Once the deduction records are sorted by employee key, the DBMS can find the cluster of Larry Dunn's deductions efficiently (see Figure 6.3). The price seems high; the DBMS must read the entire file into the sort, and perform the sort itself, always a hefty task. This technique may, however, provide the most efficient way of handling infrequent processing of payroll programs requiring as input all employee and deduction records.

3. Indexing specified data fields. This is the most common way to bridge tables based on important foreign keys. With this mechanism, the system designer

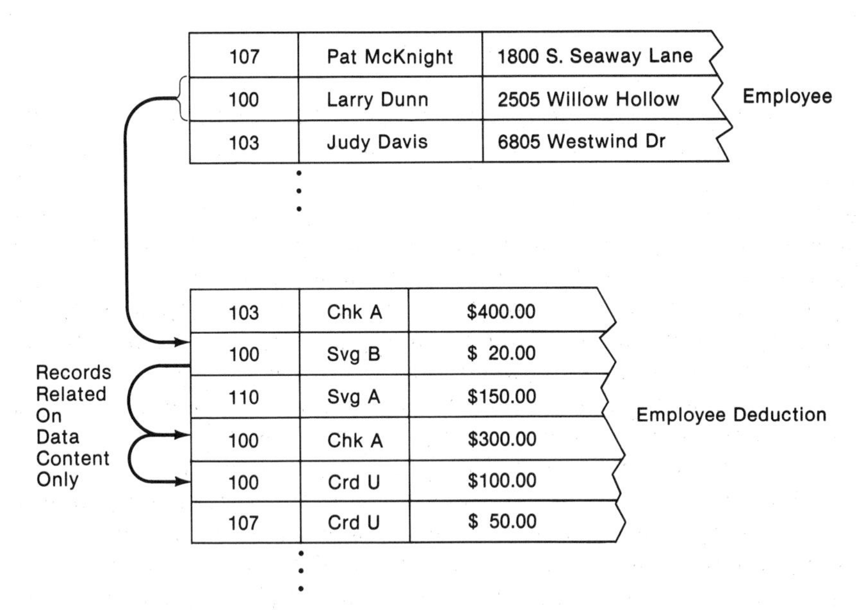

Figure 6.2 Employee and Employee Deductions in Unsorted Tables

Employee

100	Larry Dunn	2505 Willow Hollow
103	Judy Davis	6805 Westwind Dr
107	Pat McKnight	1800 S. Seaway Lane

Employee Deduction

100	Chk A	$300.00
100	Crd U	$100.00
100	Svg B	$ 20.00
103	Chk A	$400.00
107	Crd U	$ 50.00

Figure 6.3 Employee and Employee Deductions Sorted by Key

declares a system-maintained index based on that foreign key. Each entry in the index specifies where on disk the associated row is stored and provides direct access to the row having the specified value.

100	Larry Dunn	2505 Willow Hollow	Employee
103	Judy Davis	6805 Westwind Dr	
107	Pat McKnight	1800 S. Seaway Lane	

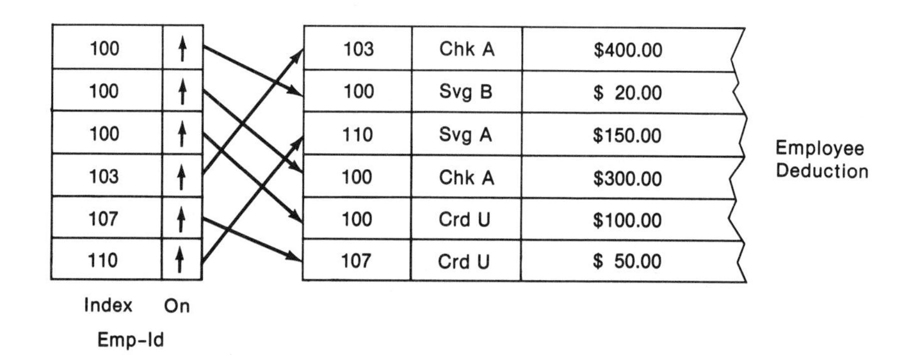

Figure 6.4 A Sorted Employee Table and an Employee Deduction Table with an EMP-ID Index

Figure 6.4 shows an index bridging two employee and deduction tables. The index directly locates each deduction record that has the specified employee key. Indexing speeds access, but it requires overhead. Note that (1) for every index (and you need one for every field which needs high performance on a join), you need more disk space; and (2) every deduction record added to or deleted from the data base requires extra I/Os for index maintenance for each index defined. In addition, modification of existing records would generate index maintenance requirements if the change affected fields for which indexes were established.

4. Pointer paths across records. Some vendors provide a mechanism for the implementation of pointer chains linking, in this example, deduction records for a specific employee. In this way, fast access is provided to the deduction records without incurring the overhead of an index.

The primary problem with this mechanism is that implementations, using this technique, normally require that the data base be unloaded and reloaded in order to implement new linkage paths (pointer chains). Because this operation costs CPU time, disk and table space and operator time, and even more because it violates the intent of flexibility of the relational system, pointer paths aren't too useful. In order to successfully implement them, it takes so long to do the detailed analysis and planning that the result is rarely worth the time spent planning.

To gain a better understanding of how these functions might be implemented, let's look briefly at how IBM's DB2 relational data base product is implemented.

6.6 AN OVERVIEW OF DB2 DATA BASE INTERNALS

To create a DB2 table, you must first define a table space to store data in. This table space must be implemented using a VSAM Entry Sequence Data Set, or VSAM(ESDS), which is VSAM's version of a physical sequential data set. Within the table space you may store rows for a single table, or for multiple tables if physical clustering of rows across a 1:M relationship is desired.

As you might suspect, DB2 tables are more sophisticated than simple physical sequential data sets. Tables normally contain some distributed free space for the insertion of new rows, with a sophisticated free space map being maintained by DB2 in order to effectively locate and use this free space.

Within each page, DB2 first loads rows sequentially, using any contiguous space remaining as free space. DB2 automatically compresses data as rows are deleted, and adjusts a mini-directory at the end of the page to maintain addressing for the rows that are still active (see Figure 6.5). Note how each entry in the mini-directory gives the offset of the corresponding row in each page.

Within the page, each DB2 row is divided between a prefix and a data component. The prefix contains information on the length of that row, as well as a row identifier indicating which kind of row is stored at that location.

One important point to note is that, by design, only 127 rows can be stored within a single page. This causes a great deal of wasted space if a large page size is chosen to store short rows.

Index structures may be used to address data in a DB2 table. Each entry in an index addresses the target row in terms of page and row number. As a matter of

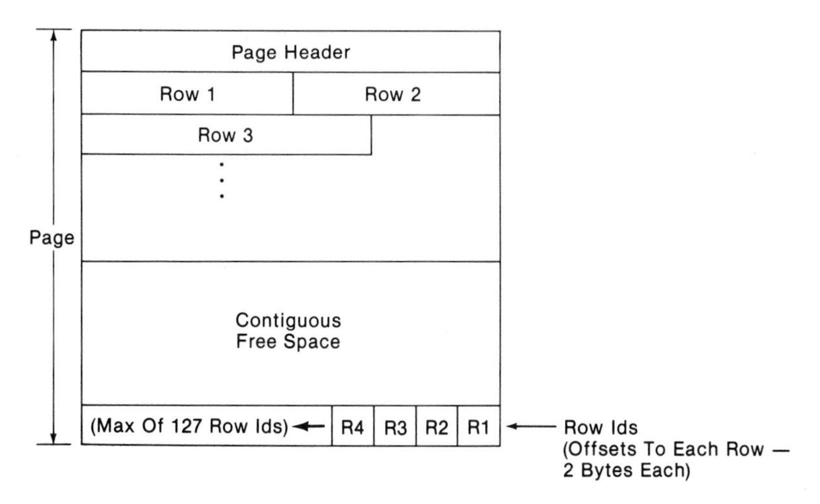

Figure 6.5 The General Page Layout Used by DB2

interest, it should be noted that DB2 index structures are stored physically inside VSAM(ESDS) data sets, using logical data structures similar to those found in normal VSAM Key Sequence Data Sets (VSAM indexes). There is no mechanism linking rows within a table or across a 1:M relationship. This bridge is performed dynamically at run time based on the data content of the rows themselves. For example, a Department-to-Employee bridge would be made based on the department's key appearing as a foreign key within the Employee table. There is no way of implementing a pointer chain to provide that access path. Instead, the relevant data rows for a specified department key would be located by searching the Employee table, by sorting the Employee table first and then searching the sorted data, or by using an index based on the department number attribute or column. Even if the index does exist, the choice of which method to use will be made by DB2's optimizer, based on its determination of the most efficient access.

6.7 DESIGNING A RELATIONAL DATA BASE

1. Develop the data model (or relational view).
2. Using the data model developed, perform a usage analysis for the required application programs.
3. Compare the usage analysis results to the original data model to identify heavily-used 1:M access paths. For each such path, create an index based on the foreign key used in that path.

As with other types of data base systems, this information should be shared with a local technical review staff in a design review to insure no oversights were made, as well as to provide additional technical tips for efficient use of the particular software used in your shop.

6.8 SUMMARY

Without a true relational system, you must make up for the lack of relational function(s) by doing more work within your application programs (that is, you must write more code). On one hand, this won't bother some experienced data processing professionals, for after all, they've done things this way "forever." On the other hand, it would certainly be easier and more productive if they didn't have to concern themselves with having to continually implement "home grown" methods of performing these functions.

Relational technology does have significant advantages to offer over more traditional, nonrelational technologies. Like many things, however, the real advantages of relational technology are obtained only when properly used. Certain applications lend themselves to this technology, while others do not. Successful implementations are based on an understanding of the capabilities and restrictions of the software being considered, and by the proper use of this technology.

REVIEW QUESTIONS

1. Assume that a new column needs to be added to the Customer table. What must be done to implement this change? Is a reorganization of the table necessary?
2. Assume that a new application system is going to be rewritten using a relational DBMS. What is the importance of normalization in the analysis of the system's requirements? To what extent should usage analysis be performed?
3. Consider the list of characteristics of relational systems given in the chapter. Which of these characteristics would you consider essential if you were responsible for the selection of a relational DBMS for your company?
4. In the migration to the use of relational technology, how important is it for new application programs to have the capability of accessing older file systems concurrently with the new relational tables?
5. Under what circumstances or conditions would it be appropriate for a company to convert to relational data base technology?

REVIEW PROBLEMS

The following problems are a continuation of those first described at the end of Chapter 2. Refer to those descriptions for an overview of the data environment involved, and derive a relational model for each. Your solution should indicate any indexes required for frequently used access paths.

1. Inventory system
   - a. For each purchase, first verify a customer's credit status. Then record the sale of an item by decrementing the quantity on hand, and update the customer's history of items purchased (on line).
   - b. Enter price data for items after price increases are received from a supplier (on line).
   - c. For a specified item, check the price information for all suppliers, and identify the supplier with the lowest purchase price (on line).
   - d. List the items purchased by each customer, including the item name (batch).
   - e. List, for each supplier, the items available with the price for each (batch).
2. Library system
   - a. Check to see what items a patron has currently checked out (on line).
   - b. Record that a specified book or article is being checked out to a library patron (on line).
   - c. Find all books and articles written by a specified author, or on a specified subject (on line).
   - d. Produce a listing of all books and articles available in the library (batch).

   e. Search all subscribers to check for loaned items overdue by more than 30 days (batch).

3. Project tracking
   a. List the skills that a specific employee possesses (on line).
   b. Find all employees with a specified skill (on line).
   c. Assign a specific employee to a project for a specified skill type (on line).
   d. Enter, for each employee, project activity (by skill type) (on line).
   e. List, by project, the skills required, the employees assigned, and the total hours worked by each (batch).

4. Magazine publication house
   a. Enter new subscribers for magazines (on line).
   b. Enter information on new ads placed by advertisers (on line).
   c. Verify the credit rating of specified advertisers (on line).
   d. Produce a list of subscribers whose subscriptions are about to expire (batch).
   e. Produce a list of magazines available, and the advertisers placing ads within each (batch).

5. Wholesale mail order
   a. When a customer calls in, check the price of desired equipment given in the specified magazine ad (on line).
   b. Check the status of orders for customers (on line).
   c. Enter new advertised items, given the magazine, issue, page of the ad, and the equipment advertised (on line).
   d. List the status of customers and orders placed during the past month (batch).
   e. List, for each type of equipment, the details of each ad in which that equipment type is listed (batch).

7

Structural Design

7.1 INTRODUCTION

Structural design is the bottom line of the data base design process. It transforms the application's access requirements, developed during the usage analysis phase, into a physical solution that satisfies those requirements. This transformation process is the subject of this chapter.

The techniques used in this phase of design apply to hierarchical, network, and relational data base systems. If you follow these procedures, they will lead you to a good, first-cut physical design for whatever DBMS you choose in a minimal amount of time. Of course, any final physical design will include a number of parameters that are DBMS specific. To get these details, as well as to check your first-cut solution, share the information you have gathered with one of your data base specialists. If you did your job well, the details of the physical solution should be a simple task for your specialist.

One topic that is not addressed is which type of DBMS to choose. Frankly, many of you won't have a choice. You will have only one DBMS in your shop, or your management will have dictated the one you are to use. If you do have a choice, such as IMS shops beginning to use DB2, the information you have gathered in developing your first-cut solution is the same information your data base specialist will need to complete performance predictions as input to DBMS selection. Section 12.4 provides additional insight into making such a decision.

7.2 MERGING ACCESS PATH REQUIREMENTS

1. The analysis begins by creating the working diagram shown in Figure 7.1. This is done by redrawing the data model previously developed (Figure 2.8) with all of the original 1:M linkage lines as dotted lines. These lines represent all of the possible access paths that you can ask a DBMS to support.
2. The list of entities accessed for Program 1 follows.

```
Find Customer (CUST-TELNO)
<20%> Add Customer (CUST-TELNO)
Add Order (ORDER-NO)
Find Item (STOCK-NO)
Find Advertised Item (STOCK-NO, MAG-CODE, ISSUE-DATE)
Add Item Ordered (ORDER-NO, STOCK-NO)
```

Draw lines representing each access on this diagram, using the following rules.

(a) The first entity accessed requires that the data model (or data base) be entered on that entity. In this example, this is the Customer record. To illustrate this direct entry, add a 'I' or a 'II' (for batch or on-line programs, respectively), terminating at the entity named.

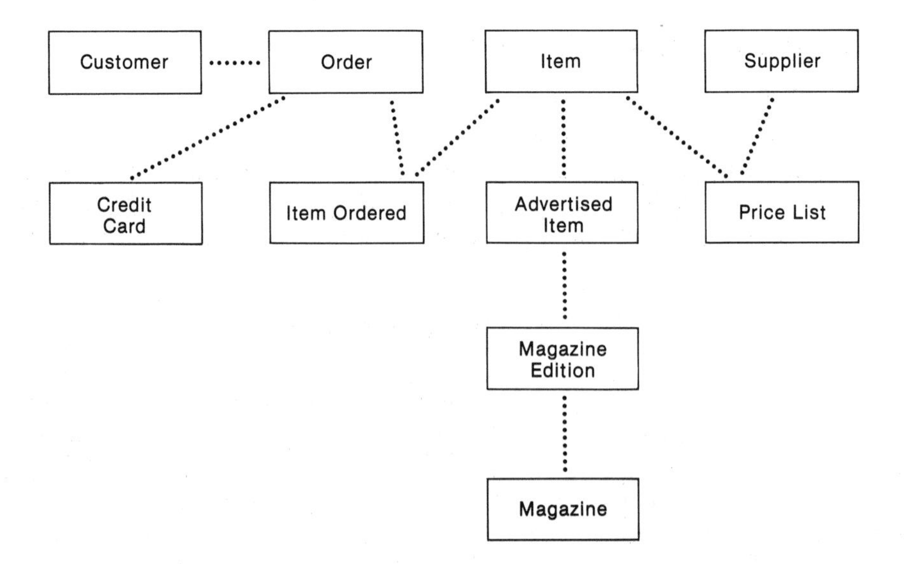

Figure 7.1 Possible Linkage Paths in the Data Model

(b) Once positioned in the data model, show any movement across a dotted line path by drawing a line between the two entities involved, with an arrowhead indicating the direction of movement. As an additional visual aid in determining the relative impact of access paths, connect entities for on-line usages with a double line, and those for batch usages with a single line.

If the next entity listed in the usage path analysis can be reached by moving across a dotted path from a previous record accessed, draw a connecting line as described earlier. This is shown in Figure 7.2 as the line between Customer and Order.

Always move from a prior position (or entity) whenever possible; when it isn't, show another direct entry point into the data model.

3. Repeat Step 2(b) with each entity in the access list for that program or usage.

Figure 7.2 shows the resulting worksheet, reflecting the first program's access requirements. The additional lines added were:

- a direct entry at Item;
- movement from Item to Advertised Item;
- movement from Item to Item Ordered.

Steps 1 through 3 should be completed for each remaining program or usage path. Use the same approach, with one added detail: when you find an access path

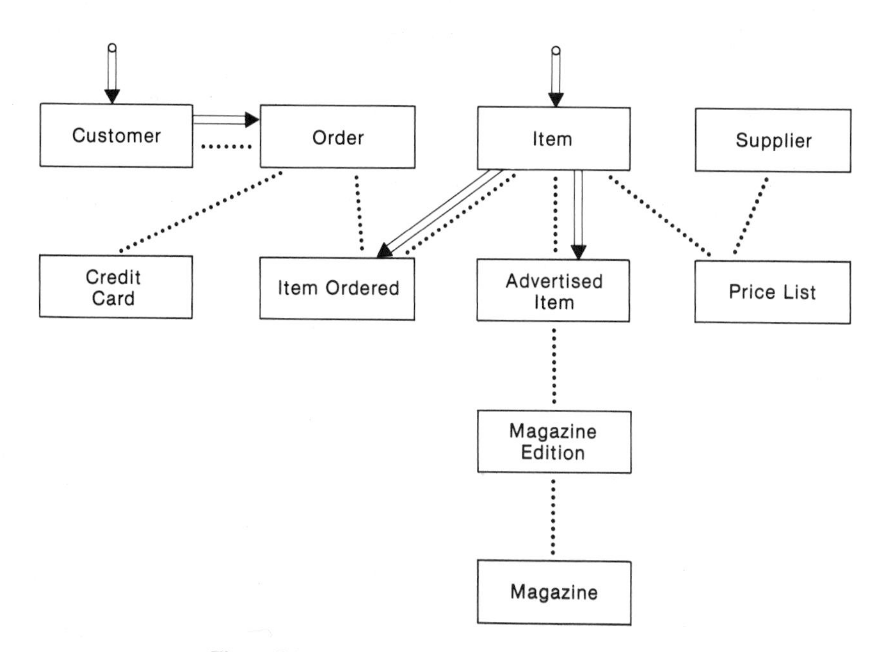

Figure 7.2 The Required Access Paths for Program 1

requirement that has already been identified by a previous usage (a single or double line already exists), update a count of the number of programs using that path. For example, if three batch programs and five on-line programs use a path from Item to Price List, with two batch programs requiring access from Price List to Item, the resulting diagram would appear as follows:

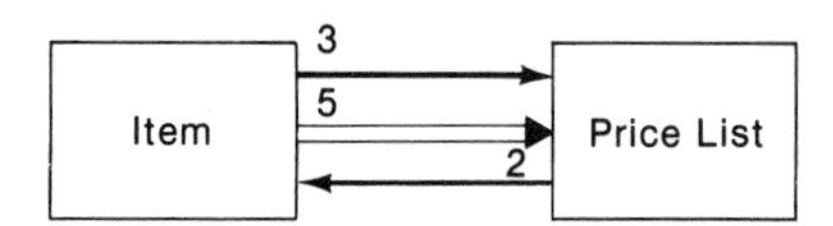

Using this technique, create a diagram reflecting the programs discussed in Chapter 3. Use Figure 7.3 to check your results.

Can you see a data base structure evolving from this diagram? If not, the following technique should help visualize the evolving solution.

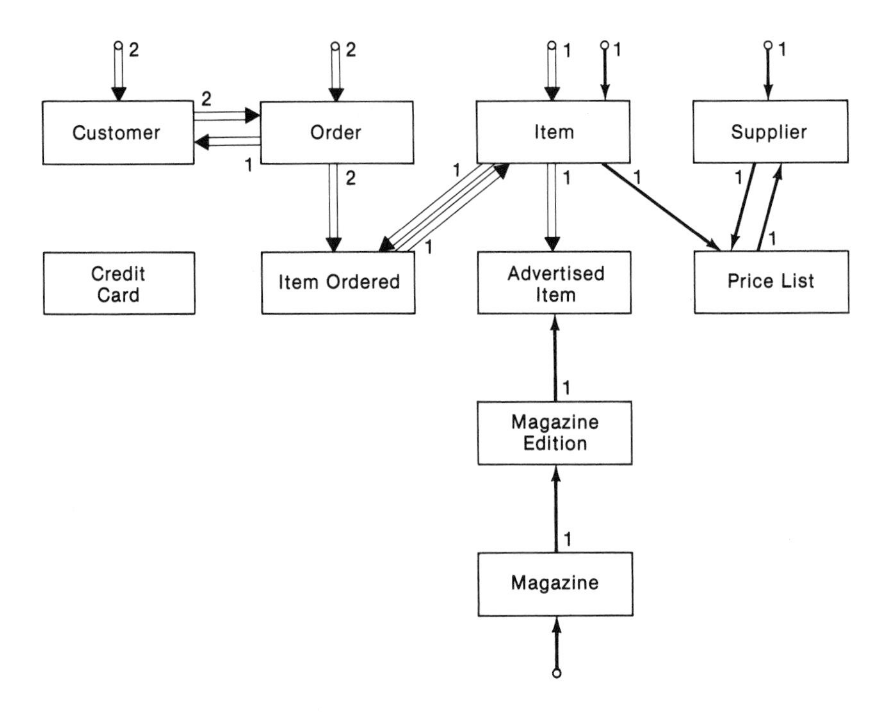

Figure 7.3 The Proposed Access Paths for Programs 1 - 6

7.3 VISUALIZING DATA BASE STRUCTURES

You are now ready to make a quantum leap to a first-cut data base solution for your access requirements. The following technique should be particularly useful to illustrate hierarchical or network solutions.

Take another look at the consolidated access path diagram shown in Figure 7.3. Imagine yourself looking down on a table, with this information displayed on the table top.

Now imagine, for each entity, the entity name being written on a separate piece of cardboard. All pieces of cardboard are then arranged as in the data model.

Wherever access paths are required between two entities (denoted by single or double lines), mentally connect the two pieces of cardboard (representing the two entities involved) with a piece of string.

For each entity requiring direct access, (having a 'I' or 'II' symbol), imagine a piece of string with one end attached to the cardboard, where the other end of the string is loose.

With this model in mind, picture the end result if each piece of loose string (denoting direct entry points) were lifted up in the air (see Figure 7.4).

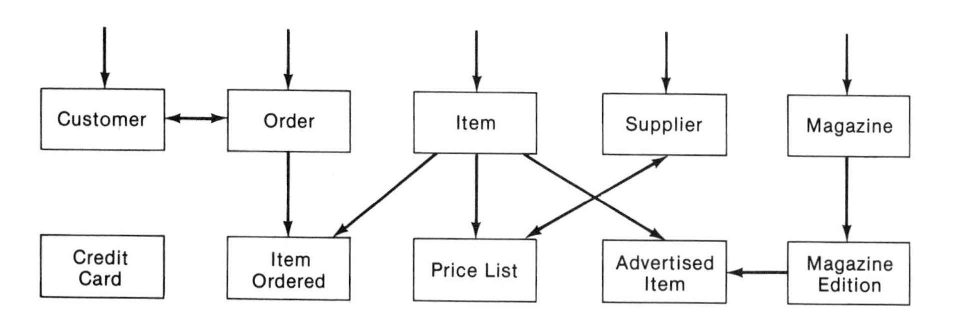

Figure 7.4 An Alternative View of Linkage Requirements

7.4 ADDITIONAL IMPLEMENTATION CONSIDERATIONS

To this point, all of the emphasis has been on consolidating initial access path requirements and forming an initial structure that would support them. Before deciding on a final configuration, however, you need to consider other factors, particularly those related to performance. Many of these factors illustrate points which need to be considered regardless of the type of DBMS chosen.

7.4.1 Avoiding Excessive Linkage of Physical Data Bases

In the simple problem developed earlier, the current state of the solution, developed through the high-tech imagery of cardboard and string, shows (in IMS terminology) three possible bi-directional implementations.

1. Price List ties Item to Supplier;
2. Item Ordered links Item and Order; and
3. Advertised Item relates Magazine Edition to Item.

Although technically possible (IMS will support all of these), it's best not to go heavily into linkages such as this for *any* DBMS, primarily for reasons of performance as well as operational practice and ease. The various bi-directional linkages in IMS (or the sets implemented in a network DBMS) would require numerous cross-data base pointers to provide those linkages. As a result, you, as the designer of this system, will be very unpopular in your data center because:

1. Every time the item data base is reorganized (an unload/reload operation to reclaim and redistribute free space), significant extra work, effort, and time are required to identify and resolve the cross-data base chains. In this example, three different sets of cross-data base pointers must be resolved.
2. Cross-data base pointers can lead to scheduling problems when a piece of the overall structure is taken away from an on-line system, for example, for data base recovery to resolve a hardware failure. Any function using a view of the data base tied to the failing component will be unavailable for scheduling purposes until the recovery is complete. On the other hand, if stand-alone physical structures are used, the odds are great of scheduling on-line work against available data bases.

7.4.2 Proper Clustering of Data

Consider the following simple network requirement, where you have on-line requirements to move from Item to Price List to Supplier, as well as from Supplier to Price List to Item.

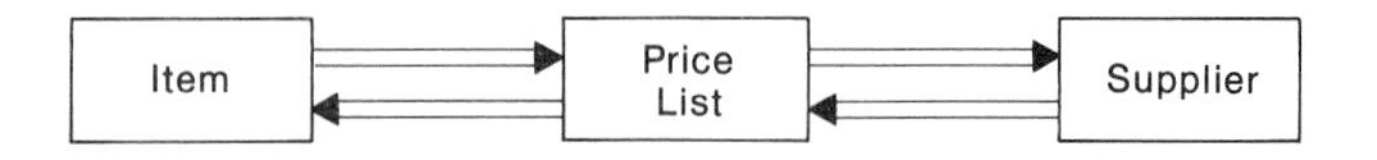

The options are simple. You may, as an implementer, use clustering mechanisms to provide:

1. Fast access from Item to Price List by clustering, on physical storage, Price List records close to Item records. This causes slower access from Supplier to Price List as a result of performing random I/O, because Price List records are stored physically with their Item owners/parents.
2. Conversely, by making a "reverse" decision, fast access from Supplier to Price List can be provided, with slower access from Item to Price List.
3. Slow access from either direction by providing direct entry capability to all three record types. This provides flexibility, but it definitely has its price!

One final concern is the length of the nonclustered path. If Item to Price List is most important, and you cluster Price List close to Item, you should check the length of the Supplier to Price List path. Although that path may be used less frequently, if it is too long, it could easily introduce a serious performance problem. The potential for this problem exists regardless of the type of DBMS chosen.

7.4.3 Blocking Up Records

In performing an I/O, three distinct types of delays are encountered: (1) disk arm movement (the positioning of the heads at the required point), (2) rotational delay (waiting for the disk to rotate to proper location for the I/O), and (3) data transfer. The most significant of these three is the component for rotational delay, but it can also be one that may be addressed as a design issue.

As one example, clustering of records results in more useful data being retrieved in a single I/O, and reduces the total number of I/Os needed to retrieve a given amount of data.

Another technique, referred to as blocking, is useful in cases where a great many records must be stored or retrieved.

Assume that 100,000 records, each 100 bytes, need to be retrieved. Consider two different ways of performing this task:

1. Issue 100,000 read requests for records 100 bytes each.
2. Assume that application code will create "blocked up" data records that are 10,000 bytes long, each containing 100 of the original 100-byte records (as in a COBOL "OCCURS" clause). With this configuration, the same original amount of data can be accessed with only 1,000 I/Os.

Comparing these two approaches, the second method requires 100 times fewer I/Os to retrieve the same amount of data. There are 100 times fewer I/O instructions required, 100 times fewer rotational delays, and less chance for channel contention. The same amount of data is transferred, but in larger pieces or buckets. Method 2 therefore provides a significant performance edge over the first.

What do you lose? You no longer have the ability to use standard data base or query software products to analyze records and generate ad hoc reports. Special application-written routines must be used to deblock records and scan those deblocked records in the program's buffers. Is the performance gain worth the extra effort for a loss of function that you may not need? Like everything else in the world of data bases, it depends. Quite often it is, depending on the numbers involved. If the volume of data records is sufficiently high, blocking techniques such as this may be the only practical way to go.

7.4.4 Alteration of the Access Paths or Data Model

Usage paths were originally created as initial proposals on how to access data. Once these paths have been consolidated into a composite view, several changes might be considered.

As one example, assume that a number of detail records must be retrieved online to add up some total value. If the equivalent total field were carried somewhere else in the data base, perhaps in the parent/owner of the detail record, the sequential access of detail records can be avoided.

Assume you find a requirement to search a lengthy dependent record chain to locate one unique record occurrence. If this happens frequently enough, consider altering the data base design to make this dependent record type the entry point of its own structure in IMS; or in network terms, use a location mode of CALC or INDEXED. This allows for direct entry at that record type rather than require a sequential search of that record type. In other words, look for potentially high I/O requirements and be creative. Don't just say, "That's the way it is...".

A final hint for network users: Choose implementation options to make the network structure be managed like IMS (that is, heavy use of VIA location modes for dependent record types). Make the most effective use of clustering on physical storage. The original data model could be implemented with a completely flexible solution by using nothing but CALC and INDEXED location modes, allowing direct entry to the data base on any record type desired. However, this means doing random access when crossing every link path, creating a much higher I/O rate than if clustering were used with the choice of the VIA location mode.

Let's take all of these things into consideration, and develop solutions for the sample problem in each DBMS. For each, we start with the first-cut solution in Figure 7.4.

7.5 AN IMS SOLUTION

In developing a hierarchical solution for IMS, you are dealing with the most restrictive of the three data base systems. Specifically, some points of note are:

1. A number of possible bi-directional implementations are indicated.
2. Some accesses, such as denoted in Figure 7.5, are not a "natural" capability of hierarchical structures. Specifically,
   (a) A Customer-to-Order hierarchy could be created, but this does not permit direct entry at Order (unless secondary indexes are used).
   (b) On the other hand, if Customer and Order are roots of separate data bases, how will the Customer-Order paths be implemented?

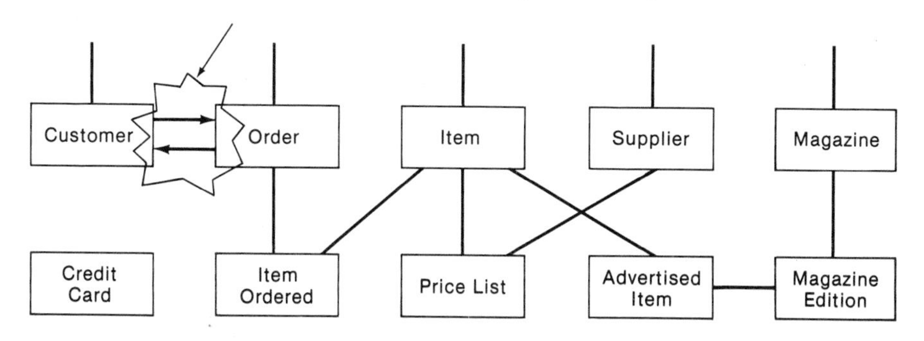

Figure 7.5 Access Requirements that Cannot Be Satisfied by Hierarchical Structures and Logical Relationships

Several things can be done to handle this requirement. These points are mentioned here to illustrate typical items addressed in any final solution. There are, of course, other issues as well.

Take a few minutes and determine what type of hierarchical solution you would propose to satisfy Figure 7.4. Keep in mind that you, at long last, are now "getting physical," and you can do anything reasonable or necessary to satisfy access path requirements in an efficient manner. When finished, compare your solution to that of Figure 7.6. The logic for specific decisions follows.

For a choice of access methods, it was assumed all data bases had sufficient update activity to warrant use of one of the HD mechanisms. In deciding between HIDAM and HDAM, in each case an assumption was made that the data base did, or did not, require a significant amount of key-sequential processing, respectively.

The Credit Card entity is unused at this time. It was therefore eliminated from the proposed solution. If, at some future point, this information is required, a separate data base can be created at that time without altering existing programs.

Adjustments in access path sequences are as follows:

1. *Customer-to-Order*. This path is provided by the Secondary Index on Order's CUST-TELNO field.
2. *Order-to-Customer*. Whenever Order is accessed, CUST-TELNO is available and can be used for a direct access of the required Customer record/segment.

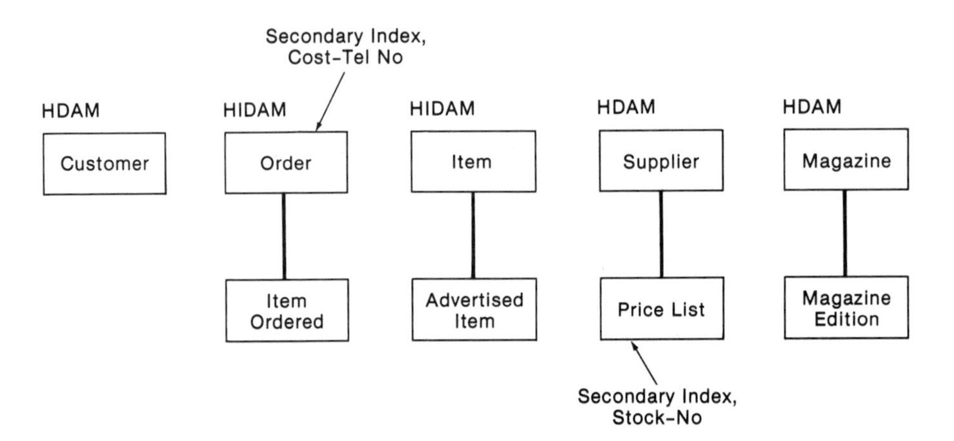

Figure 7.6 An IMS Solution

3. *Item-to-Item Ordered.* Program 1's access path was changed to access Item Ordered directly from Order, rather than Item.
4. *Item Ordered-to-Item.* When Item Ordered is accessed, the ITEM-NO field is available and can be used for a direct access of the corresponding Item segment.
5. *Magazine Edition-to-Advertised Item.* The access path was changed to move from Magazine Edition directly to the next Item segment (using STOCK-NO), and from Item to Advertised Item.
6. *Item-to-Price List.* Note the secondary index on Price List. With IMS, ADVER-PRICE can be placed in the secondary index, allowing the index to be accessed as a stand-alone data base to choose the Supplier with the lowest cost for the item.

7.6 A NETWORK SOLUTION

To create a network solution, begin again with Figure 7.4. Identify sets required for a solution, and assign appropriate location modes to each record type. When finished, compare your solution to Figure 7.7.

The logic for implementation choices of note are as follows:

All records requiring direct entry to the data base have location modes of either DIRECT or CALC. The choice between these two was made on an assumption that sufficient key-sequential processing either did or did not exist, respectively. They correspond to the HIDAM versus HDAM decisions made in deriving the IMS solution.

Clustering was implemented wherever feasible with the use of VIA SET location modes.

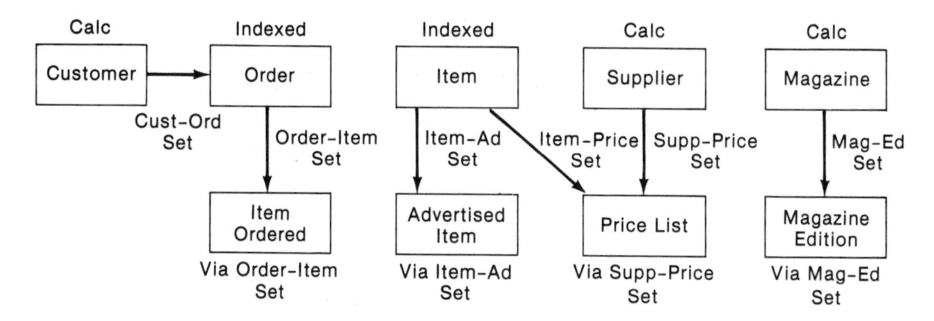

Figure 7.7 A Network Solution

Most linkages identified in the composite usage diagram were implemented. However, the Item-to Item Ordered, Item Ordered-to Item, and Magazine Edition-to-Advertised Item links were omitted by making the corresponding revisions as noted in the preceding IMS solution.

7.7 A RELATIONAL SOLUTION

To devise a relational solution, consider once again Figure 7.4. Assume that all record types identified are to be implemented as their own relational tables. Identify what indexes might be implemented initially to support these access paths, and compare your list to the following information.

Figure 7.8 illustrates an initial solution to this problem in relational terms. Indexes will be initially created to satisfy all on-line linkages, except for the same list of changes given previously. It is assumed that batch programs will be monitored for performance, with additional indexes defined as needed to obtain satisfactory performance.

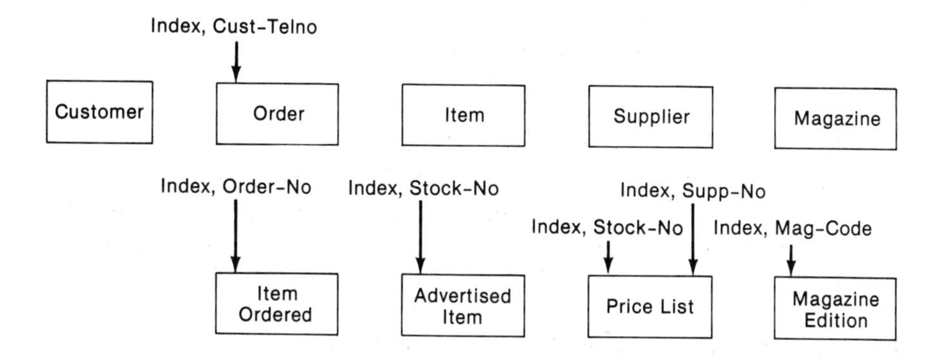

Figure 7.8 A Relational Solution

REVIEW QUESTIONS

1. How would your approach toward structural design vary, based on the type of DBMS (hierarchical, network or relational) to be used?
2. What other analytical techniques have you used in moving from program requirements to data structures?
3. Assume that a new project for a system to run under IMS is under development with extremely short due dates. What steps would you take in managing the project to insure the most effective use of the time available?

8

A Case Study: The Job-Shop Model

8.1 INTRODUCTION

In the previous chapters, a relatively simple data model was taken, step by step, through the various phases of data base design. The last chapter ended this process by developing first-cut data base solutions for each of the three classes of data base management systems.

This chapter repeats this series of steps, using a data model that is much more complex. Each stage of the analysis contains a problem, with an explanation of how to solve it. A first-cut solution is proposed for each class of DBMS.

8.2 DEVELOPING THE DATA MODEL

Put yourself in the role of managing projects for a software consultant. Your client, Buildem Right (B-R), needs a new job costing system to monitor the effectiveness of their shop's operation. As a metal fabricator, they run a "job shop," building metal products to order based on customer specifications.

A customer requests a bid from B-R to build a specific piece of equipment. B-R's engineers study the plans for the equipment, and submit a bid for the job. If B-R is the low bidder, they get the job.

In summary, B-R uses standard material parts to build equipment. Managing jobs in process requires ordering material as well as taking some from inventory. Shop labor is recorded and tracked as the job is built.

The new system must track labor and material costs for each job. As each job is completed and shipped, it will be "costed," summarizing labor and material charges for the fabrication process.

In developing the initial entity/attribute list, a need for the following entities has been identified.

Job. The name for a customer's order, created when B-R is the low bidder and they are contracted to build the equipment specified.

Employee. Shop personnel who perform the fabrication of the equipment.

Material. The parts used in the fabrication process. Material types can vary considerably in description. However, the concatenation of four fields uniquely identify one kind of material used. These fields are:

- material class (stainless steel, carbon steel, and so on)
- material type (bar, plate, pipe, and so on)
- nominal thickness
- size

To simplify the explanation of the data model, the concatenation of these fields is referred to as a unique part number. This simplifies the analysis without altering the true function or meaning of the data.

Supplier. Companies from whom B-R purchases raw material (parts).

Shop Time. Records for labor expended in the building of a job. Employees fill out a time card daily while they work. A different line on the time card is completed every time they perform a unique function on a single job. If the employee paints equipment for five different jobs, five lines would be recorded, one for each job. If, on the other hand, an employee performs three functions for a single job, (for example, welding, inspection, and cleanup), three lines would be recorded.

This level of detail, recording what kind of work, on which job, by employee by day, is required for auditing purposes as well as for jobs built on a "time and material" basis. The initial entity/attribute list reflecting these requirements appears in Figure 8.1.

The next step in the analysis is to review the entity/attribute list and resolve any problems in terminology. Figure 8.2 shows a modified entity/attribute list, containing these revisions: under Job, JOB-NUMB was changed to JOB-NO, and CUST-NUMB to CUST-NO.

Item	Description	Domain
Job		
JOB-NUMB	A unique numeric identifier for each job	1000-9999
JOB-DESC	A description of the basic unit to be built	50AN
CUST-NUMB	A number uniquely identifying each customer	6N
CUST-NAME	The standard spelling for that customer's name	30AN
JOB-STATUS	A code classifying the overall job status	2AN
LABOR-EST	The job's estimated dollar cost for shop time	6N
MATL-EST	The job's estimated dollar cost for material	
SALESMAN	The initials of the salesman handling this job	3A
START-ASSY	The scheduled date when shop assembly begins	6N
COMP-ASSY	The scheduled date for assembly completion	6N
SHIP-DATE	The sched date for shipping the job to the cust	6N
DEPT-CODE	The department assigned for unit assembly	2N
SELLG-PRICE	The total cost of the job to the customer	
QUAN-ORD	The quantity of units to be built on this job	2N
Employee		
CLOCK-NO	A unique identifier for each employee	3N
EMP-NAME	2 initials and last name for this employee	30A
SOC-SEC-NO	This employee's social security number	9N
ADDRESS	The home mailing address for this employee	30AN
BIRTH-DATE	This employee's birth date	6N
NUM-DEP	The total no. of deductions claimed for payroll	2N
DEPT-CODE	A code for the dept where the emp is assigned	
DEPT-NAME	The name for the dept where the emp is assigned	
HOURLY-RATE	The current hourly wage for this emp	99v99
Material		
PART-NO	A unique identifier for this matl type/size	10AN
UNIT-COST	The price of one unit of this matl type	50AN
SUPP-CODE	A unique identifier for a particular supplier	6N
STATUS	A flag signifying reserved matl for a job	1A
JOB-NO	A unique identifier for a job	4N
STG-LOC	A unique code for the specific storage location	
PO-NO	A unique identifier for each order placed	5N
LEAD-TIME	The wait time for delivery of matl from a supp	
REORDER-LVL	The quan of units on hand for an auto reorder	
REORD-QUAN	The number of units to be ordered on a reorder	
INV-QUAN	The actual number of units in inventory	
Supplier		
SUPP-CODE	A unique identifier for each supplier	6N
SUPP-NAME	The standard spelling for this supplier's name	30A
SUPP-ADDR	The mailing address for this supplier	
PO-NO	A unique identifier for each order placed	5N
Shop Time		
CLOCK-NO	A unique employee identifier	3N
EMP-NAME	2 initials and last name for this employee	
DATE	The date this work was performed	6N
NUM-HOURS	The hours worked for this emp/date/lbr code	
LABOR-CODE	A unique code classifying the type of work perf	2AN
JOB-NO	A unique identifier for each job	4N

Figure 8.1 The Initial Entity/Attribute List

Item	Description	Domain
Job		
JOB-NO	A unique numeric identifier for each job	1000-9999
JOB-DESC	A description of the basic unit to be built	50AN
CUST-NO	A number uniquely identifying each customer	6N
CUST-NAME	The standard spelling for that customer's name	30AN
JOB-STATUS	A code classifying the overall job status	2AN
LABOR-EST	The job's estimated dollar cost for shop time	6N
MATL-EST	The job's estimated dollar cost for material	
SALESMAN	The initials of the salesman handling this job	3A
START-ASSY	The scheduled date when shop assembly begins	6N
COMP-ASSY	The scheduled date for assembly completion	6N
SHIP-DATE	The sched date for shipping the job to the cust	6N
DEPT-CODE	The department assigned for unit assembly	2N
SELLG-PRICE	The total cost of the job to the customer	
QUAN-ORD	The quantity of units to be built on this job	2N
Employee		
CLOCK-NO	A unique identifier for each employee	3N
EMP-NAME	2 initials and last name for this employee	30A
SOC-SEC-NO	This employee's social security number	9N
ADDRESS	The home mailing address for this employee	30AN
BIRTH-DATE	This employee's birth date	6N
NUM-DEP	The total no. of deductions claimed for payroll	2N
DEPT-CODE	A code for the dept where the emp is assigned	
DEPT-NAME	The name for the dept where the emp is assigned	
HOURLY-RATE	The current hourly wage for this emp	99v99
Material		
PART-NO	A unique identifier for this matl type/size	10AN
UNIT-COST	The price of one unit of this matl type	50AN
SUPP-CODE	A unique identifier for a particular supplier	6N
STATUS	A flag signifying reserved matl for a job	1A
JOB-NO	A unique identifier for a job	4N
STG-LOC	A unique code for the specific storage location	
PO-NO	A unique identifier for each order placed	5N
LEAD-TIME	The wait time for delivery of matl from a supp	
REORDER-LVL	The quan of units on hand for an auto reorder	
REORD-QUAN	The number of units to be ordered on a reorder	
INV-QUAN	The actual number of units in inventory	
Supplier		
SUPP-CODE	A unique identifier for each supplier	6N
SUPP-NAME	The standard spelling for this supplier's name	30A
SUPP-ADDR	The mailing address for this supplier	
PO-NO	A unique identifier for each order placed	5N
Shop Time		
CLOCK-NO	A unique employee identifier	3N
EMP-NAME	2 initials and last name for this employee	
DATE	The date this work was performed	6N
NUM-HOURS	The hours worked for this emp/date/lbr code	
LABOR-CODE	A unique code classifying the type of work perf	2AN
JOB-NO	A unique identifier for each job	4N

Figure 8.2 The Corrected Entity/Attribute List

The rules for first normal form are:

1. All entities must have a key, composed of a combination of one or more attributes which uniquely identify one occurrence of the entity.
2. For any single occurrence of an entity, each attribute must have one and only one value.

Figure 8.3 illustrates the data model with key fields identified with '**', and repeating groups with 'rg'.

Most key fields should be obvious with the possible exception of shop time. Recall that detailed labor records are created each day any time an employee does any specific kind of work on a job. Therefore, the key for this entity contains four fields, including WHO did WHAT on which JOB and on which DATE.

To remove the repeating groups, consider first the purchase order number attribute in Supplier. This is a 1:M relationship. One supplier may have many purchase orders from B-R, while one specific purchase order applies to only one supplier.

A repeating group must be removed from the entity in which it appears. However, you can't remove the information until you are sure it exists in the data base where it belongs.

Does purchase order number exist "where it belongs"? The answer is "no," so you must create an appropriate entity. The real question, then, is what does purchase order number describe? It identifies purchase order activity, so you must create Purchase Order as a new entity that describes an order placed with a supplier. Attributes of PURCHASE-ORDER-NUMBER (key field) and SUPPLIER-CODE (describing the supplier with which it is associated) will be associated with it.

You can now remove the PURCHASE-ORDER-NUMBER attribute from Supplier.

The remaining repeating group elements are in Material; there are quite a few. In handling these, identify and treat attributes which appear to be key fields of related entities. The nonkey repeating elements will just "follow along" if these keyed attributes are treated first. The adjustments necessary to correct these problems include the following:

1. The attribute SUPP-CODE is a key attribute of Supplier, and denotes an M:M relationship between Material and Supplier. The new intersection element required, Supplier-Material, indicates a new entity which is essentially a price list of what a part costs if purchased from a specific supplier. It has attributes of LEAD-TIME and UNIT-COST associated with it.
2. PO-NO is the key of Purchase Order, which also has an M:M relationship with Material. The intersection element created, MATERIAL-PO, represents material on order, and has attributes reflecting the quantity of parts ordered, the purchase price, and the job they were ordered for.

```
Item           Description                                    Domain
Job
 **JOB-NO      A unique numeric identifier for each job       1000-9999
   JOB-DESC    A description of the basic unit to be built    50AN
   CUST-NO     A number uniquely identifying each customer    6N
   CUST-NAME   The standard spelling for that customer's name 30AN
   JOB-STATUS  A code classifying the overall job status      2AN
   LABOR-EST   The job's estimated dollar cost for shop time  6N
   MATL-EST    The job's estimated dollar cost for material
   SALESMAN    The initials of the salesman handling this job 3A
   START-ASSY  The scheduled date when shop assembly begins   6N
   COMP-ASSY   The scheduled date for assembly completion     6N
   SHIP-DATE   The sched date for shipping the job to the cust 6N
   DEPT-CODE   The department assigned for unit assembly      2N
   SELLG-PRICE The total cost of the job to the customer
   QUAN-ORD    The quantity of units to be built on this job  2N

Employee
 **CLOCK-NO    A unique identifier for each employee          3N
   EMP-NAME    2 initials and last name for this employee     30A
   SOC-SEC-NO  This employee's social security number         9N
   ADDRESS     The home mailing address for this employee     30AN
   BIRTH-DATE  This employee's birth date                     6N
   NUM-DEP     The total no. of deductions claimed for payroll 2N
   DEPT-CODE   A code for the dept where the emp is assigned
   DEPT-NAME   The name for the dept where the emp is assigned
   HOURLY-RATE The current hourly wage for this emp           99v99

Material
 **PART-NO     A unique identifier for this matl type/size    10AN
   UNIT-COST   The price of one unit of this matl type        50AN
rg>SUPP-CODE   A unique identifier for a particular supplier  6N
rg>STATUS      A flag signifying reserved matl for a job      1A
rg>JOB-NO      A unique identifier for a job                  4N
rg>STG-LOC     A unique code for the specific storage location
rg>PO-NO       A unique identifier for each order placed      5N
rg>LEAD-TIME   The wait time for delivery of matl from a supp
   REORDER-LVL The quan of units on hand for an auto reorder
   REORD-QUAN  The number of units to be ordered on a reorder
   INV-QUAN    The actual number of units in inventory

Supplier
 **SUPP-CODE   A unique identifier for each supplier          6N
   SUPP-NAME   The standard spelling for this supplier's name 30A
   SUPP-ADDR   The mailing address for this supplier
rg>PO-NO       A unique identifier for each order placed      5N

Shop Time
 **CLOCK-NO    A unique employee identifier                   3N
   EMP-NAME    2 initials and last name for this employee
 **DATE        The date this work was performed               6N
   NUM-HOURS   The hours worked for this emp/date/lbr code
 **LABOR-CODE  A unique code classifying the type of work perf 2AN
 **JOB-NO      A unique identifier for each job               4N
```

Figure 8.3 The Entity/Attribute List with Keys and Repeating Groups

3. STG-LOC brings a new perspective to the data model. It is associated with information on physical inventory, which has not yet been identified. B-R stores parts in marked areas within a large storage yard; STG-LOC is the unique identifier for one of these locations. As parts come in for a job, they are placed together, as much as possible, in one location.
   To reflect this relationship, a new entity is created for Location which represents these storage areas. Location has an M:M relationship with Material, which causes the Material-Location entity to be created. This intersection element contains additional attributes reflecting the quantity of parts stored here, and the job the parts are to be used on.
4. Finally, JOB-NO identifies an M:M relationship with Job. An intersection element for Job-Material is created, reflecting material used in building a job, with an additional attribute to indicate the number of parts used.

The first normal form solution for this problem appears in Figure 8.4.

```
Job
  *JOB-NO
   QUAN-ORD
   JOB-DESC
   CUST-NO
   CUST-NAME
   JOB-STATUS
   LABOR-EST
   MATL-EST
   SALESMAN
   START-ASSY
   COMP-ASSY
   SHIP-DATE
   DEPT-CODE
   SELLG-PRICE

Employee
  *CLOCK-NO
   EMP-NAME
   SOC-SEC-NO
   ADDRESS
   BIRTH-DATE
   NUM-DEP
   DEPT-CODE
   DEPT-NAME
   HOURLY-RATE

Material
  *PART-NO
   REORDER-LVL
   REORD-QUAN

Supplier
  *SUPP-CODE
   SUPP-NAME
   SUPP-ADDR

Shop Time
  *CLOCK-NO
  *DATE
  *LABOR-CODE
  *JOB-NO
   LBR-COST
   EMP-NAME
   NUM-HOURS

Purchase Order
  *PO-NO
   SUPP-CODE

Location
  *LOC-KEY

Job-Material (Matl Usage)
  *JOB-NO
  *PART-NO
   QUAN-USED

Supplier-Material (Price List)
  *SUPP-CODE
  *PART-NO
   LEAD-TIME
   UNIT-COST

Material-Location (Inventory)
  *LOC-KEY
  *PART-NO
   INV-QUAN
   JOB-NO

Material-PO (Matl Ordered)
  *PO-NO
  *PART-NO
   QUAN-ORD
   UNIT-COST
   JOB-NO
```

Figure 8.4 The First-Normal Form Solution

For second normal form, an entity must be in 1NF, and each non-key attribute must depend on the key and all parts of the key. Moving to second normal form requires making these adjustments:

1. Shop Time has two attributes not in second normal form, EMP-NAME and LBR-COST. EMP-NAME is dependent on CLK-NO (given CLK-NO, you know the EMP-NAME), and must therefore be removed. EMP-NAME does exist elsewhere in first normal form (in Employee). As a result, it can be removed from Shop Time. Because the relationship between Employee and Shop Time is 1:M, no further adjustments are necessary.
2. LABOR-COST does not exist anywhere. It could, however, be derived as a calculated cost if the hourly rate were available. The employee's current hourly rate is in Employee, but to calculate labor cost at a future date, you need to have a table of hourly salaries, reflecting any pay raises. Therefore, for each detail record, you can look up the rate that was effective on the day the work was performed, and then calculate the labor cost.

Figure 8.5 reflects the second normal form solution.

For third normal form, an entity must be in 2NF, and each nonkey attribute must not depend on any other nonkey attribute. The changes required to the second-normal form solution are as follows:

1. CUST-NAME appeared in Job and is dependent on CUST-CODE. To adjust it properly for third normal form, a new Customer entity is created. Since Customer and Job have a 1:M relationship, no intersection element is required.
2. DEPT-NAME appeared in Employee but is dependent on DEPT-CODE. As a result, a Department entity is created, with DEPT-CODE as a key. Because Department and Job have a 1:M relationship, no intersection element is necessary.
3. Unit cost attributes were added to several entities. Recall that the objective of the system is to track labor and material costs. The second normal form solution had no way to track the cost of material ordered.

This adjustment was used to illustrate that this process requires more than just mechanical adjustments. You need to continually check the data model to insure that it contains sufficient elements to meet the goals of the project.

The third normal solution appears in Figure 8.6 with the corresponding data model in Figure 8.7.

8.3 USAGE PATH DEVELOPMENT

The initial phase of the B-R project requires developing twelve programs. The following section gives a description of each program, and translates these require-

```
Job                    Material                Job-Material (Matl Usage)
  *JOB-NO                 *PART-NO                *JOB-NO
   QUAN-ORD                REORDER-LVL            *PART-NO
   JOB-DESC                REORD-QUAN              QUAN-USED
   CUST-NO
   CUST-NAME
   JOB-STATUS           Supplier                Supplier-Material (Price List)
   LABOR-EST              *SUPP-CODE              *SUPP-CODE
   MATL-EST                SUPP-NAME              *PART-NO
   SALESMAN                SUPP-ADDR               LEAD-TIME
   START-ASSY                                      UNIT-COST
   COMP-ASSY
   SHIP-DATE            Shop Time
   DEPT-CODE              *CLOCK-NO             Material-Location (Inventory)
   SELLG-PRICE            *DATE                   *LOC-KEY
                          *LABOR-CODE             *PART-NO
                          *JOB-NO                  INV-QUAN
Employee                   NUM-HOURS               JOB-NO
  *CLOCK-NO
   EMP-NAME
   SOC-SEC-NO                                   Material-PO (Matl Ordered)
   ADDRESS              Purchase Order            *PO-NO
   BIRTH-DATE             *PO-NO                  *PART-NO
   NUM-DEP                 SUPP-CODE               QUAN-ORD
   DEPT-CODE                                       UNIT-COST
   DEPT-NAME                                       JOB-NO
   HOURLY-RATE

                        Location                Wage Rate
                          *LOC-KEY                *CLOCK-NO
                                                  *DATE-RAISE
                                                   HOURLY-RATE
```

Figure 8.5 The Second-Normal Form Solution

ments into a description of proposed record accesses. The resulting usage paths are shown for each.

Program 1. Order material (on line)

The purchasing agent is given material requirements which list, by job, the type and quantity of required parts. The data base is searched to identify, for each part, the supplier who can provide the required material in the required lead time with the least expense. This information will then be used later to consolidate purchase requirements for a given supplier, at which time a purchase order will be issued (see Program 2).

```
Job
  *JOB-NO
   QUAN-ORD
   JOB-DESC
   CUST-NO
   JOB-STATUS
   LABOR-EST
   MATL-EST
   SALESMAN
   START-ASSY
   COMP-ASSY
   SHIP-DATE
   DEPT-CODE
   SELLG-PRICE

Employee
  *CLOCK-NO
   EMP-NAME
   SOC-SEC-NO
   ADDRESS
   BIRTH-DATE
   NUM-DEP
   DEPT-CODE
   HOURLY-RATE

Department
  *DEPT-CODE
   DEPT-NAME
   FOREMAN

Material
   *PART-NO
    REORDER-LVL
    REORD-QUAN
    AVG-UNIT-COST

Supplier
   *SUPP-CODE
    SUPP-NAME
    SUPP-ADDR

Shop Time
   *CLOCK-NO
   *DATE
   *LABOR-CODE
   *JOB-NO
    NUM-HOURS

Purchase Order
   *PO-NO
    SUPP-CODE

Location
   *LOC-KEY

Customer
   *CUST-NO
    CUST-NAME
    CUST-ADDRESS

Job-Material (Matl Usage)
   *JOB-NO
   *PART-NO
    QUAN-REQD
    QUAN-USED
    CUM-COST

Supplier-Material (Price List)
   *SUPP-CODE
   *PART-NO
    LEAD-TIME
    UNIT-COST

Material-Location (Inventory)
   *LOC-KEY
   *PART-NO
    INV-QUAN
    JOB-NO
    UNIT-COST

Material-PO (Matl Ordered)
   *PO-NO
   *PART-NO
    QUAN-ORD
    UNIT-COST
    JOB-NO
    LINE-ITEM
    DUE-DATE

Wage Rate
   *CLOCK-NO
   *DATE-RAISE
    HOURLY-RATE
```

Figure 8.6 The Third-Normal Form Solution

Program Functions. Use the part number to access the Material record to verify the material name. Next, get all Price List records for this part to identify the one containing the least expensive unit cost which has an acceptable delivery time. Once the least-cost supplier is identified, read the Supplier record to get the supplier's name, and address.

```
Find Material (PART-NO)
Find Price List (PART-NO)
Find Supplier (SUPP-CODE)
```

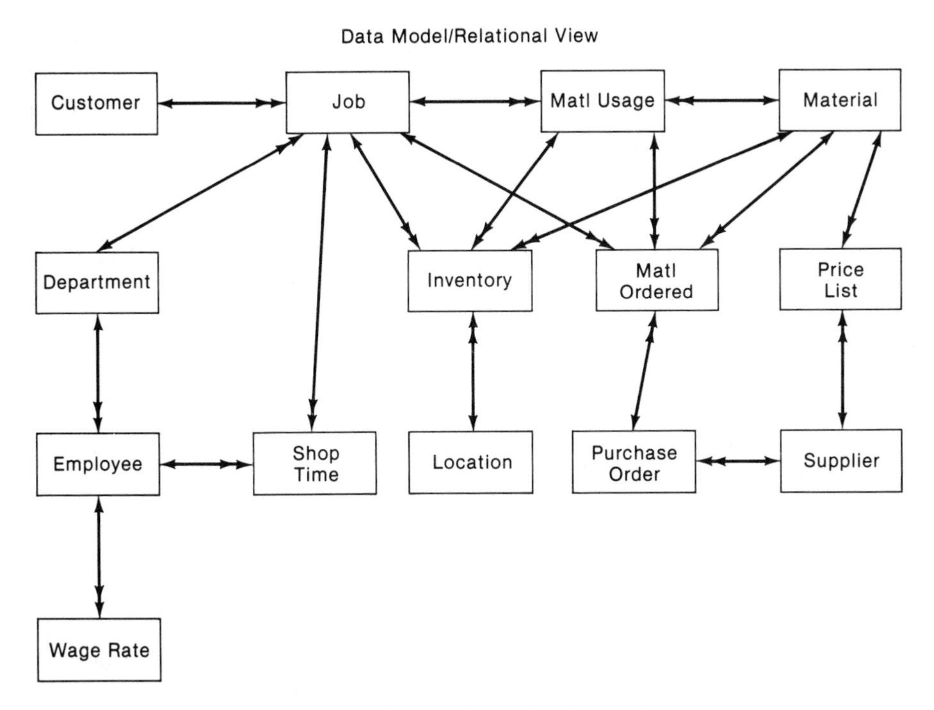

Figure 8.7 The Data Model/Relational View

Program 2. Enter new purchase order information (on line)

The purchasing agent has been given a list of parts and quantities required for various jobs. These items are periodically consolidated, and, for each supplier, a purchase order is created for all known parts requirements. The purpose of this program is to enter this information into the data base.

Program Functions. Using the order information, create a new Purchase Order record in the data base. Then create new Material Ordered records for each line item on the order. Print a report showing the information in each of these new records, including the part name.

```
Add Purchase Order (PO-NO)
Add Material Ordered (PO-NO, PART-NO)
Find Material (PART-NO)
```

Program 3. Update data base upon receipt of ordered parts (on line)

The shipping department receives a shipment of parts, and decides (externally from the data base) where the parts are to be stored. The data base is updated to reflect the receipt of the parts, as well as the updating of inventory data to reflect where they are stored.

Program Functions. Material Ordered records are read and checked for the quantity ordered. The line item is complete 90 percent of the time, and the Material Ordered record is deleted. Inventory records are added to reflect where the parts have been stored.

```
Find Material (PART-NO)
Find Material Ordered (PO-NO, PART-NO)
(90%) Delete Material Ordered
(10%) Modify Material Ordered
Add Inventory (LOC-NO, PART-NO)
```

Program 4. Report on the quantity and location of required parts (on line)

Frequently inventory data are checked to identify the location and quantity of a specified part.

Program Functions. Given the specified part, locate all inventory records to obtain the location, quantity and job number information.

```
Find Material (PART-NO)
Find Inventory (PART-NO)
```

Program 5. Update inventory to reflect parts used for a job (on line)

As each phase of assembly begins, parts are required. The data base is used to identify the location of that kind of part in inventory.

Program Functions. For the specified job and quantity of parts, access all inventory records applicable and display the inventory location and quantity. Update the inventory records to reflect the reduced quantity on hand.

```
Find Job (JOB-NO)
Find Inventory (JOB-NO, PART-NO)
Modify Inventory
```

Program 6. Check status of customer jobs (on line)

Customers often call B-R for a general status check on jobs which are active in the shop. All Job records for that customer must be read to obtain scheduling information maintained there.

Program Functions. The customer's code is used to access customer information to verify authorization for the request. All Job records for this customer are then accessed to obtain the schedule dates for the job.

```
Find Customer (CUST-CODE)
Find Job (CUST-CODE)
```

Program 7. Process shop time records (batch)

On a daily basis, all shop employees fill in a time card as they work. They record a one-line entry every time they complete a specific kind of work on a job, indicating the number of hours applicable.

At the beginning of the next day, all of the time cards are collected. The data processing department uses a key-to-disk system to key the data from these cards. This, then, becomes a sequential file which is read by this program.

For each time card line item, the corresponding labor cost is computed, and a report is produced for review by the shop managers. The shop time records are then added to the data base.

Program Functions. The sequential input file is sorted and read in clock number order. For each employee, the hourly salary is obtained and a work file is produced which is used to produce the daily shop work reports.

The input file is then sorted by job number and read again. For each job, the job record is accessed, after which the relative shop time data are added to the data base.

```
Phase 1 (CLOCK-NO sequence):
Find Employee (CLOCK-NO)
Find Wage Rate (CLOCK-NO, DATE)

Phase 2 (JOB-NO sequence):
Find Job (JOB-NO)
Add Shop Time (JOB-NO, DATE, LABOR-CODE, CLOCK-NO)
```

Program 8. Upon job completion, cost out the job (batch)

Each day a list is produced of the jobs to be costed and removed from the system. This involves producing summary reports showing, for each job, the quantity and value of material used on the job, and summarizing all of the shop time records for the job.

Program Functions. For the specified job, obtain all Material Usage information and the Shop Time data. For each Shop Time record, Wage Rate records are accessed to get the employee's salary at the time the work was performed so the cost of shop time may be calculated.

```
Find Job (JOB-NO)
Find Matl Usage (JOB-NO)
Find Shop Time (JOB-NO)
Find Employee (CLOCK-NO)
Find Wage Rate (CLOCK-NO, DATE-RAISE)
Modify Job
Modify Matl Usage
Modify Shop Time
```

Note that the Modify operations are performed to turn on a "logical delete" flag which is set to indicate costing of the job. You could perform deletes here, but experience has shown that jobs are sometimes costed in error, and this Modify can be reversed easily to reactivate the job's status. You want to note the requirement for a periodic cleanup job which passes the data base sequentially and, when the logical flags are found to be "on," issue a true (physical) delete.

Program 9. Produce a list of material on order (batch)

On a weekly basis, a list of all material on order is produced, where each item on order is shown as a line on this report. In addition to showing the part's name and the date the item is scheduled to be received, various job scheduling information is shown to determine if the part will be received by the time it is needed in the shop.

Program Functions. Find each Material Ordered record, as well as the Part record, to obtain the part name and create a work file containing this information. After sorting this work file by job number, access the Job record to obtain the scheduling information for the job, adding this information to the work file. This work file is passed through several sort/print sequences to produce the required reports.

```
Phase 1:
Find Material (PART-NO)
Find Material Ordered(PART-NO)

Phase 2 (sorted by JOB-NO):
Find Job (JOB-NO)
```

Program 10. Print bill of material data (batch)

Frequently questions come up requiring, for a specific job and kind of part, information pertaining to quantities required or used for that part and job.

Program Functions. For a specified job, print all related bill of material/job usage information.

```
Find Job (JOB-NO)
Find Material Usage (JOB-NO)
Find Material (PART-NO)
```

Program 11. Produce a monthly employee list (batch)

On a monthly basis, produce an employee list by department.

Program Functions. For each department, produce a list of employees assigned to that department.

```
Find Department (DEPT-NO)
Find Employee (DEPT-NO)
```

Program 12—List material available by supplier (batch)

Periodically produce a list of all materials available from each supplier.

Program Functions. For each supplier, access each item in the Price List, then obtain the part name from Material.

```
Find Supplier (SUPP-CODE)
Find Price List (SUPP-CODE)
Find Material (PART-NO)
```

Figure 8.8 was created by drawing the usage paths from Programs 1 through 12 on one picture of the data model.

8.4 DEVELOPMENT OF AN IMS SOLUTION

Using the visualization techniques described in Chapter 7, Figure 8.9 was created as a first-cut data base solution. These results represent data base requirements for this system regardless of the kind of DBMS chosen for physical implementation.

For a hierarchical solution, the following adjustments would be made, resulting in the solution shown in Figure 8.10:

1. *Choice of Access Methods.* Most data bases are assumed to have significant insert/delete activity, and therefore to justify one of the HD access methods. The further choice of HIDAM versus HDAM was based on the assumption of a significant need for key-sequential processing.
2. *Customer-to-Job.* This path was provided by placing a secondary index on Job, based on the CUSTOMER-NO field.

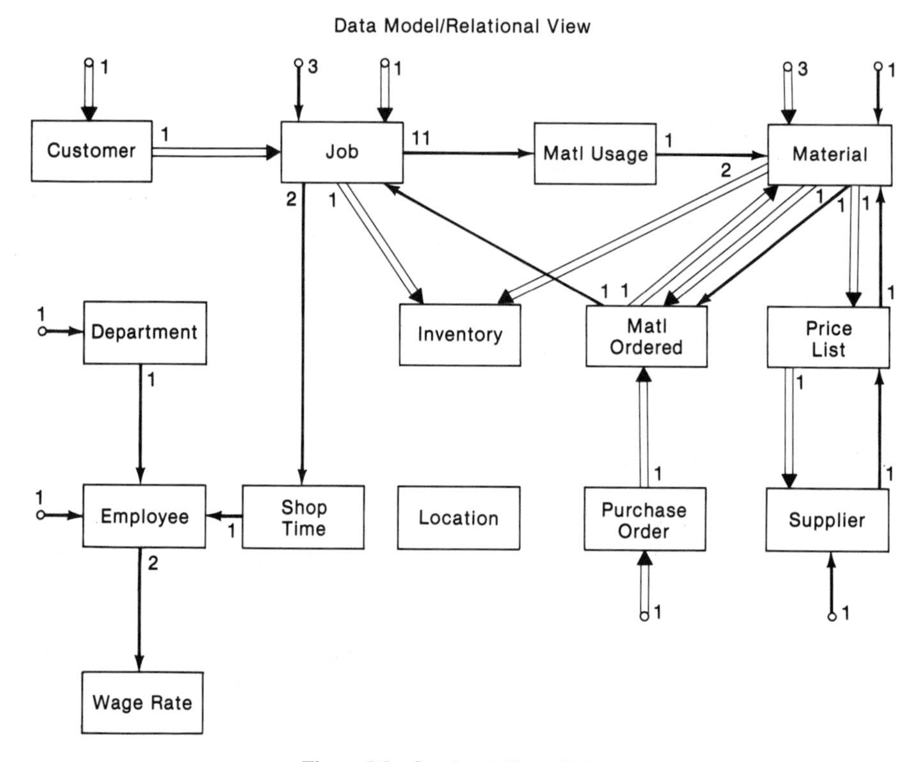

Figure 8.8 Overlayed Usage Paths

3. *Material Usage-to-Material.* With the PART-NO field in Material Usage, Material may be directly accessed without the use of any additional structural connection or pointer path.
4. *Job-to-Inventory.* This path is provided by placing a secondary index on Inventory, based on JOB-NO.
5. *Material Ordered-to-Job.* With the JOB-NO stored in Material Ordered, Job may be accessed directly without the use of any structural connection or pointer path.
6. *Purchase Order-to-Material Ordered-to-Material.* Program 1's access path was changed to go from Purchase Order to Material to Material Ordered. This avoids the need to implement a logical relationship between Purchase Order and Material.
7. *Department-to-Employee.* This requirement, from Usage 11, can be satisfied by sorting the Employee file into DEPT-NO sequence to produce this report.
8. *Shop Time-to-Employee-to-Wage Rate...The Elimination of Wage Rate.* The Wage Rate entity was created in the normalization process because the cost of each Shop Time entry could not be stored there without a violation of third

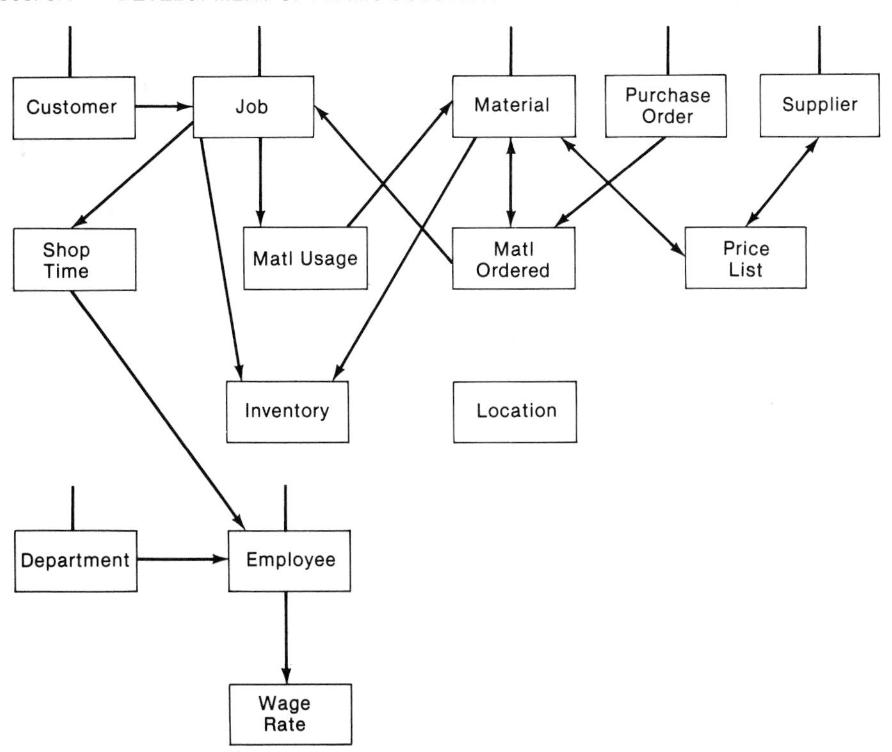

Figure 8.9 First-Cut Data Base View

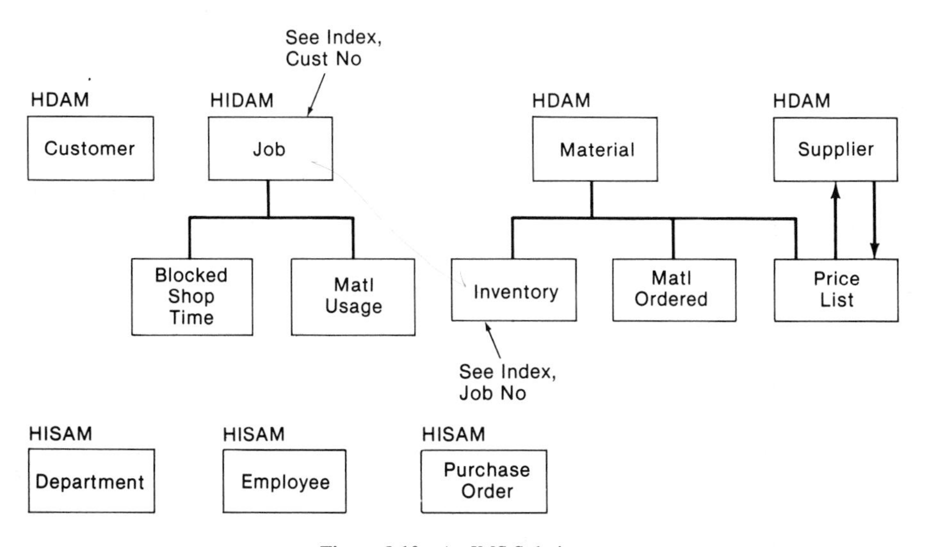

Figure 8.10 An IMS Solution

normal form. This, however, would require a tremendous amount of I/O when summarizing Job costs, because each Shop Time record would require an Employee-to-Wage Rate lookup for that day in order to recalculate the cost of that labor record. This overhead can be avoided by revising Shop Time to contain this salary cost. Although it would no longer be in third normal form, this avoids having to create a Wage Rate record, and makes several processes much faster.

9. *Blocking Up Shop Time.* In looking at volume statistics, there are, on the average, several thousand shop time records for each job. In order to more quickly add new records each day, and to retrieve these records quickly when removing jobs from the system, they will be programmatically blocked up into variable-length records which each contain up to 50 sets of Shop Time information.
10. *Elimination of Location.* The Location entity type was never used by any process, since it was created to satisfy third normal form criteria.

8.5 DEVELOPING A NETWORK SOLUTION

In deriving a network solution, the same reasoning would be applied as when deriving the IMS solution. The one difference is that additional set types were implemented in place of using secondary indexing as shown in the IMS solution. Finally, the choice of Location Modes was based on the same assumptions as used in the IMS solution for the need for key-sequential processing. The network solution is shown in Figure 8.11.

8.6 DERIVING A RELATIONAL SOLUTION

In a similar manner, the relational solution shown in Figure 8.12 was developed. Here, again, most of the changes made in deriving the IMS-based solution were used, showing indexes which are required to bridge the required 1:M linkages. The only additional modification needed is the artificial definition of a unique key for the blocked-up Shop Time records.

8.7 SUMMARY

As you undoubtedly have recognized, each of the preceding solutions used basic adjustments in either the initially proposed access paths or the data model itself. Keep in mind the reason for these adjustments was not simply to circumvent restrictions in what a DBMS can do, but to identify and implement high-performance access paths wherever possible. In this way, unnecessary overhead is

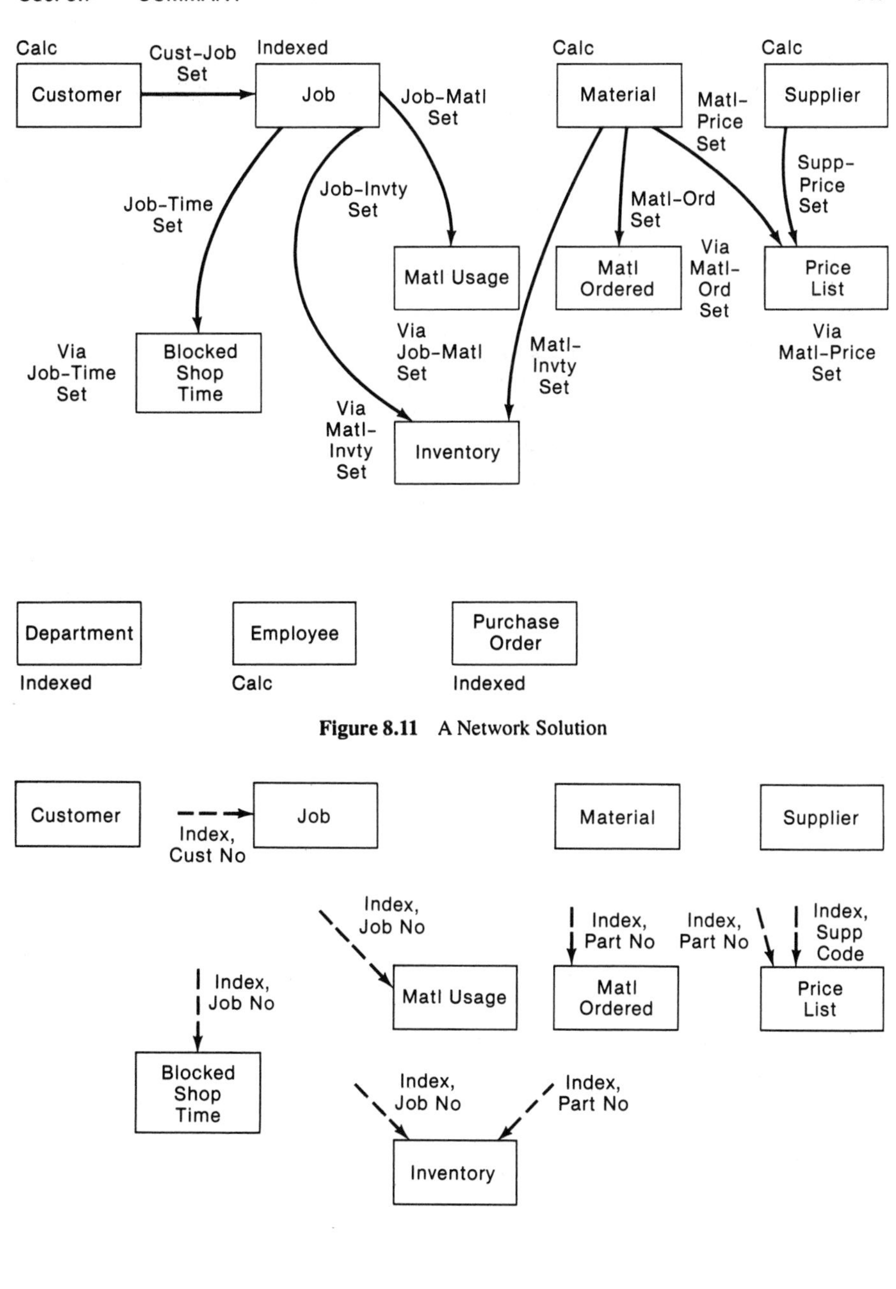

Figure 8.11 A Network Solution

Figure 8.12 A Relational Solution

avoided for the DBMS, and whatever implementation options are available may be used to the advantage of as many application processes as possible.

REVIEW QUESTIONS

For each type of DBMS, describe the work required to implement each of the following types of changes in a production data base.

1. Expand the data model to incorporate payroll record changes for employees. Next, decide how to incorporate these changes into the existing structures. Finally, how could these changes be implemented into the production system?
2. Add the quantity-required information to the Job-Material record.
3. Add the capability of a fast retrieval of Customer based on customer name.
4. Add the capability for on-line access to Material-PO status information.

9

Data Administration

9.1 INTRODUCTION

Chapter 1 introduces the term *data administration*, and includes a general discussion of a data dictionary. In this chapter, we look more closely at data administration:

- what it is,
- what it consists of,
- its potential benefits, and
- typical problems found with its implementation.

To begin, here are terms which are so similar they are often confused with each other, although they really represent different things.

9.2 TERMINOLOGY

Data administration. The job function which provides centralized identification and tracking of data elements used within corporate data structures. Through the use of automated data entry and tracking tools (usually a data dictionary), this knowledge of "what data are stored where" is essential to the effective development of any new or revised system. New data elements can be identified and integrated into new or revised structures. Additional support services are also provided, including the generation of standard I/O areas for application programs as well as certain control blocks required by the data base management system used.

Data base management systems include control mechanisms that protect access to data by permitting program access to only those data elements for which they have authorization. Such controls are commonly produced as an output product of a data dictionary. Essentially, the organization which controls the dictionary has the ability to provide and control the access to all data elements within corporate data bases.

Data Base Administration. A related, but more technically oriented, function. This responsibility includes the more technical aspects of data base definition, defining and reviewing parameters that specify pointer selection, addressing mechanisms, space utilization, and so on. Since this information is contained within the data base description, this function is often confused with data administration. Keep in mind, however, that data administrators define and track data elements, their meaning and usage, while data base administrators (DBAs) manage the technical aspects of data base definition, tuning, and maintenance.

Operational DBA. Holds responsibility for the day-to-day "care and feeding" of data bases in the data center. They run backup and recovery utilities as needed, monitor data base growth and performance, tune data bases to obtain better performance, and control changes to data base structures when doing tuning or as a result of application conversions.

Of course, in a small company a single person may have all three responsibilities. As a company grows in size and complexity, however, these job functions become the responsibility of separate groups. This chapter deals only with the narrower issue of data administration, with the more technical responsibilities of Operational DBAs reviewed in Chapter 10. Figure 9.1 summarizes the major responsibilities in these areas.

Let's begin by looking in detail at how the data administration function can serve in the data base design process.

9.3 DATA DEFINITION

The data administration role can be a vital part of the data base design phase. As data requirements for new or revised systems are defined, the data dictionary should be checked to see if new data requirements can be satisfied by an existing corporate data base, and, if so, to establish access to the data. If the data elements

	DATA ADMINISTRATION
Planning Identification Control Tracking	• Centralized identification and tracking of data content of corporate data bases. • Insure standard definition and entry of descriptive information. • Define and enforce naming conventions for data elements. • Create I/O areas and data base control blocks for applications.
	DATA BASE ADMINISTRATION
Physical Design Implementation Options Tuning	• Define parameters required for physical data base definition. • Analyze data volume and space requirements. • Perform data base tuning.
	OPERATIONAL DBA
Operational Use Backup Recovery Reorganization	• Execute data base backup and recovery functions as required. • Monitor space requirements. • Install parameter changes for data base tuning. • Verify integrity of data bases.

Figure 9.1 Data Administration vs. Data Base Administration Functions

are new, they enter the entity/attribute definitions into the dictionary as hypothetical records and fields. This data definition, created by using corporate standards for field names and title information, is reviewed and revised if necessary, using the standard reporting features of the dictionary. These reports are used in subsequent discussions with the user group to assure an understanding of, and agreement on, the definitions for the data elements.

Later, these entities evolve into record formats for the new system, and the dictionary can generate standard I/O areas needed by application programs, as well as any data base control blocks required.

9.3.1 The Importance of Standards

It's important to use standard naming conventions when entering data into a data dictionary. In identifying each new data attribute, descriptive information must be created using a consistent set of terms and abbreviations that describe what this element represents. Reports are then generated for review by the design team to insure a common agreement of the definitions. Vague or unclear definitions must be identified and corrected to assure agreement on what each attribute really in fact represents.

```
Employee
        Field Name         Field Description
        SOC-SEC-NO         The employee's social security number
        EMP-SALARY         The employee's salary       <=== very vague and
                                                            confusing
```

In this example, the design team recognized that they needed information on the employee salary. The attribute defined, however, reflects the level of fuzzy feeling or understanding about what the salary should be. This is corrected in the following report. If there is any doubt at a future point as to what the element is, or what it means, this information is available for clarification.

```
Employee
        Field Name        Field Description
        SOC-SEC-NO        The employee's social security number
        EMP-SALARY        The employee's weekly salary <=== more specific
```

Of course, this information will only be available if the design team chooses to document it originally and enters it into the dictionary. Too often design teams are so rushed that data definitions are not properly documented, and are not available when needed at a future point in time.

The first job in defining a new attribute (as a field) to the dictionary is to create a field name and a title or description, as illustrated in the previous example. In creating the field name, descriptive abbreviations are often used to create a name consistent with the requirements for the application language to be used. Standards for field names are important because the programming staff should, wherever possible, "speak the same language." Common field names in I/O areas make it easier for any member of the programming group to read and understand another's program. This is critical for those within the same programming group, and desirable for any groups who share access to common data bases.

The standards for the description or "title" field are less obvious, but more important and far-reaching. Assume that you have just finished the design and implementation of a data base system dealing with customer-related marketing information which contains information on customers, customer purchases, and customer requests for the manufacturing of custom equipment. Then, at a later point in time, your management has the need to run ad hoc queries against these data to do marketing research for new business opportunities.

```
Customer
        Field Name       Field Description
        CUST-CODE        A unique code identifying a customer
        CUST-NAME        The customer name used in correspondence

Customer Purchase     (from a second data base)
        Field Name       Field Description
        CUSTMR-CODE      A code identifying a cust purchasing equip
        EQUIP-CODE       A code identifying equipment sold to cust's

Custom Equipment       (from a third data base)
        Field Name       Field Description
        CUSTM-EQ-CODE    A code identifying equip custom designed
        CUS-REQUEST      A code for a custmr requesting design
```

To perform this research, they need to see all information in the data base related to customers. However, because of the careless and inconsistent way in which these titles and field names were created, a query to "show all records containing the word CUSTOMER in the title field" will fail. It can't identify all records with customer information because of the variation in the abbreviations used. Unfortunately, once the data are entered, it's essentially too late (or too expensive) to make changes in data definitions. On the other hand, if standard abbreviations were used to describe the data elements, then you could use those same abbreviations to search the title fields for matching expressions or terms. You must recognize the need for standards for descriptive or title fields before entering the data into the dictionary, and not several years later when someone has a need to identify what your data bases contain.

It would appear, from the preceding discussion, that the data administration function provides a wide variety of services. Why, then, does this topic remain controversial, and a continual subject for articles in literature? Let's review some common problems, and take a look at alternative available solutions.

9.3.2 Problems with Naming Conventions

A common problem encountered by many data administrators is in the creation of field names for I/O areas in application programs. Discussions reviewing proposed names are often characterized by disagreements on the details of how the COBOL or PL/I name should be constructed. For example:

1. An application which is being redesigned finds that the old existing standards for COBOL or PL/I names don't comply to the standards of the data administration group. This usually happens after the data administrators create new standards for naming fields, and now an older application needs to be updated.

If these standards are to be followed, all programs must be rewritten, even those not affected by the modification.

2. Two application program groups share access to a common set of data bases. However, each application group has an existing, but different, set of naming conventions for fields.
3. The data administration staff keeps changing the standards for naming conventions.
4. A design team simply can't agree on naming conventions.

As one example, I heard a story of how someone attended a meeting where the participants did nothing but discuss a COBOL name for one data field. The particularly amusing (or distressing!) thing was that the entire discussion revolved around the choices of CUST-REQDEQUIP-OPTION, CUST-REQD-EQUIP-OPTION, or CUST-REQD-EQUIPOPTION. At the end of an hour, he found an excuse to leave. Can you blame him?

What can be done about these issues?

1. Insure that standards (and particularly enforcement of standards) must revolve around reasonable objectives. While standardized names are a good objective, they alone do not justify the rewriting of all application programs. As an alternative, insure that a given application group uses consistent naming conventions for all programs, rather than trying to have standard names across all applications.
2. Whenever design meetings take place, agree in advance on a moderator for the discussion, and establish a time limit when discussing new data elements. Whenever that time passes without agreement on how to name the subject element, the moderator interrupts, the item is noted and shelved temporarily to be reviewed again at a future session. This technique helps keep the discussion moving.

9.3.3 Checking Data Fields on Data Entry

When adding a new data field to the dictionary, the new field should be checked against existing data to avoid creating multiple entries for the same attribute where each has a different description. In theory, this check is made by choosing key terms from the proposed description for the field, then using dictionary query facilities to look up all fields having those terms as part of their description. Each potential match should be checked to see if it is the same as the field that is about to be entered. If no duplicates are found, the new field is created in the dictionary, and the process repeats itself for the next field.

As the amount of data defined in the dictionary grows, this checking process will become increasingly more time consuming, yet some type of checking must be done if you are to avoid data duplication.

As an alternative, check for duplicates through entity/attribute comparisons. Identify an entity to which the new attribute(s) are associated in third normal form, then query the dictionary to see if this entity has been previously defined. If the entity is, in fact, new, then no further checking is necessary, and the normalization process will prevent problems or errors across the newly defined attributes associated with it. On the other hand, if the entity being defined does already exist, then a report of its associated attributes can be used to check each of the proposed attributes. In this way, the effort to check for duplicates is greatly reduced.

Another effective way to address this problem is to develop data specialists from within each application group. These individuals serve in an ongoing support role to their application programmers by providing all data-related services. If these job functions have been implemented, these individuals can be consulted to check their "data awareness" about the data their application uses. If your company has not consistently defined data fields on entry to the dictionary, these data specialists may be the only hope you have of finding information about data when you need it.

9.3.4 The "True Meaning" of Data Elements

With all of the standards in the world, naming conventions for fields simply are not sufficient, in themselves, to clearly identify and describe what a data field represents.

With any given data element in mind, and with a list of standard naming conventions as a reference, any analyst can construct a field name and title description for that field. However, another analyst, using the same information as a starting point, would construct a similar "solution" for a field name and title, but *the two solutions would be different.*

Put yourself in the role of trying to determine if a specific data field currently exists within a data base. Using the standard abbreviations previously referenced, queries can be run to produce a list of potential matches for the data element in question. However, based simply on field names and descriptions, the odds are extremely high that you cannot clearly determine if you have found "a match."

Fortunately, this problem is easy to solve. At the point in time that the data field is defined, a paragraph-style, clear English description of what the data field represents should be stored in the data dictionary. This description can also include anything that's relevant regarding update rules or edits, data security restrictions, and so on. After running a query, this information would be used to clarify if you have found a match in what you're looking for.

This is a simple, but critical, component in the identification of data elements. Yes, it takes more time and effort to capture this information at data entry time. If not done then, it's very difficult (or impossible) to do at a later point in time. But if it's not done at all, then you have no hope of later using the data dictionary to clearly provide the meaning of the data elements stored within the data base.

9.4 PERSONNEL STAFFING FOR DATA ADMINISTRATION

Another problem concerns adequate staffing of the data administration section. Quite often others view this type of service organization as strictly overhead because the members don't "write any code," or because the end product cannot be measured in terms of dollars. As a result, this organization has at most only a sufficient number of personnel to handle the immediate data entry functions. As a result:

1. If too many projects become active simultaneously, they cannot all be adequately serviced. This leads to providing an inadequate level of service to all, or to providing no service at all for some projects.
2. As new projects become active, the data entry for design support moves to new projects. However, projects previously serviced are being expanded through continued design or maintenance work, generating a continued support requirement. The data administration staff is hard at work on a new project, and has no time to support the modifications.

One approach to this problem would be to justify, somehow, an adequate staffing level for the maximum level of activity that could exist. Besides being difficult to do, this presents the problem of keeping this larger number of people productively occupied during slower periods of design or maintenance work.

A second and more practical approach is to redefine the specific roles and activities of the participants in the following way:

1. Make the data administration group responsible for defining, creating, and teaching the use of any required standards or processes for the definition and entry of data into the dictionary by the application groups.
2. The application group assigns a member(s) of their staff the responsibility for providing support for that application's data definition and data entry. These personnel will serve as contacts to the data administration staff and, after obtaining the appropriate training in methods and tools, can service their own organization's data entry needs throughout the life of the application system.

Using this approach has two obvious benefits. Because the application staff is servicing their own group, response time in handling changes is fast; there's nothing better than having dedicated local support. Second, the data administration manager no longer must staff in advance for an undetermined, uncontrolled, and unknown work load. Any project that becomes active will automatically need to include staffing considerations for its data definition/data entry requirements from within the application group, but the benefits obtained through internal data administration support will far outweigh the minimal staffing required.

Figure 9.2 summarizes the major problems that data administrators deal with most.

Insuring new data elements are described using a consistent set of keywords or abbreviations.

Checking for duplicate entries on initial input requires an excessive amount of time.

Obtaining agreement across multiple application groups for standards for field names.

Inadequate staffing levels to provide proper support to client organizations.

Figure 9.2 Problems Facing Data Administrations

9.5 THE INFORMATION CENTER

By definition, the purpose for an information center is to provide assistance to end users in identifying and using local computer resources to accomplish their jobs. As one aspect of this process, data administration issues surface quickly as a requirement in assisting end users to identify and gain access to corporate data. As such, the information center becomes the natural interface between the end users and the informational resources available through the data dictionary. With the establishment of the proper environment, the information center can assist users in identifying how data requirements can be met with access to data from production data base systems. They can tell where and how to download the production data.

As users come to find which data they need, the next step is to allow end user access to the production data. This sounds relatively simple, and from the technical standpoint it is. However, with all due respect to the end user community, each end user cannot arbitrarily be given access to anything he or she asks to see. It is one thing to provide access to information about employee names, titles, assigned departments, and so on, downloaded for the purposes of performing a personnel profile study. On the other hand, a slight, “minor” expansion of data requirements to include salary information brings a much greater level of concern.

Must application groups deal with these concerns when designing application systems? In a minor way, yes. However, it is reasonable to grant a payroll systems programmer access to all data within an employee record whenever the record must be accessed. But this is much different than providing complete field-level authorization to end users who have a need occasionally to perform an ad hoc search.

Let’s restate the problem. Whenever end users have the need to gain access to production data bases, either to support queries, or for downloading to other systems, a mechanism must exist to: (1) identify where the data are located; and, (2) grant or control access to the data.

We have already covered how data dictionaries can assist in locating what data are stored where. With proper standards and use, the dictionary is the central storage location for this information and control. Making this information available to end users can be accomplished through a combination of responsibilities between the data administration staff, the information center, and end user representatives.

Granting access to the data, on the other hand, presents a situation of a different nature. This issue may seem trivial, based on the way your particular shop operates today. What will happen, however, when the time comes that production data bases are implemented under a relational DBMS? These systems are, by nature and design, flexible and powerful, with an emphasis on ease of access to data as data access requirements change. Using IBM's DB2 system as an example, control mechanisms exist to create user views that permit access to only those data which are required. But who will make that determination? An operational DBA may have to have the final technical ability to grant the required access but be in no position to deal with requests from users on changes to data access requirements. Even the information center personnel may not have the knowledge to properly deal with end-user access requests. One solution is for the end-user department to establish a coordinator who serves as the "clearinghouse" for access requests. The coordinator passes change requests on to the operational DBA, who performs the required authorization steps to permit that capability.

9.6 DATA ADMINISTRATION AS A SERVICE ORGANIZATION

A key element in all aspects of data administration support is responsiveness. Active design work will cause the generation of a great deal of new attributes which must be entered promptly into the data dictionary. Those definitions discussed and tentatively agreed upon in yesterday's work sessions will be reviewed and built upon in today's sessions. Standards for naming conventions, program names, and for the construction of title fields must be agreed upon in advance and available for use in the data entry phase. New or unforeseen factors requiring standards must be handled quickly; any prolonged discussion or "second thoughts" about what the standards should be are extremely counterproductive. The "name of the game" in making data administration an effective, positive function is to provide a service to those involved in the design. A lack of responsiveness or uncertainty over standards detracts quickly from a service-oriented posture, and can quickly lead to dissatisfaction on the part of the design team with the data administration staff, perhaps even by bypassing them whenever possible just to, in the application's eyes, "keep things moving."

REVIEW QUESTIONS

1. Your company has just acquired a DBMS as well as a data dictionary system. You have been asked to lead the development of corporate standards for naming data elements. How would you approach this task (that is, what steps taken in what sequence)? How would you create standards for field descriptions? For each field defined, for which languages will you create standard names?
2. In trying to get different application groups to move toward corporate standards for data elements, what arguments would you use?
3. What is the single biggest problem of data administrators? Assuming that this problem exists within your company, how would you handle it?
4. What procedures would you use for describing new data elements in the data dictionary? What would you do to insure adherence to your company standards?
5. Describe the various job responsibilities that you feel should be performed by a data administration function. What background is desirable for each position? What type of career path would you recommend to help implement this?

10

Backup/Recovery Mechanisms

10.1 INTRODUCTION

Data bases contain the key operational data upon which a company relies to run its business. It is vital, therefore, that these data be available when needed, as well as be accurate in terms of data content. Should data be lost or destroyed due to hardware or software failures, data base management systems contain backup/recovery mechanisms that have the ability to restore the affected data base to the point of failure.

Those individuals responsible for defining and establishing backup/recovery plans for applications, or in managing data center operations, must have a clear understanding of the capabilities and restrictions of these backup/recovery mechanisms to insure both the integrity and availability of these data bases.

10.2 RESTORING TO A POINT OF FAILURE

Let's explore the concept of "restoring to a point of failure." First, the data base is *rebuilt* by backup/recovery utilities; you don't have to reexecute update jobs since the last backup. Second, after recovery the data base will contain all updates applied to it, right up to the instant of failure. Recovery mechanisms are not limited to recovering, for example, only to the way the data base looked last night.

To provide this level of protection in a batch environment, a good recovery system includes a utility to automatically reverse a series of data base updates to a logical checkpoint. This checkpoint occurs at a logical point in time when the application program can commit all changes previously made as being irreversible in status. For example, the program has just completed processing all updates for a customer account, and is ready to begin updating the next account. If the system were to fail in the future, backout processes would reverse updates made after the checkpoint was taken, in a reverse sequence, to reestablish the data base(s) at that point in time. Standard checkpoint/restart procedures would restart the application process from the checkpoint, rather than require reexecution of the entire job.

In an on-line environment, the on-line system automatically manages control of the backout and reexecution of programs active at the time of a system failure.

The IMS on-line and batch environments contain probably the most comprehensive set of backup/recovery facilities available. They are used here as a model in describing what can be done to guarantee data base integrity.

To provide recovery of a data base to the point of failure, the following must take place (See Figure 10.1):

1. Periodically, take a master backup of the data base. Note the date and time of the backup in a tracking file as reference should recovery be necessary. IMS calls this master copy an "image copy," being a snapshot of the data at that instant in time.
2. Application programs then process updates against these data bases. A log file is automatically created, containing information on the changes made.
3. When recovery becomes necessary, the recovery utility uses the master backup copy to restore the data base to when the backup was taken. Then, by reading the log files, further updates are made by reapplying the changes recorded in the log records.

   Note that this process does *not* require the reexecution of application code or logic. It merely reapplies the results of decisions previously made by the data base on the behalf of the executing program(s).
4. Other types of hardware and software failures may require a backout to reverse uncommitted updates to the data base.

In an on-line environment, backout is automatically invoked when the system is restarted after a system failure. The on-line system's log data set is used as input to reverse everything that was "in flight" at the time of the system's failure. These transactions can then be requeued for reprocessing.

In batch, a batch utility reverses updates to either a specified checkpoint or to the beginning of the job (See Figure 10.2).

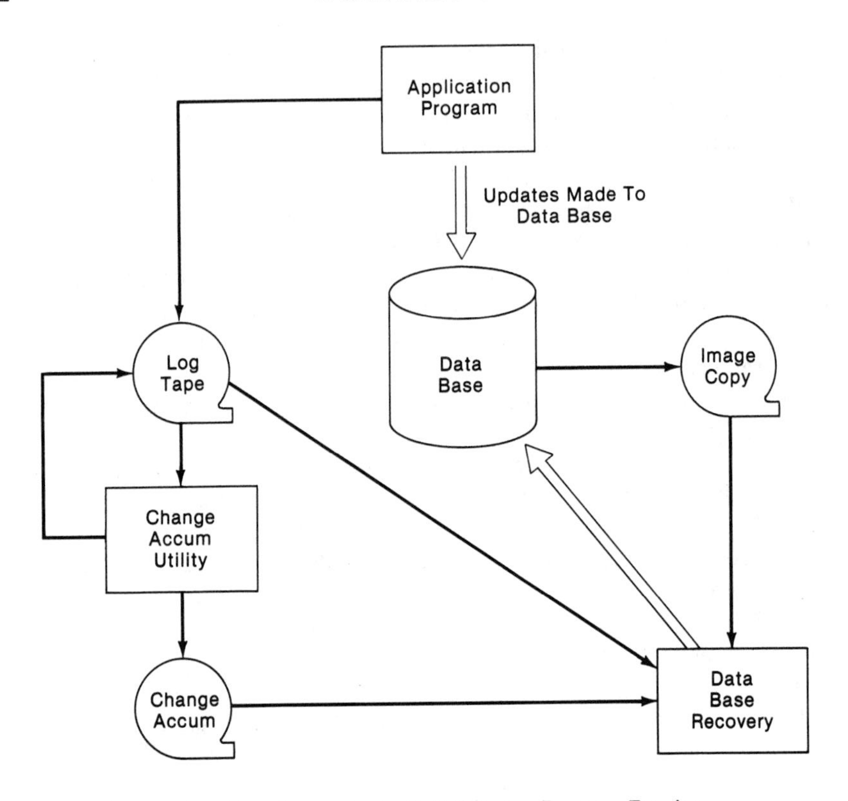

Figure 10.1 Data Sets Involved with IMS Backup/Recovery Functions

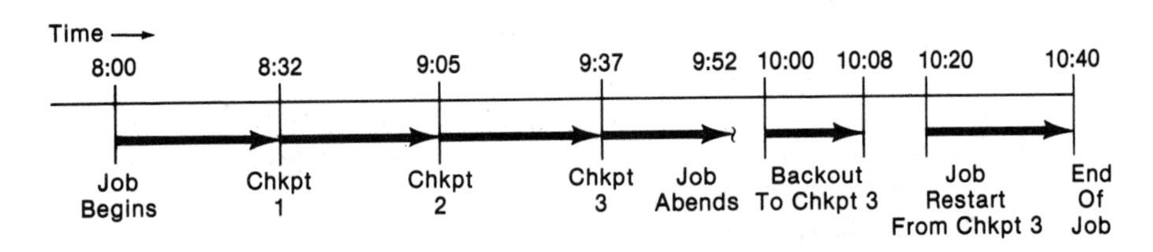

Figure 10.2 Using Backout and Restart Facilities

In both cases, the backout processes themselves create log files which must be included in any subsequent data base recovery.

10.3 MANAGING BACKUP/RECOVERY

To minimize data base downtime during recovery operations, special utilities are often available which can reduce the processing required. IMS provides several ways in which this might be done.

10.3.1 Tracking Log Data Sets

IMS's Data Base Recovery Control (DBRC) software has the capability to automatically track and control all recovery-related data sets. These functions are activated for specified data bases through a process called *registration*. Although this may seem trivial, performing this tracking manually, and having to manually edit and submit recovery JCL when needed, could easily add 30 minutes or more to downtime for someone to manually set up and check the required input data sets for the job. In addition, DBRC also insures the accuracy of this information. Errors made in the generation of recovery jobs can go unrecognized for days, and are *very* expensive to correct in terms of time and effort. Finally, DBRC produces a much higher level of data base integrity by preventing "dual updaters" and other operational errors.

10.3.2 Change Accumulation Data Sets

The Change Accumulation utility reduces the time for data base recovery by consolidating log tape input. Individual log records are summarized to create one composite set of changes per data base block. In this way, only the latest version of a particular data segment or record need be retained. In addition, these changes are created and stored in ascending sequence by block number, and therefore can be quickly applied to the data base in the recovery process.

Change Accum jobs will be automatically generated by DBRC for all registered data bases.

The recovery utility can use, as input, a combination of a complete copy of the data base, a Change Accumulation data set, and individual log data sets (see Figures 10.1 and 10.3).

10.3.3 On-line Image Copies

More and more, today's on-line systems require longer on-line days. As a result, the time the data base is off line (the "batch window") continues to shrink, and less time is available for batch processing as well as for taking backups.

The on-line image copy utility works particularly well in an extended on-line environment. It creates a new master backup of the data base concurrently with the data base being updated on line. This is an essential component for any shop where data bases are on line 24 hours per day, seven days per week.

The advantages of this kind of utility extend beyond the value of simply taking a backup copy of the data base. Once a new copy is taken, the related Change Accumulation data set will be reduced in size because it reflects only changes since the latest image copy was taken. As a result, the run time for the Change Accumulation jobs will be shorter.

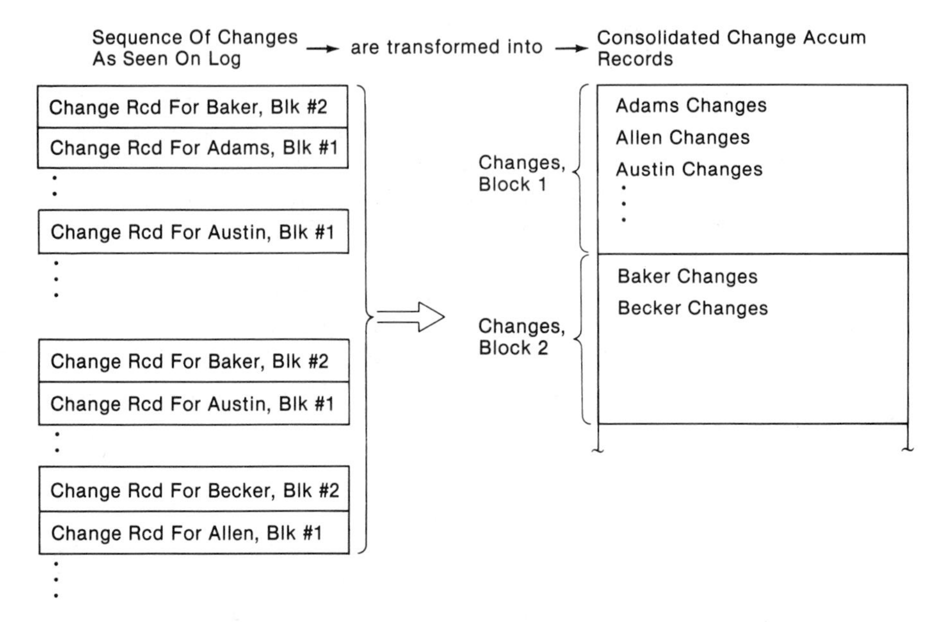

Figure 10.3 The Change Accumulation Process

10.3.4 Verifying Data Base Integrity

Although not directly related to recovery, periodic integrity checking is an essential part of a data base environment. This process verifies the accuracy of the internal pointer chains, and confirms that no failure condition or event has damaged the data base.

To perform an integrity check of an IMS data base, the data base is read by a batch utility which analyzes and verifies the internal data content of the data base. IMS uses an addressing mechanism where pointers are used to link associated data segments together. These pointers are found and verified by the utility, with any improper linkages reported through error messages. In addition, numerous reports are produced which are extremely useful in data base tuning.

The utility that performs this function is the Data Base Tools "HD Pointer Checker," or, to use the more popular name from an earlier version, SMU (Space Management Utility). It can read the data base directly, or use as input an image copy of the data base.

Whenever a problem occurs in a data base, the SMU reports will normally contain sufficient information to permit an experienced DBA to recognize the cause for the error condition. This knowledge is tremendously valuable in reacting to the problem in a timely and effective way.

Given the fact that integrity checking is possible, how does it effect the backup/recovery strategy for your installation? **An essential part of this strategy must be to perform integrity checking in a time frame to permit recovery of**

a data base using an image copy that has been verified by SMU, in addition to all subsequent log tapes. In other words, if and when a recovery is necessary, you know in advance that the input data sets are clean and contain no errors.

This requirement stands even if the Change Accum utility is used in a non-DBRC environment. It is very easy to omit a log tape to a Change Accum run when operating outside of DBRC's control. Using SMU to verify the image copy also verifies the readability of the tape data set, in addition to verifying the integrity of the data base.

Your recovery plan needs to consider other factors, as well. Check the expiration dates of each log tape data set to insure they will be available when needed. Also, many shops like to run more frequent Image Copies, but don't have time to run SMU against them (fpr example, they take nightly image copies). This is an acceptable practice, and these data sets should be used without question in recoveries because of a disk failure or application requirement. They *cannot*, however, be assumed to be error free unless checked by SMU.

The unload phase of a reorganization of the data base provides an alternative way of performing an integrity check. Although this approach technically checks only the forward pointers, it's essentially impossible for significant damage to occur to any data base without affecting the forward path through it.

10.4 METHODS FOR EXPEDITING RECOVERY

When deciding on the specific details of a new backup/recovery strategy, you need to first determine the cost of not having the data bases available for processing. After gaining this perspective, compare the cost of not having the data bases available against the increasing costs for strategies to expedite recovery. Acceptable recovery times should be documented in "service agreements," formal agreements with end user departments detailing the data processing services they are to be provided. These agreements include such things as response times, availability requirements, and acceptable downtime in the event data base recovery is required.

Assuming that you have identified the required recovery time for your application data base systems, let's now review various techniques which can reduce downtime. Although this will be done in terms of facilities in an IMS environment, most of these concepts apply to any DBMS.

10.4.1 More Frequent Backups (Image Copies)

The recovery process begins from the basic backup copy of the data base, the image copy. All changes made to the data base since the backup was taken must then be applied to make the data base current.

The more current the data base is, the fewer changes need to be applied and the faster the recovery. Many shops take nightly image copies, whenever the batch window permits. In addition, many batch systems having significant batch updates take full images between major job sequences to expedite recovery and restart when problems occur.

10.4.2 Keep Change Accumulation Data Current

As previously described, individual log data sets can be used as direct input to the recovery process. However, log tapes generated from on-line systems contain change records with updates against random positions in the data base, causing recovery to run more slowly. Because Change Accumulation data sets are sequential, the recovery process can apply these updates in the same sequential pass as the image copy. Therefore, whenever recovery is required, as much data as possible should be input via the Change Accum data set.

Using Change Accumulation as a recovery mechanism does not in itself assure efficient processing. To update a Change Accumulation data set, each new log is read, and the new data are sorted. This process could extend downtime sufficiently if the Change Accumulation process were allowed to fall too far behind. On the other hand, if the Change Accum were kept relatively current, (for example, never more than one or two log tapes from being totally current), it should be relatively easy to bring the Change Accum up to date.

Change accumulation can be used in a variety of ways.

1. Run Change Accumulation whenever two or three new log data sets become available. When recovery is required, begin the recovery using image copy-only input while simultaneously running a final Change Accumulation for any unaccumulated logs. Then run recovery again with only the Change Accumulation data set as input.
2. Run Change Accumulation each time a new log is available. When recovery is required, for one execution of the recovery utility, use the image copy, Change Accumulation, and the very latest log tape.

10.4.3 Maintain "Warm Copies" of Data Bases

"Warm copies" of data bases can be maintained to provide faster recovery over what is available through the more standard techniques outlined earlier. You would create extra copies of the data base, with slightly different data set names, on spare disk packs. Periodically, you would run recovery as a background job using the latest Change Accumulation data set as input to update the copy. In the event recovery is required, you would apply the very latest changes to the copy, followed with renames of the data sets to "flip-flop" the status of the two copies of the data base.

This approach also provides flexibility on how current either the Change Accumulation or the warm copy should be at any point in time.

10.4.4 Maintain Simultaneous Copies of Data

The application programs can be designed to process against two copies of each data base, applying identical updates simultaneously to both. Then, if one data base requires a recovery operation, the "good" or usable one is input to a copy operation to recreate the second.

Each technique described gives some incremental advantage in speedier recovery operations. Of course, using any combination of these techniques requires additional resources of some kind. In determining the optimal strategy for your environment, you must weigh the need for the time saved against the cost for the extra effort required in providing that capability.

10.4.5 Deferred Recovery

IMS has always used sophisticated mechanisms in handling I/O errors. Earlier releases allowed deferring recovery operations for write errors until after the on-line session ended. IMS Version 2.1 introduced significant enhancements on how I/O errors were handled *across* on-line sessions. This feature allows updated data bases buffers to be reestablished in core even though those corresponding blocks could not be written to disk. These buffers would then be used to satisfy all requests for, and updates to, the corresponding data. Recovery processing, therefore, can be deferred for some time.

10.5 RECOVERY ISN'T ALWAYS POSSIBLE

Using the recovery facilities described, backup/recovery strategies and polices can be developed to minimize downtime and avoid loss of data in the event of hardware or software failure. This is what I suppose you would call the "good news"; the facilities are there, and they work. The "bad news", however, is that circumstances can occur to put you in an unrecoverable position. By this I mean the only options available are to reprocess all updates from some point in time (on-line as well as batch) or to "repair" a damaged data base.[1]

Let's take a look at examples of how this might happen, and see what can be done to avoid this possibility.

10.5.1 Recovering from System Software Problems

A system software failure can create the need for recovery. Although these failures are extremely rare, they *can* take place, either as a result of bad software maintenance, or

---

[1] Hogan, Rex. *Diagnostic Techniques for IMS Data Bases* (Wellesley, MA: QED Information Sciences, Inc., 1986).

due to an error in applying the maintenance. The failing software component might even be part of the operating system itself rather than the DBMS. For example, the data base might have applied updates to a buffer correctly, but a subsequent error occurred in altering this buffer or in the process of writing it to disk.

This kind of problem can be handled by the normal recovery utilities, if you recognize what happened. Unfortunately, there are normally no error messages produced. The fact that a problem state exists in the data base will only be recognized by a subsequent application process failing when trying to retrieve the now damaged data, or by running an integrity check.

Under these circumstances, you must begin with an image copy of the data base *before the damage was incurred*, and apply to it all changes made since that point. Keep in mind that an image copy taken after the point of failure would simply contain a snapshot of the damage, and therefore be useless in the recovery process. That sounds like, and should be, a relatively straightforward process, as long as you find the problem quickly enough.

Under these circumstances, you often find that either image copy or log tape data sets have expired (and you need both). Also, be careful about relying on the Change Accumulation utility. Change Accum is based on all changes since the latest image copy, and therefore may not contain all updates since the point of failure. When that happens, it needs to be fully recreated using log tapes. In addition, if you don't use DBRC for recovery control and you have made an error in maintaining the Accum file (for example, forgetting to input one or more log tapes), the Change Accum is useless.

Another serious problem is the volume of data that must be processed to recover the data base. If the problem state occurred two weeks ago and you did not find it until today, recovery is technically possible but would require a very significant amount of time and resources to accomplish. The number of log tapes required for recovery would be a major problem.

Based on the nature of the data in the data base, it may be easier and more feasible to "repair" the data base. The damage is represented by pointers in error; they are addresses to data that no longer exist. To repair them, they can be "zapped," or set to a value of zero, which eliminates that path to data. Application programs can then process the data base without error, but data are missing. With luck, application and user groups can work together to reinstate lost data.

The point of this review is not to convince you that mistakes will happen or that your organization must experience significant problems in trying to utilize data base technology. The ability to handle these problems depends on the frequency of integrity checking which is done to assure the data integrity of data bases. Your shop's maintenance schedule should include periodic integrity checks, perhaps run immediately against new image copy data sets, to establish a recovery-based synchronization point. Your remaining recovery strategy should be based on assuring the ability to forward recover, using log tapes as input, since the last successful integrity check.

10.5.2 Recovering from Operational Errors

System software very rarely damages data bases. However, extensive damage can easily result from a variety of data center operational errors.

Typical examples of operational errors are:

1. Allowing batch update jobs to run simultaneously against the same data bases. Shops having multiple CPUs sharing disk drives and data bases are particularly vulnerable to this problem.
2. Making an error in recovery operations (for example, omitting a required log tape), and then processing updates to the data base. This produces a situation where recovery cannot be used to restore any updates after the error condition occurred.
3. Accidentally back-leveling a data base to a prior point in time, followed by a series of updates. Once again, recovery facilities cannot preserve updates to the data base after the error occurred.

The proper use of technology can help prevent errors. DBRC provides excellent protection against human error in recovery operations, and prevents operational errors, including those that can occur across CPUs. Integrity checking should be performed frequently enough to detect any error conditions quickly enough to permit a timely reaction.

Application design can also provide protection against certain kinds of operational errors. For example, a special data base record can be included in the design to contain date and time fields indicating when updates were last made to the data base. As a standard practice, an application initialization program checks these control records to verify that all data bases are at the same logical point in time before any updates are processed.

10.6 SPECIAL PROCESSING REQUIREMENTS

Other issues such as reorganizations, data base size, and the length of the on-line day affect both data base availability and integrity.

10.6.1 Reorganization Issues

A reorganization requires, in its simplest form, an unload, reload and image copy sequence to rearrange data base segments, and reestablish the physical clustering of the segments to gain a higher level of performance. Additional steps in the reorg sequence will be required if the data base has any secondary indexes or is involved with logical relationships. Although this type of maintenance is fairly routine, several problem areas need to be addressed to avoid mistakes.

First, an image copy needs to be taken after the unload/reload sequence to serve as a starting point for any subsequent recovery. Time to take this image must be included in the planning of the maintenance cycle to insure completion of the entire job before any updates take place.

Second, care must be taken in managing the unload data set itself. Because of the time requirement for the unload/reload/image copy sequence, at times a data center may begin a reorg job and later realize there is not sufficient time to complete the entire job before the on-line system needs the data bases. Under these circumstances, the unload step might be cancelled, or the reload operation might not be submitted if run as a separate job. This in itself causes no immediate problem, except for the handling of the unloaded data set. If referenced as a "new, cataloged" data set, a potential trap has been laid. The next time the reorg is executed, the new unload will have a "not catalogued" status, since the data set name already exists in the system's catalog from the previous unload. If this goes undetected, the reload step, referencing the unload data set by name, will use as input the older (earlier) version. The reload will run without error. If the data center personnel aren't checking the segment counts between the separate unload and reload steps, the error will go undetected. At this time the data base has been back-leveled. It may be some time before the mistake is discovered. This problem scenario presents another situation which normal recovery procedures cannot correct without loss of updates.

Finally, a third concern with reorganizations is the potential for access and modification of the unload data sets themselves. Many applications routinely use these data sets as an input file when doing massive conversions against the data base. However, all access and use of these data sets are strictly outside of the integrity provisions of IMS. Because of this, the access and modification of unload data sets within any installation deserves the same controls, security checks, or audit requirements that are deemed necessary for the data bases themselves.

10.6.2 Large Data Bases

The physical size of a data base can cause a number of problems. Backup and recovery are done at the data set level; the larger the data set, the more time required to perform a backup or recovery operation, or to perform an integrity check.

Data base compression routines enable a given amount of data to be stored in a significantly smaller amount of space than it logically appears in an application program's I/O area. They are implemented transparently to the application, and are invoked automatically by the DBMS when moving data to or from the data base's buffers. Using this technique, data set size may be reduced by as much as 50 to 70 percent.

10.6.3 Extended On-Line System Hours

When user requirements call for extended on-line availability, the batch window, that time available for off-line processing, shrinks. The reduced time remaining can cause problems in scheduling time to obtain image copies, integrity checks, or data base reorganizations.

Under these circumstances, the on-line image copy utility may be required, in addition to use of the Change Accumulation utility. The issue of integrity checking becomes more complex, however, because an on-line image copy, taken while a data base is concurrently being updated, cannot be used as input for an integrity check. This is because the data on the on-line image do not represent data at a static point in time. An on-line update could easily have run while the image was taken, updating pointers in a block at the beginning of the data base (not reflected on the image—that block was already copied) as well as at the end of the data base (which will be copied).

10.7 DEVELOPING A BACKUP/RECOVERY STRATEGY

Let's try to summarize points for establishing an effective backup/recovery strategy for data bases. Once again, this is done in terms of facilities available within IMS.

1. Identify the maximum amount of time which the application and user community will accept for downtime should a data base recovery be required. Using this time requirement as a guideline, design a plan for the use of image copy and Change Accum utilities to permit execution of recovery within this time frame.
2. Define and schedule a time sequence for periodically taking image copies of data bases. Using the image copy tape as input, perform an integrity check with SMU. When considering the frequency for performing this integrity check, remember to assure the ability to recover with log tape input from the last image copy which has been verified with SMU. Change Accum data sets, as an alternate input to recovery, should not be considered as valid input to recovery unless they are produced under the control of DBRC.

   Keep in mind that you can't rely on nightly images, though otherwise desirable, to guarantee recovery unless SMU has verified the data base integrity. It is perfectly acceptable to take nightly images, and you can use them without question to recover data bases because of hardware failure. However, for the purposes of guaranteeing recoverability using previously verified inputs, they "don't count."
3. Insure that you have solid procedures for recording information about all recovery-related data sets (image copies, Change Accums, logs, and so on).

4. Verify the expiration date of all recovery-related tape data sets with the time frames used in the recovery plan.
5. Monitor data set space requirements and growth.
6. Review your reorganization schedule for the proper level of maintenance. Review the access controls which exist for the access and use of the unload data sets.
7. Insure that working JCL exists for the execution of SMU diagnostic runs, or the equivalent diagnostic software if another DBMS is used.
8. Insure that knowledgeable data base administrators have been identified and are available to read and interpret SMU diagnostic reports when required to provide input to problem scenarios.
9. If you work in an IMS shop that does not use DBRC to manage recovery control, develop a testing and conversion plan to move toward the registration of data bases. Today's environment is difficult enough to manage without DBRC being actively involved to manage recoveries. Tomorrow's more complex environment will be virtually impossible to manage effectively without DBRC. DBRC conversion is no minor overnight effort. The sooner this is acknowledged and addressed, the sooner you will be able to take advantage of the automatic controls and increased level of integrity protection.

   If you work in a non-IMS shop (or if you use IMS without registering data bases to DBRC), insure that you have solid manual procedures in place to track and record information for all recovery-related data sets.

10.8 SUMMARY

Data base technology includes the most sophisticated and advanced capabilities and technology for sharing access to data across a number of processes. As updates take place, log records reflect all updates. These log tape records can be used to rebuild the data base in the event of a hardware or software failure. However, the proper and effective use of this technology, or in fact having the ability to simply recover from a failure scenario, depends on advance planning and design of an overall backup/recovery strategy. This strategy should include use of available utilities in a coordinated way to allow early and timely identification of a problem, while providing all of the required inputs to permit the recovery utilities to resolve the problem.

REVIEW QUESTIONS

1. Under what circumstances do you feel a data base should be repaired, as opposed to being recovered?
2. What are the tradeoffs in taking more frequent image copies?

3. Why is integrity checking necessary? Does the use of a facility such as DBRC make this more or less important?
4. How can integrity checking be performed for a data base that is continually on line? How frequently should this be done?
5. Describe alternative methods of backing up, or integrity checking, data bases.
6. Assume that an application program abends with a code that indicates a pointer error. Devise a plan that indicates the proper diagnostic approach to take and the various courses of action available for the possible conditions that might be found.

11

Application Development Strategies

11.1 INTRODUCTION

Of all the different types of problems or challenges facing application groups, the most significant is the amount of time it takes to design and implement new application systems. The tools and programming languages traditionally used are certainly capable of producing application systems that meet user requirements and provide satisfactory performance levels, but the design, development and implementation effort takes time. When upper management mandates a reduction in a project's development time, planning and analysis are reduced to a minimum, and the resulting system will normally require major redesign or enhancements shortly after being placed in production. If this situation isn't bad enough, in most companies user requirements evolve faster than the development staff can handle them.

Managers of the application development process must insure that all phases of the development effort are performed as efficiently as possible in order to provide satisfactory service and support to clients in the end-user departments. You simply can't afford to waste time and effort at any phase of system design and implementation. This requires sound managerial judgment on when and how to use the technologies available so that the system's overall design objectives can be met in a timely manner.

In this chapter, common problems found in various stages of a system's design are reviewed, and, wherever possible, alternative approaches for handling them will be suggested.

11.2 IDENTIFYING USER REQUIREMENTS

This is the oldest problem that system designers have faced. Application programmers work and think in terms of records, I/O areas, reading and writing records, and so on. These terms are totally foreign and meaningless to the end user.

As a member of the application team, your role is to satisfy the requirements of your clients, the end users. If you aren't identifying and meeting their needs, there is little, if any, justification for your job. Fortunately, most application developers recognize this; unfortunately, most aren't too good in communicating with end users in defining these requirements.

The first thing that must be done is to eliminate technical jargon and terms in any discussion with users. The project's requirements should be discussed in terms of the information needed to do specific tasks. This information, expressed in terms of entities and attributes, defines the project by describing data and how they are to be used. Of course, these discussions need to begin with an introduction and definition to the terms entity and attribute. After the proper orientation, the entire design should move forward based on a discussion of the user's data requirements.

Once the basic terminology issue has been addressed, the next problem is to derive and maintain a consistent understanding and interpretation of the meaning of each data element. There may initially be as many interpretations of a given attribute as there are people on the design team. Fortunately, this problem is one of the easiest to address. Your company's data dictionary is the logical place to store entity/attribute definitions as they are derived, with the information stored as hypothetical records and fields. Standard dictionary reporting facilities can be used to produce reports on the definition of these data elements, which can be reviewed by the design team and changed if necessary.

To strengthen and insure communications between end users and application groups, many companies have established full-time positions with knowledgeable, experienced users who serve as permanent liaisons to the development staff. Their job responsibilities are to communicate the data requirements of the user department to the application's analysts; for example, "here are our entity/attribute elements, and this is how we need to use them." Because these individuals know the user environment as well as the capabilities and restrictions of computer systems, they provide invaluable input on the objectives for the new system, as well as in the accurate translation of data requirements.

11.3 ACCURACY OF THE DATA DICTIONARY

A word of caution: If you happen to be developing your application using a relational DBMS that does not have an active dictionary, you have an additional problem to solve. The relational system, under these circumstances, "knows" the descriptive characteristics (for example, length and data type) of each data element as columns are defined in the relational tables, but will not have knowledge of what the column or field *represents*. Your dictionary has the capability of storing this knowledge, but at best has only some off-line download link to update the relational catalog's pictorial view of data fields. As a result, information about your data exists in two locations. The problem is in keeping the dictionary current when it is so easy to make design changes directly in the relational catalog, bypassing the dictionary. Every time that happens, the dictionary becomes further out of date, and may never again catch up with the reality of the relational catalog.

Your organization may try to address this issue by defining a standard practice for using the dictionary as the front end for catalog updates. That might even work. However, a more proactive approach would be to either purchase or develop internally an extension to your relational catalog to capture and maintain this descriptive information in the catalog itself. This information can be extracted and downloaded periodically to the dictionary. In this way the application can do all development work directly with the relational catalog, avoiding the overhead and delays inherent in using the dictionary as a front end to the catalog.

11.4 LACK OF USER EXPERIENCE

It isn't always possible or practical to use knowledgeable, "data-wise" user contacts to communicate data requirements. It's very difficult for first-time users of computer systems to identify their needs for data processing services. They don't know what can be done, therefore they don't know what to ask for. In many cases, they and the application group simply do the best they can in designing the new system. After the project is operational, the user begins to understand the broad capability of computer systems. The typical reaction is "Gee, if I had known that we could do that, I would have asked for...". Despite all the honest efforts and intentions, a system has been designed and implemented that does not meet the true requirements. In this case, the users simply needed to go through that first learning experience before they could begin to understand what computer systems can do.

The most effective way to address this problem is to use a micro-based relational data base system to create an early prototype. The system can be dynamically designed and modified, with full user participation in creating changes to reports and screens. The result should be a complete (although scaled down) image of what the full system should contain.

Keep in mind that micro-based systems are becoming extremely powerful. It's possible that some of the prototype can be used "as is" in a micro-based solution for the system. At the very least, it should provide the development staff with complete and accurate specifications of the system's requirements.

11.5 PROLONGED REQUIREMENTS ANALYSIS

Delays in analysis can also be caused by managerial, not technological, problems. Attempts to perform detailed analysis by a central design or support staff normally adds a considerable amount of time to the project. As competent as the central staff might be, it takes time to bring them "up to speed" on the new data environment. In addition, participation by staff members who have a full-time profession of performing analytical functions can lead to "paralysis by analysis."

To avoid this trap, the responsibilities of the central data base design staff should be redefined to one of a technical sounding board or consulting group. In this role, they become coaches and leaders in all design aspects, while leaving the data analysis phases to those who best understand the data environment—the combined team of application group and users. This approach permits the support group's expertise across as many applications as possible, and allows the application development staff to handle routine design questions and issues.

11.6 CHANGING USER REQUIREMENTS

One further complication in defining requirements stems from unforeseen or unpredictable changes. They could be caused by changing federal or state laws, or simply by a very dynamic business environment.

Change is more difficult to deal with when using traditional systems and methodologies. Hierarchical or network data bases are quite good for providing a high level of performance in accessing static, well-defined data bases. However, the price for this performance lies in the rigidity of the system. Changes in the data base structure must be introduced in a specific, controlled manner and sequence.

Application systems that involve a dynamic or evolving data environment should strongly consider using relational technology for the data bases. Relational systems were created to provide the highest possible degree of flexibility. Table definitions can be modified "on the fly," making it easy to add new data elements as they arise. Productivity tools are also becoming widely available to permit faster application development. These systems do not provide the performance or "throughput" of the more traditional data base systems, but they offer a new dimension in terms of flexibility for future revisions to the data base's structures.

11.7 DESIGN REVIEWS

A design review process should be an integral part of the application development process. These reviews includes a basic statement of what the user requirements are, how the application will meet those requirements, and what data elements are involved. This serves as a checkpoint to verify the goals and direction of the project. Other items reviewed include the anticipated hardware and software requirements for the project, and anticipated conversion dates.

This process could be managed by having one formal review of a master document, where each participating member of the review team would sign an acknowledgment specifying that their area of responsibility had been reviewed. In this way the design review would assure that the application group is developing a system that the user community wants and needs.

In practice, many companies do not conduct design reviews in this way. Participants often feel the extra documentation effort required is not worth the benefits obtained by holding the review, or the project development dates don't allow for this time.

When designing an application, a design review process can be structured to be a series of checks on the various stages in a system's design. The formal review should be handled not in one large, formal meeting, but as a series of working sessions with only the pertinent participants involved in each. The documentation reviewed is the same as what would be naturally developed as part of the design process. Handled in this way, the design review process becomes a combination road map and checklist for things that should be done and information that needs to be collected while assuring that no critical steps are missed.

Here's one final thought on design reviews. If you're using a relational system, you might feel the DBMS's ease of use and dynamic capabilities for change might eliminate the need for such reviews. That is not true. At the application level, the definition, scope and content of the project still needs to be verified. Further, at the program level, the proposed call patterns still need to be verified to avoid subtle mistakes that can cause serious performance problems; for example, the difference between an index lookup versus a data base scan.

11.8 PERFORMANCE ESTIMATION

If the new system requires high-performance on-line processing, each program must be reviewed in terms of the anticipated data base calls and the resulting I/O. For a specified operating environment, which consists of a combination of hardware, software, and general load running on the system, an on-line program will have a limited number of I/Os that may be performed while still keeping the run time within the desired limits. I/O, then, becomes the limiting factor that an application designer must use to control run time (and the response time) for the new system.

During the usage analysis phase, the anticipated call patterns of each program can be used to forecast I/O requirements for each program. Monitor your existing system to accumulate historical data on calls issued versus the resulting number of I/Os. If treated at a high level, these numbers can be used to approximate the I/O requirements for new programs by predicting a range of I/Os the new program will require to satisfy the planned data base calls.

This is not a highly accurate process; attempts to make it so will, in most cases, fail. This is because the same program, executing calls for identical data, but running at different times during the day, will require a different number of I/Os. The on-line system's buffer pools will, at any particular instant, contain data base records that may be accessed without incurring additional I/O. However, because of the very dynamic and transient nature of system activity, the exact content of those buffers is unpredictable. The best that can be done is to accumulate statistics giving the average cost for an indexed lookup, or for a sequential access. When used against the number and types of calls planned for a new program, the result should be a rough ballpark figure for the number of I/Os required.

For example, you may find from statistical analysis that your programs can execute 25 to 30 I/Os within a five-second response time. A new program predicted to take 30 to 35 I/Os *might* run in five seconds; however, one that is forecasted for 100 I/Os will run considerably longer than that. If a longer run time is unacceptable, perhaps the design could be altered to reduce I/O, or the program can be subdivided into programs that can be independently scheduled and executed, where each can execute in the required frame. The point is to identify and address performance problems in the design stage, not after they have become a reality as part of a production environment.

In other words, preplanning for high performance systems is required to insure satisfactory performance levels. This does take work and extra time, which might create a problem in meeting the project's deadlines. Regardless, this phase of analysis should not be ignored. As an alternative, it may need to be restricted to programs that have a higher anticipated frequency for execution, or that you know have higher response time requirements. Simply try to do the best you can in the time available.

One final thought for this estimation process. A lot of people have gotten in trouble by being too optimistic in predicting performance results. Keep in mind that any number of things can make a process run slower than anticipated, but very few things can be done to make them run faster. Forecast times in broad ranges, with cautious pessimism as the underlying theme. If a program is later found to run at the high end of the anticipated range, fine. If it runs faster than predicted, everyone is pleased and you may become a hero. You simply want to avoid unpleasant surprises.

11.9 TIME REQUIRED FOR CODE GENERATION

The time required to code and test a new application program has been a continuing problem. While being well known and understood, at the same time it's probably the least often addressed. Who can disagree about the time and effort required to design, code, and test a complex COBOL program? This has been used as an excuse all too often.

Many times performance or transaction volumes dictate that the solution be implemented with traditional languages such as COBOL or PL/1. However, there are an increasing number of alternatives becoming available to provide reasonable solutions for application requirements in a much shorter time than with traditional languages.

1. Fourth-generation report generators have been used to handle queries for a number of years. These should be considered to produce reports, even though any programs performing data base updates are written in a traditional language.
2. Another option that should be considered involves the use of a fourth-generation *language*, as opposed to a report generator. Such a language is capable of performing data base updates in addition to simple report generation. Entire systems can be developed and implemented in a greatly reduced time frame. The advantages, of course, include ease of use and greatly reduced development time. Here, however, you are faced with additional execution-time overhead which can often be significant. A system written entirely in a fourth-generation language may not be able to provide the performance requirements necessary for the application. Once again, the best answer for a specific application environment may involve a mix of traditional and advanced technologies. All high-performance "bread and butter" maintenance programs can be coded in a traditional language to provide the highest performance characteristics possible, while the remaining programs would be developed in the fourth-generation language to obtain productivity gains wherever practical.
3. The most promising innovation in this area concerns the increasing availability of Computer-Aided Software Engineering (CASE) tools. They are software packages that combine the capabilities of a dictionary-like facility with that of code generators to provide an integrated platform for data definition and application development with which to automate the entire system's life cycle. Using these products, typically an English-like macro language is used to specify the desired operations. The code generator uses this information as input, and produces the source code equivalent for these functions. This source, in turn, can then be compiled and link-edited in the traditional manner.

The advantage of this approach is that the programmer can think and specify functions in a shorthand-type language, greatly reducing the amount of input required to create a working program. On the negative side, this often requires redundant data definitions, as these generators normally use their own internal dictionary-like system. In addition, these generalized systems normally produce results that are much less efficient than a program containing explicit data base calls. These issues, and how to integrate these tools with your company's standard dictionary facilities, are matters that need to be evaluated in determining the potential use and selection of a CASE tool.

11.10 SUMMARY

Let's review the major points discussed in this chapter.

1. Analyze the system's requirements in terms of data and data requirements of the user.
2. The application development team should discuss the project with the user representatives in terms of entities and attributes (that is, data definitions), not in technical jargon.
3. The data dictionary should be used to contain a description of the data elements as they are derived.
4. Experienced users should be utilized as liaisons with the application groups in describing data, data definitions, and data access requirements.
5. For new end-user groups with no data processing experience, use a microcomputer-based relational system to produce an early working prototype of the proposed system.
6. Have the application groups do their own data entry and data maintenance functions with the data dictionary.
7. Consider the use of relational data base technology for implementing systems having undefined or evolving data definitions and access requirements.
8. The design review documentation and review process should be created as an integral by-product of the system analysis and design process.
9. Application analysts should check the anticipated I/O requirements for all high-volume or high-performance programs while these programs are still in the design stage.
10. Consideration should be given to alternative approaches to conventional programming languages, including:
    (a) using report generators for generating reports required;
    (b) using fourth-generation languages to generate as many programs as practical;

(c) using CASE tools to manage the entire development of the system's life cycle, including the generation of application programs.

The timely and accurate development of application systems is a difficult task at best. The use of the proper tools and methodologies, however, can significantly reduce development time as well as producing an end product which comes closer to meeting true user requirements.

12

Putting It All Together

12.1 INTRODUCTION

The previous chapters cover a wide variety of topics and issues that involve development of application systems using data base technology. With each topic, a number of potential problem areas are reviewed which seldom involve black-and-white decisions or actions for any specific set of circumstances. In order to deal effectively with today's technology, managers must have a basic understanding of these issues so that they can deal with them more effectively. Let's review the major concerns and options of each topic.

12.2 THE ANALYSIS OF DATA REQUIREMENTS

The first step of the project is to identify the data requirements of the proposed system. Obtain full user participation to insure these data accurately reflect true user requirements. In this analysis, avoid technical phrases and jargon, discussing data requirements in terms of entities and attributes. Put the emphasis on what needs to be done in terms of accessing and using data elements, without discussing the technical aspects of how that is done.

After defining the initial set of entities and attributes, normalize these data, placing the result in third normal form. Draw a data model or relational view, illustrating all of the relationships and dependencies across the data elements. Check this data model carefully for completeness in terms of data definition; that is, verify that it contains all data necessary to satisfy the required application processes. In addition, the one-to-many relationships depicted must be logically consistent in terms of accurately reflecting all parent-child relationships.

As the final step in this phase, develop first-cut, proposed access paths for how the data model will be accessed to satisfy each program's data requirements. Verify that all data requirements are included in the data model, and identify attributes necessary for record selection in data access. Show the access paths required to provide access to these data.

If the project is sufficiently large or complex, have one or more users serve as full-time coordinators whose sole job is to translate data definitions and access requirements to the application design team. Use a micro-based relational DBMS to implement a micro-based version of the proposed system. This will more fully illustrate to the user community the capabilities of the proposed system. Above all, encourage open and active participation and communication between all members of the design team to insure that the new system will identify and meet true user requirements.

12.3 DATA ADMINISTRATION

In defining and deriving the new system, your corporate data dictionary can store the detailed definitions for the elements in the data model. However, you must resolve several problems before your dictionary can be effectively used.

Chapter 9 reviews standard naming conventions for data elements and their associated descriptive information. You must create field descriptions in a consistent way when the field is entered in the dictionary. In order to later use a dictionary's search capabilities to perform queries, standard terms or abbreviations must be developed and used "up front" for all data elements.

There are a number of related questions that must be answered.

- How will these standards be enforced?
- Is one support group going to do all data entry work for all applications? If so, are they adequately staffed to provide timely entry and modification requests for all applications?
- If data entry is supported within the applications themselves, how will the standards be taught and later enforced? All groups doing data entry and modification of dictionary information must be following the same set of procedures.

Other questions involve standards for creating field names for programs.

- What is your company's standard for field names? Some uniformity or standardization should exist, at least within a given application.
- Do all applications use the same field name for a given element?
- Are standard names already in place? If so, how are they enforced?
- For a given field, how many languages do you generate program names for?

Answering these questions "up front" allows data definitions to be developed quickly and effectively, and avoids later rework efforts when a forgotten issue surfaces.

12.4 THE DESIGN REVIEW PROCESS

As part of your company's system development strategy, you need to have a design review procedure built in to assure that no errors or omissions are made in designing the new system. In designing this process, identify all of the normal effort or work that should be incorporated as part of designing any system. Build your reviews around the project's natural sequence of events and documentation, so they may be done as part of the normal project workload. Keep in mind that the objective of the design review process is to insure that the user needs match the functional capability which the application plans to provide, as represented in the data elements identified.

The user and application groups must jointly perform the data analysis and design. As far as possible, this is done independently of a centralized support staff. This technical staff should be included as an integral part of the design review process to handle questions. They are a resource and "sounding board" for assistance on an as-required basis. In this way the analysis can proceed as quickly as possible, yet with all appropriate checks being made at the proper times.

12.5 DATA BASE TECHNOLOGY

In selecting which data base technology to use (hierarchical, network, or relational), the choices don't get any easier. The more traditional hierarchical or network structures use pointer mechanisms for data linkage, usually in addition to clustering of data records within a block or page, to provide a high level of performance in gaining access to data. However, these mechanisms are more costly when implementing changes. Hierarchical structures in particular are less flexible in providing alternative access paths to data. Both hierarchical and network structures require more up-front analysis to assure the complete and accurate identification of access requirements.

A truly relational system, by definition, provides 1:M linkages across record types based on data content within the data records themselves, and not through the use of pointer paths. This provides the basis for a much more flexible and dynamic environment, allowing a basis for the data model to continue to dynamically grow and evolve in complexity and use as data requirements change. This technology will enable you, over time, to approach the development of the infamous "corporate data base."

The questions involving selection of a DBMS are more difficult.

- When is a relational strategy appropriate?
- Should you arbitrarily switch to the exclusive use of relational technology?
- Is relational technology for everyone?
- Assuming that you understand the considerations for not using relational technology, what is the price if you do use it?

Remember that the more traditional hierarchical or network data base management systems achieve a high degree of performance by using clustering techniques to store multiple associated record types together. Because of this, related data records are typically stored within the same data block or page, which requires a minimal amount of I/O when later retrieving the data in response to application calls. Of course, the fewer I/Os performed, the faster the process will run. IMS does this clustering automatically by storing dependent segments physically close to their parents. In network systems, the data base designer would chose options that cause member records to be stored physically close to the owner record for that set. These systems, then, are best for well-defined data definition and structures requiring a high level of performance, generally your "bread and butter" production applications.

A relational solution, on the other hand, should be considered when flexibility is required for the further definition and expansion of increasingly complex access paths across the data base. The data base designer would implement the data base as one record type per table. While most relational systems allow clustering mechanisms in creating tables, clustering should be avoided in order to achieve maximum flexibility.

The result of the decision to avoid clustering in relational data bases will require many more I/Os to retrieve the equivalent amount of information than in a hierarchical or network DBMS. This higher I/O rate will necessarily result in a lower performance level. The reduced performance may, or may not, be acceptable in your environment.

As a manager, then, you are confronted with a number of complex, nontrivial issues.

- Is a relational solution appropriate for your particular environment?
- If so, how can you determine that a relational solution can provide a satisfactory performance level for your application system?

To consider the processing capability of a relational solution, translate your solution into relational terms: the number of tables, the number of 1:M links or "joins" required, and the number of rows accessed per transaction. Investigate the required transaction rate for the new system, as well as the proposed hardware to be used. With this information, talk to current users of the proposed DBMS, using these data as a basis to obtain a rough estimate as to the kind of performance level you might expect from your system.

Relational systems do require more I/O than hierarchical or network data bases to access the equivalent amount of data. However, as hardware becomes faster and the DBMS software becomes more powerful, the cost of that additional I/O will be reduced. When choosing between alternative DBMSs for an application, you must be continually aware of what these various systems can, and cannot, provide in terms of performance. Any DBMS can and will provide significant payback if chosen and used wisely.

12.6 APPLICATION DEVELOPMENT STRATEGIES

Use of the more traditional programming languages such as COBOL or PL/I produces program modules that are more efficient and require less system resources for execution. However, these languages require more time to design, code, and implement.

Fourth-generation report generators are also commonly available for use with most simple files and data base systems. While flexible and simple to use, they are generally restricted to read-only processes. True full-function fourth-generation languages are becoming more common, but these are generally found to require more resources for execution. Even if an acceptable fourth-generation language could be found, compatibility with the preferred data base management system might not be possible. Fortunately, these languages are becoming more readily available for all major data base management systems.

Investigate and select a CASE tool that can be integrated into your existing environment and that will also support the direction your company is headed in terms of data base technology. Look carefully at the integration issues involved with that tool and your existing data dictionary system. Develop plans to integrate these systems together so that your company has one central source of information for data definitions.

12.7 MANAGING DATA BASE BACKUP/RECOVERY

The design and implementation of an application system requires a considerable amount of planning and management, particularly to assure timely and efficient implementation. The data center in which this application is to be run then picks up the responsibility for installing and maintaining the system. Considerations involve not only the more mechanical aspects of installing and backing up software libraries, but proper management of the actual data base data sets.

A critical component of any backup/recovery plan is to predetermine the maximum time allowable to recover each data base. Using this as input, a strategy can be developed which will permit recovery within the specified time frame. This strategy will result in the specification of how often each of the recovery-related utilities must be used.

Effective backup/recovery strategies include not only procedures to backup data bases, but include periodic integrity checking. They must also include provisions for monitoring space utilization and growth, and include considerations for whatever reorganization runs are appropriate. Also, the backup/recovery plan needs to include the retention period of all recovery-related data sets (backup copies, log tapes, and so on).

12.8 SUMMARY

Application development using data base technology is rich with function and full of promise to provide powerful systems requiring a minimum amount of software maintenance. Capabilities exist to design data bases with little or no data redundancy. The proper design of data records will permit growth and expansion of the data base without impact to the application community.

However, simply having access to, or using, a data base management system is not in itself sufficient to obtain these benefits. Data base systems are simply tools which, if used properly, can provide significant payback and dividends to applications. However, if used improperly, the use of data base technology can be very costly without providing any of the possible benefits. Today, as never before, more choices are available to the development team. Many productivity tools packaged together as development "toolkits" require a major commitment in terms of time and expense. Decisions with regard to the proper use of any phase of this technology must be made by clearly identifying your application development requirements, identifying the desired data base technology, and mapping out a migration strategy to move toward this environment. Conflicting requirements or objectives will be found and need to be evaluated by reviewing and prioritizing objectives.

The design and implementation of a new data base application requires a number of issues to be addressed. Some are nontechnical in nature, such as naming conventions and standards for describing data in a dictionary. Others, such as establishing a plan for backup/recovery operations, are quite technical. The successful implementation of this application requires a solid understanding of both the technical and nontechnical issues, leading to more informed decisions being made, and resulting in the development of the best possible overall solution.

Index

F

H

I

J

K

L

M

N

O

P